I0011259

The Rise of the AI Author:

The Complete Guide to Writing with AI

Eldar Haber

Copyright © 2026 by Eldar Haber

All rights reserved. No part of this book may be reproduced, stored, or transmitted by any means without the author's prior written permission.

Printed in the United States of America

Fourth Edition (March 2026)

First edition published March 2025

This book is for informational purposes only. The author and publisher assume no responsibility for errors or omissions.

Table of Contents

—

Preface

Imagine standing at the edge of a technological tsunami, watching as it reshapes the landscape of human creativity. The horizon pulses with possibility, crackling with the energy of a new dawn. That's where we find ourselves today—perched on the threshold of a revolution that promises to redefine not just how we write, but how we think, create, and connect with one another. I'm inviting you to ride this wave with me.

Throughout history, certain pivotal moments have tilted the world on its axis—when everything we thought we knew is suddenly cast in a new light. The invention of the printing press, the Industrial Revolution, and the birth of the Internet weren't mere technological advancements; they were profound paradigm shifts that fundamentally altered the trajectory of human civilization. Each revolution not only changed how we operated but transformed how we understood our own potential.

I've had the extraordinary fortune to witness two such transformative eras. The first was the emergence of the Internet in the late 20th century. I remember the distinctive screech of a dial-up modem, the wide-eyed wonder of sending my first email, and the sudden realization that the world was at my fingertips. It was a time of unprecedented connectivity, a digital Big Bang that expanded our universe of knowledge and communication.

Now, barely a generation later, we stand at the threshold of another seismic shift: the rise of Generative Artificial Intelligence. This isn't just another step forward; it's a quantum leap into a future we've only glimpsed in our dreams. We're not talking about faster computers or smarter algorithms. We're talking about machines that can create, innovate, and—in some remarkable ways—think.

As a law professor specializing in technology, I've spent years studying and teaching about AI. I've parsed the theories, debated the ethics, and speculated about potential impacts. I'd been anticipating the AI revolution with equal parts excitement and trepidation. But when it finally arrived, it wasn't what I expected.

When I first interacted with ChatGPT, I knew we'd crossed an invisible threshold. It wasn't the sci-fi vision of sentient robots or omniscient supercomputers. Instead, it was something far more subtle and, ultimately, more powerful: a tool that could augment and amplify human creativity in unprecedented ways. Here was a system that could generate content seemingly from thin air, challenging everything I thought I knew about the creative process.

For someone who lives and breathes words, who has built a career on the power of language, this was both exhilarating and unsettling. Writing has always been my passion, my vehicle for influencing the world. It's how I've expressed ideas, shared research, and hopefully, made a difference. I've authored numerous articles, book chapters, and an academic book, amassing well over a million words. Each project was a labor of love, a testament to both the joy and struggle of translating thoughts to paper.

But let's be honest: writing is rarely a walk in the park. We've all faced the tyranny of the blank page, the frustration of writer's block, the tedious process of editing and refining our work. There are days when words flow like a river, when you can sit at your desk for hours, lost in the pure joy of creation. And there are days, many days, when every sentence is a battle, when you question every comma, every turn of phrase.

And for those of us who aren't native English speakers, there's an added layer of challenge. We compete in a linguistic arena where others have had a lifetime's head start. Every sentence becomes a tightrope walk between expression and accuracy, between what we want to say and what we know how to say.

Enter AI, and suddenly the game transforms. The barriers that once held us back begin to crumble. With these new tools, we can write more efficiently, more eloquently, and more prolifically than ever before. It's like having a brilliant writing partner who never sleeps, never spills coffee on your manuscript, and never judges your 3 AM bursts of inspiration.

But here's the crucial twist: AI isn't a magic wand. You can't simply say "Abracadabra, write me a bestseller!" and expect miracles. I learned this the hard way, spending countless hours experimenting with almost every AI writing tool available. There were frustrations, dead ends, and moments of sheer bewilderment. But there were also breakthroughs, eureka moments, and the thrill of creating something genuinely new.

This book distills that journey. It's a guide for anyone curious about navigating this brave new world of AI-assisted creativity. Whether you've never written a word beyond school assignments, you're already sharing your thoughts online, or you dream of crafting stories that move others—this book is for you. Already an experienced writer? Even better. AI can give you the creative superpowers to finally write all those books you've dreamed of but never had the time to finish. I'll show you how to harness AI's power to amplify your voice without losing the unique perspective that makes your ideas distinctly yours.

We'll explore legal and ethical considerations, demystify the technology, and mainly dive into practical techniques for collaborating with AI. You'll learn how to use these tools to overcome writer's block, polish your prose, and expand the boundaries of your creativity. We'll address potential pitfalls and how to avoid them, ensuring you remain in control of your creative process.

More than anything, this book is an invitation to join the revolution. We stand at the dawn of a new era in writing, where the only limit is our imagination. The possibilities stretch endlessly before us, and the future remains unwritten—quite literally. Together, we'll explore how AI can help us tell stories never before told, express ideas never before articulated, and push the boundaries of what we once thought possible in literature.

Are you ready to reshape the landscape of writing? To challenge conventional wisdom about what it means to be an author? To ride the AI wave and discover where it takes us? To join a movement that could redefine creativity for generations to come? Turn the page, and let's begin the adventure.

The future of writing awaits, and it's more exhilarating than anything we've ever imagined.

Introduction

You're somewhere on the writing spectrum, aren't you? Maybe you've already published books or articles with your name proudly displayed. Perhaps you're midway through a manuscript that's been your passion project. Or you might be someone who's just toyed with the idea of writing something—anything—that captures what's in your head and heart. The beauty of this moment we're in is that wherever you fall on that spectrum—published author, regular blogger, occasional journaler, or just someone with thoughts to express—AI can meet you exactly where you are. For the veterans among us, it's about amplifying what you already do brilliantly. For the newcomers, it's about bridging the gap between what you imagine and what you can create. And for everyone in between, it's about making the whole process more fluid, more intuitive, and frankly, more fun. The playing field is leveling, and that's something to get excited about.

Yet, for many of us, there's still that next book, that dream project, that story that remains unwritten. Why?

The reasons are likely as diverse as they are familiar. Life, with its relentless parade of obligations—work, family, endless responsibilities—has a way of crowding out our deepest aspirations. You've probably told yourself you'll start writing "when things calm down" or "when the time is right," but that elusive perfect moment seems forever out of reach. The thought of writing an entire book can feel overwhelmingly daunting, like standing at the base of Everest without a map or gear. Perhaps you've grappled with self-doubt, questioning whether you're truly "good enough" to be an author. Or maybe it's the specter of criticism, rejection, or failure that has held your pen at bay, preventing you from even taking that first, crucial step.

If any of this resonates with you, take heart—you're far from alone. Countless aspiring authors have stood where you are now, brimming with ideas yet uncertain how to bring them to life. You've picked up this book because something within you still yearns to write, even as doubts and uncertainties cloud your path. Deep down, you know there's a story or message inside you that deserves to be shared with the world.

So, how do you take that first step? How do you transform your long-held dream into a tangible reality, especially when time is scarce and confidence feels like a luxury?

Here's my promise to you: By the time you finish this book and apply its strategies, you will possess the tools, techniques, and—most crucially—the confidence to write the book you've always dreamed of creating. Whether it's a gripping novel, a comprehensive non-fiction work that establishes your expertise, a heartwarming children's story, a life-changing self-help guide, or a touching memoir—all of these are within your grasp.

The key that unlocks this world of possibilities? AI, specifically Generative AI.

We are living in an era of unprecedented technological advancement. AI tools can now generate text, images, and ideas with capabilities that were unimaginable just a few years ago. It's not quite a magic box (yet), but it's remarkably close—a digital genie that can help bring your book to life, regardless of your chosen genre or writing experience.

Let me be clear: AI won't write your book for you, at least not in a way that truly matters. Attempting to rely solely on AI to generate a book from scratch will likely result in a short, incoherent collection of words lacking depth, coherence, and soul. And even if some fancy apps or websites promise to produce a "complete book" for you in just minutes, what they actually deliver is, at best, a somewhat coherent timeline or skeleton— never a genuinely good book with your unique perspective. These shortcuts simply can't replace real input from you, the author. However, when used effectively, AI can be an incredible ally in your writing journey. It can help you brainstorm ideas, overcome writer's block, refine your prose, and even enhance your unique writing style. With AI as your partner, you can become an AI author, capable of producing work that rivals the best in the business (maybe).

When I first encountered ChatGPT, I was both amazed and intrigued, even as its early writing capabilities were still evolving. As I continued experimenting with it over the following months, it became clear that we were on the brink of a textual revolution. The technology was advancing at breakneck speed, and those who learned to navigate this new landscape would find themselves at the forefront of a new era in writing and creativity.

In this book, I'll take you along on my writing journey with AI. I've made countless attempts, adapting as the technology rapidly evolved. The path has been bumpy—sometimes entire sections needed rewriting when new updates or tools rendered previous work obsolete. Many of my AI-authored books will never see the light of day. But each attempt taught me something remarkable: with AI as your writing partner, anyone can craft quality content on any topic. The possibilities are limitless.

As mentioned earlier, this book is more than just a guide—it's an invitation to explore the boundless possibilities that AI brings to the craft of writing. We'll examine the intricacies of AI-assisted writing, addressing the challenges you might face and uncovering best practices for making the most of these powerful tools. We'll explore how to unlock your creativity, streamline your writing process, and ultimately bring your ideas to life in ways you never thought possible.

By the time you reach the final page, you'll have more than just theoretical knowledge—you'll have practical, actionable strategies that will empower you to finally write the book you've always dreamed of. Whether you're crafting fiction, non-fiction, memoirs, or anything in between, AI can help you transform your ideas into a finished work that you can be proud of.

So, are you ready to turn your writing dreams into reality? Are you prepared to take that first step and discover what you're truly capable of as an author? Let's embark on this journey together. The tools are in your hands, the possibilities are endless, and the time to begin is now.

Let's begin.

Chapter I: Where to Begin

By acquiring this book, you've already taken a significant step towards becoming an AI author. Now comes the exciting part—diving into its contents. Let's be clear: this isn't a page-turner novel; it's mainly a practical guide for writers exploring AI-assisted creation. While it may not keep you up at night with suspense, it will arm you with powerful tools to transform your writing process. It's important to absorb these concepts before starting your project, but don't worry about memorizing every detail. This guide will be your companion throughout your AI authorship journey.

With time and practice, you'll internalize the process, and the need to constantly refer back will diminish. Like mastering any new skill, there's an initial learning curve, but once you've conquered it, AI-assisted writing will become second nature, opening up new realms of creative possibility. Remember, the journey of becoming an AI author is not about instant perfection, but about growth and discovery.

One of the most valuable lessons I learned when first exploring AI-assisted writing was the importance of patience. It's easy to fall into the trap of thinking this technology will magically automate everything, producing perfect projects, reports, or presentations at the push of a button. Believe me, I tried to do exactly that. However, the reality is far more nuanced and, in many ways, more exciting.

I want to emphasis this: many people mistakenly assume that AI can produce a complete, publishable book at the click of a button. This is not the case. While AI can generate text, the raw output rarely meets publishing standards without significant human input. It's essential to understand that quality work still demands your time, effort, and creativity. The notion of writing a polished book in a single day remains firmly in the realm of science fiction—at least for now.

But here's the exciting part: with AI assistance, you won't need to spend years or even months on your project. By following the well-structured approach and guidelines I'm about to share, you could potentially complete your book in a matter of weeks. The key is to approach the process thoughtfully. Take the time to absorb the information in this book, develop a solid plan, and then begin your writing journey with confidence. Remember, AI is a powerful tool to enhance your writing, not replace you– when used effectively, it can significantly boost your productivity and help bring your creative vision to life.

I must caution you that even when following my guidelines, you're likely to face frustrations along the way—and quite a few of them. While current AI is undeniably impressive, it's far from perfect. Creating a lengthy, coherent book remains a challenging task for AI, due to limitations in areas like context management and maintaining long-term narrative consistency. Some might describe this as a "computationally costly" endeavor for AI systems. But regardless of the exact reason, the reality is that AI can't produce a complete book as effortlessly as you might initially imagine. It's a powerful tool, but not a magic wand that instantly conjures up bestsellers. Understanding these limitations from the outset will help you set realistic expectations and approach your AI-assisted writing journey with patience and perseverance.

Additionally, the process of communicating effectively with AI—often referred to as prompt engineering—isn't always straightforward. It requires practice, creativity, and sometimes a bit of trial and error. But don't let the term "engineering" intimidate you; it's not as technical as it sounds. Essentially, you'll be learning how to craft effective textual commands to guide the AI.

We'll explore prompt engineering in detail later, but for now, it's important to understand that current AI systems may perform differently across languages. While you can interact with AI in various languages, English currently has an advantage due to the more advanced development of English-language AI models. Don't let this discourage you if English isn't your first language. One of the main advantages of this technology is that it democratizes writing, regardless of your native tongue. Perseverance is key as you navigate these initial challenges in your writing journey. I can assure you that with practice, these hurdles will become easier to overcome. The results of your efforts will be well worth it, as you'll gain the ability to leverage AI effectively in your writing process, no matter what language you call your own.

So, where do you begin on this exciting journey of AI authorship? Do you already have a book idea burning in your mind, or are you still exploring possibilities? Perhaps you have multiple ideas competing for your attention.

The first step in writing is deciding on your book's topic and type. This choice will shape your entire writing process, influencing everything from the AI tools you'll use to how you structure your work. Take some time to reflect on your passions, your expertise, and the stories or knowledge you're eager to share with the world. Consider the genres that excite you as a reader and the types of books you've always dreamed of writing. Remember, with AI assistance, you have the potential to tackle projects that might have seemed daunting or even impossible before. Whether you're drawn to fiction or non-fiction, technical topics or creative storytelling, there's an AI-assisted approach that can help bring your vision to life.

Selecting Your Book's Topic

After deciding to write a book, the most crucial step is determining its subject matter. This task might be more challenging than it initially appears. Perhaps you've harbored various ideas over the years—a science fiction epic that's been brewing in your mind for decades, a heartfelt novel inspired by personal experiences that you've always wanted to share, or an educational tome in your area of expertise that could revolutionize your field. The possibilities are as vast as your imagination, and this abundance of options can sometimes be overwhelming, especially when you're embarking on the exciting journey of AI-assisted writing.

While the temptation to tackle multiple projects simultaneously may be strong, I strongly advise against it, particularly when you're just starting your journey as an AI author. When I first ventured into this exhilarating adventure, I was like a kid in a candy store, enthusiastically attempting to juggle multiple projects. The allure of exploring various genres and topics was irresistible.

I found myself starting a new project every time words piled up in another, constantly tempted by fresh ideas and new possibilities. One day, I'd be deep into an academic book I'd wanted to write for a while; the next, I'd pivot to a self-help guide; and by the end of the week, I'd be outlining a book about the future of AI. This constant shifting felt exciting at first, like I was exploring the full potential of AI-assisted writing. I was very intrigued about which genres AI could handle better. Could I use AI to create new worlds like Tolkien's? Maybe I could finally write the novel I'd once dreamed of but never started because I didn't know where to begin? The possibilities seemed endless.

However, this approach significantly complicated the learning process and diluted my focus. I soon realized that each genre, each type of book, required a different set of skills and a unique approach to AI collaboration. By jumping between projects, I wasn't giving myself the time to truly master any one style or to develop a deep understanding of how to best utilize AI in different contexts. The steep learning curve associated with AI-assisted writing, which we'll explore in detail later, isn't conducive to managing multiple projects concurrently.

Instead, I urge you to focus on one topic—one project at a time. This focused approach allows you to fully immerse yourself in the nuances of AI-assisted writing and to develop a deeper understanding of the process without the distraction of juggling multiple narratives or themes. By concentrating on a single project, you allow yourself to explore all aspects of AI-assisted writing within that context. You'll learn how to craft effective prompts for your chosen genre, how to maintain consistency in tone and style throughout your book, and how to leverage AI's strengths while mitigating its weaknesses in your specific type of writing.

Interestingly, this singular focus doesn't necessarily mean choosing the subject you're most passionate about right from the start. Your first AI-authored book could explore lessons from your professional life, offering a structured way to reflect on your career while mastering AI authorship techniques. It might be a cookbook featuring your favorite recipes, allowing you to experiment with descriptive writing, procedural text generation, and visual creation through AI. Or perhaps a simple children's story, allowing you to work on narrative structure and character development in a concise format. The specific topic matters less than becoming proficient in the process of AI authorship itself.

Think of your first project as a learning experience, a way to familiarize yourself with this new way of creating content. It's an opportunity to make mistakes, to learn from them, and to discover your own unique way of collaborating with AI. This initial project will serve as a foundation for all your future AI-assisted writing endeavors, so it's worth taking the time to really understand the process, even if the topic isn't your ultimate passion project.

That being said, selecting a topic that genuinely fascinates you can make the learning process more enjoyable and motivating. When you're passionate about your subject matter, you're more likely to power through the inevitable challenges and frustrations that come with mastering any new skill. While the specific topic may not be crucial from a learning standpoint, striking a balance between a manageable first project and a subject that captivates you can set the stage for success in your AI-assisted writing journey. Your enthusiasm for the topic will fuel your persistence, helping you navigate the learning curve of working with AI more effectively.

Exploring the AI Writing Landscape

Selecting your topic is a personal decision, and you don't need to finalize it before finishing this book. You might even start writing your first AI-assisted book on one subject, then decide to shift to another. That's perfectly acceptable. As mentioned earlier, when I began writing with AI, I faced this dilemma, and my journey took unexpected turns. While I don't recommend this winding path, these twists not only taught me about AI-assisted writing but also uncovered new passions and abilities. Your own AI writing journey might similarly reveal hidden talents or interests, even if you take a more direct route.

I should share more about how I actually started this AI writing adventure. My first project seemed like a no-brainer—an academic book blending my expertise in AI and law. After all, I'd spent years researching and teaching at this intersection, so I had the knowledge base. I pictured creating something substantial that would connect dense legal theory with the lightning-fast evolution of AI. And initially, things clicked into place. The AI helped me organize my scattered thoughts and instantly pulled relevant case studies and precedents that would have taken me days to compile manually. It felt like having a research assistant who never slept, one who could instantly recall every legal text I'd ever mentioned in passing.

However, midway through this project, I found myself drawn to a completely different style of writing. I shifted gears to try writing a self-improvement book. After some analysis with my AI collaborator, we settled on a topic: steps to become healthier and happier. We titled it "The Longevity Blueprint," naively assuming it would be a straightforward task. After all, if AI could help me write complex legal arguments, surely it could assist with practical life advice, right?

I was mistaken. it wasn't as simple as I'd anticipated. Translating scientific research into actionable steps for everyday life proved to be a unique challenge. However, with passion and dedication, I found that it was certainly achievable. This project taught me valuable lessons about using AI to distill complex information into accessible, engaging content. I learned how to craft prompts that would generate relatable examples and clear explanations of scientific concepts. I also discovered the importance of fact-checking AI-generated content, especially when dealing with health-related information.

As I worked on "The Longevity Blueprint," I explored various ways to enhance the reader's experience. I used AI to create graphs that simplified complex data into digestible visuals. The technology also helped me generate original drawings to illustrate key concepts, teaching me how to guide AI to maintain a consistent visual style. In some chapters, I incorporated QR codes (made by AI) leading readers to interactive content or up-to-date resources, transforming the book into a dynamic, technologically interactive experience. This process not only improved the book's content but also expanded my understanding of AI's capabilities in content creation and reader engagement.

But my writing journey didn't stop there. About 70% into "The Longevity Blueprint," I pivoted again, this time to a topic I'd been pondering for years: the future of humanity and work in the AI age. This became "The Day Everyone Lost Their Jobs," a deep dive into how AI is reshaping our world and our work. The process of writing this book was particularly illuminating, as I was using AI to write about AI, creating a fascinating meta-narrative that enriched my understanding of both the technology and its implications.

This project required a different approach to AI collaboration. I needed to strike a balance between leveraging AI's ability to process vast amounts of data and trends and maintaining a critical, human perspective on the social and ethical implications of widespread AI adoption. I found myself constantly questioning and refining the AI's outputs, ensuring that the book wasn't just a compilation of statistics and predictions, but a thoughtful exploration of our potential futures.

But perhaps the most surprising turn in my AI writing journey came when I was about 80% through "The Day Everyone Lost Their Jobs." On an impulse, I set out to prove to a friend (and to myself) that I could write a complete children's book, with full illustrations, in just a few hours. This challenge pushed me to explore yet another facet of AI-assisted writing—creating engaging, age-appropriate content in a highly visual format.

While it ended up taking a bit longer than anticipated—mainly due to the challenge of creating consistent characters in the illustrations—I managed to complete it in a matter of days. This experience opened my eyes to the versatility of AI in different genres and styles of writing. I learned how to craft prompts that would generate whimsical, child-friendly language and how to guide AI in creating cohesive visual narratives. It also highlighted the importance of human creativity in the process, especially when it came to infusing the story with warmth and emotional resonance that would appeal to young readers and their parents alike.

Finally, inspired by all these experiences and the potential I saw in AI-assisted writing, I began writing this book. My goal was to share how AI is democratizing the writing process, potentially turning anyone with a story to tell or knowledge to share into a super writer. I felt I had learned so much about writing with AI that I had to share it with others. Each of these projects, with their unique challenges and lessons, has contributed to my understanding of AI-assisted writing and shaped my approach to this transformative technology. This book is the culmination of that journey, designed to guide you through the exciting world of AI authorship.

I realize this anecdote might seem to contradict my earlier advice about focusing on one project at a time. However, I share it to illustrate the exciting possibilities that AI opens up and to emphasize the importance of remaining flexible and open to new ideas as you navigate this landscape. My journey taught me that while focus is crucial, especially when you're starting out, the ability to pivot and explore new territories is equally valuable in the world of AI-assisted writing. If I had had this book you are reading at my disposal back then, before starting, the journey would have been much shorter and smoother.

As of 2025, more than two years after ChatGPT burst onto the public scene, knowing how to write with AI (and use it) isn't just useful—it's becoming essential. The funny thing is, while most people now recognize that AI could transform their work, a surprising number still use it like a fancy calculator rather than the creative powerhouse it can be.

This timing matters when you're picking your topic. Take this book you're reading right now—it's hitting at the perfect moment, when most of us are still figuring out how to ride this AI wave effectively. But let's be real: five or ten years down the road, these skills might become as second-nature as googling something is today (and by then, you might ask what is googling?). We're living in that sweet spot—the golden age of AI adoption—where understanding these tools still gives you a genuine edge.

This rapid evolution of AI technology underscores the importance of considering your book's potential lifespan when choosing your topic. The book industry, like almost all industries, is poised for dramatic change. Some types of books might cease to exist as people start creating their own personalized versions. Take children's books as an example. As a parent who has read countless such books to my children, I've often been surprised by their varying quality. Many lack coherent storylines or contain only a few words per page, yet these books often become bestsellers in their market. Now, imagine a future where parents can use AI to create personalized stories for their children, featuring their child's name, incorporating their interests, and even adapting to their reading level. What happens to the traditional children's book market in such a scenario? How does this change the role of the children's book author?

And it's more than that. As you'll discover, AI can help any author create entirely new children's books inspired by previous examples. By drawing inspiration from millions of existing works, AI can now generate brilliant children's stories that combine the best elements of countless tales (I'll address copyright issues later). Picture an AI system that has analyzed almost every beloved children's book ever written, understanding what makes each story captivating, educational, and memorable. It can identify common themes, successful narrative structures, and engaging character archetypes. Then, using this vast knowledge, it can assist authors in crafting stories that resonate deeply with young readers while maintaining originality. It will then aid in creating all the necessary book graphics, from the cover to the characters.

Similarly, consider the potential impact on educational books. AI could enable the creation of textbooks that automatically update with the latest information, or adapt their content based on the student's learning style and progress. Imagine an AI system that has analyzed millions of educational materials across various subjects and grade levels, understanding effective teaching methodologies, learning patterns, and knowledge retention techniques. This AI could then assist authors in crafting educational content that's not only up-to-date but also tailored to individual learning needs. For instance, a history textbook could dynamically adjust its narrative complexity based on the reader's comprehension level, or a science book could generate interactive simulations to illustrate complex concepts.

Moreover, AI could help create supplementary materials like practice questions, case studies, and real-world applications that align perfectly with the main content. This level of personalization and adaptability could revolutionize how we approach education and lifelong learning. The role of educational authors and subject matter experts would evolve, focusing more on curating and validating AI-generated content, ensuring its accuracy and ethical presentation, while leveraging AI to create more effective, engaging, and accessible learning materials.

These are just a few examples of how AI could reshape the book industry. And yes, I am fully aware that perhaps the very notion of books could become obsolete one day (and I further discuss that in "The Day Everyone Lost their Jobs"). But for now, as an aspiring AI author, it's crucial to consider these potential shifts when choosing your topic and approach. While predicting the future is impossible, I want to provide you with all the information I can to help you make an informed decision about your project. If you're writing for personal fulfillment, choose the project you've always wanted to pursue, even if it might have a shorter shelf life in the rapidly evolving world of AI. The joy of creation and the satisfaction of completing your book are valuable in themselves, regardless of future market trends.

If you're considering entering the book business professionally, you'll need to weigh all possible outcomes of your choice carefully. Consider the time investment required not just to write the book, but to learn and master AI-assisted writing tools. Think about the skills and software you'll need to learn: will these be transferable to other projects or industries if the book market shifts dramatically? How do you envision the industry's future in both the short and long term, and how can you position your work to remain relevant and valuable?

Remember, the journey of AI-assisted writing is as much about discovering your voice and passion as it is about mastering the technology. As you embark on this exciting adventure, remain open to possibilities, be prepared to adapt, and most importantly, enjoy the process of bringing your ideas to life in ways you might never have imagined possible before. The world of AI-assisted writing is full of potential, and your unique perspective and creativity are the keys to unlocking that potential. So take that first step, choose your topic, and let's begin this incredible journey together.

With a clear direction for your book and an understanding of the AI writing landscape, you're ready to take the next step. Chapter II will introduce you to the core concepts of AI technology, equipping you with the knowledge to harness its power in your writing process.

Now, let's talk technology.

Chapter II: Learning AI

Generative AI sits at the center of the current authorship revolution. Unlike earlier automation tools that could only retrieve or reorganize existing content, generative AI creates, producing original text, images, music, and code from nothing more than a prompt. For writers, this means a single technology can handle nearly every element of a book: crafting prose, generating illustrations, even structuring an argument. The creative process, once the exclusive domain of human imagination, now has a capable collaborator.

What is Generative AI? For the purposes of this book, the technical details matter less than the practical ones. What counts is knowing how to work with it effectively: understanding its capabilities and limitations, knowing what to expect, and recognizing where it tends to go wrong. The focus here is on application, not theory. By the end of this book, you will have a clear sense of how to use generative AI to sharpen your writing and expand what you can produce as an author.

Before we begin, a word of reassurance: you do not need to be a tech person to use AI. Many people assume that working with these tools requires specialized knowledge or a background in computing. It does not. One of AI's most underappreciated qualities is how accessible it makes technology for everyone, including those who have always found it intimidating. Using AI is often more intuitive than running a Google search. The main adjustment is learning how to "talk" to it, and that turns out to be less of a technical skill than a human one. Think of it as having a capable assistant you can instruct in plain language. No code, no manuals, no learning curve beyond your first few conversations.

Let's start with a quick overview. Until recently, practical applications of AI meant one thing: machine learning. This approach builds systems that learn from data rather than from explicit instructions, improving their performance over time by identifying patterns and using them to make predictions or decisions. The more data, the better the system gets, often surpassing what any programmer could have hardcoded manually.

Picture an algorithm working through thousands of book reviews, gradually learning to distinguish praise from criticism. Or a system analyzing years of sales data to surface patterns no human analyst would spot. Machine learning excels at exactly these tasks: classification, prediction, recognition. It is very good at finding structure in large amounts of data. What it could not do, until recently, was create. These systems could analyze and predict, but they could not generate something new.

Then came the turning point. On November 30, 2022, OpenAI released ChatGPT, and generative AI became something anyone with an internet connection could use. For the first time, the ability to generate original content with AI was not limited to researchers or engineers. It was available to everyone.

Generative AI changed the nature of human-machine interaction in a fundamental way. These systems do not retrieve or reorganize existing content. They produce something new, crafting responses that are original, contextually aware, and often surprisingly nuanced. The shift from analysis to creation opened up possibilities that had no real precedent. With that context in place, let's look at how this technology actually works.

How Does Generative AI Work?

Let's take a quick look at how generative AI functions, focusing on what you actually need to know as an author. Think of it as an assistant that has processed an enormous amount of text: books, articles, websites, code, and more. During its training phase, the model learned patterns in language well enough to generate new text that follows those patterns. When you give it a prompt, it draws on that training to produce a response that fits the context. As models improve, they get better at understanding nuance, maintaining consistency, and producing content that feels coherent and purposeful.

That is really all you need to know at this stage. You do not need to understand the underlying architecture to use these tools well. The practical questions are simpler: how do you give clear instructions, how do you push back when the output misses the mark, and how do you build on what the AI produces to make it your own? That is what the rest of this book is about.

What AI Authors Should Know About AI

As a writer using AI tools, there are several important factors to be aware of.

Language Proficiency. Most AI models have historically been trained on predominantly English text, and English still tends to produce the most reliable output. That said, the gap has narrowed considerably. By 2026, leading models like GPT-5.2, Claude Opus 4.6, and Gemini 3.1 Pro handle major world languages with impressive accuracy, and multilingual performance continues to improve with each new release. Hebrew, French, Spanish, German, and other widely spoken languages are now reasonably well supported.

This does not mean you must write in English. If you prefer to work in your mother tongue or in a language better suited to your target audience, that is a perfectly reasonable choice. Just be aware that for less commonly spoken languages, the AI may still make more errors, and you will need to review its output more carefully.

Tool Variability. Not all AI tools are created equal, and this field is advancing rapidly. Today's cutting-edge tools might be obsolete tomorrow. That's why this book focuses on teaching you a versatile approach to writing with AI rather than tying you to specific technologies. While we'll use current leaders like ChatGPT and Claude to illustrate our textual points, along with other tools for visuals, the principles we discuss should remain relevant. They'll apply to future tools as long as the fundamental way this AI operates doesn't undergo a dramatic shift (and currently, there's no reason to believe it will).

By focusing on adaptable strategies rather than specific tools (though we'll exemplify them with existing tools), we're future-proofing your skills. This way, whether you're working with today's AI or tomorrow's even shinier version, you'll be well-equipped to make the most of whatever digital writing assistant comes your way.

Potential for Errors. Generative AI is only as good as its training data, which means it is not immune to mistakes. When ChatGPT first debuted, we quickly discovered its tendency to "hallucinate," a term for producing plausible-sounding but entirely fictitious information. These models often cannot simply say "I don't know" when faced with a query outside their knowledge base. Instead, they will confidently offer their best guess, even when it is completely wrong. If you ask about a locally famous footballer from your village who has never made headlines beyond the local pub, the AI might invent an entire fictional career, complete with imaginary trophies and made-up statistics.

In other cases, the AI may decline certain requests rather than fulfill them, citing copyright concerns, potential legal issues, or platform guidelines. It might refuse to reproduce song lyrics, avoid writing a harshly negative review of a specific company, or add unsolicited caveats to sensitive content. This is different from hallucination, but it can still affect your writing process if the AI steers you away from what you actually need. Understanding both tendencies, the confident mistake and the cautious refusal, is essential for working with these tools effectively.

Resource Realities. Most leading AI tools offer both free and paid tiers, and the gap between them has narrowed considerably since these tools first launched. Free versions of ChatGPT, Claude, and Gemini are now genuinely useful for writing tasks, though they still come with limitations: slower response times during peak hours, restrictions on the most powerful models, and caps on how much you can use them in a given period. For casual experimentation or occasional assistance, a free plan may be perfectly adequate.

For serious, sustained writing projects, a paid subscription is still worth considering. It typically gives you access to the most capable models, higher usage limits, and more consistent performance. At around $20 per month for most major platforms, it is a modest investment relative to what these tools can contribute to a book-length project.

Usage limits exist for a combination of reasons: managing infrastructure costs, preventing abuse, and, increasingly, managing the environmental impact of running these computationally intensive systems. AI data centers consume substantial amounts of energy, and providers are under growing pressure to use that capacity responsibly. The practical implication for you as an author is straightforward: learn to work in focused sessions, break longer projects into manageable chunks, and avoid leaving long conversations idle. These are good habits regardless of which tier you are on.

Model Size Matters. In the world of AI, the number of parameters in a model, essentially its knowledge connection points, has a significant impact on what it can do. Larger models generally handle complex tasks more smoothly, understand context with greater subtlety, and produce writing that feels more coherent and nuanced. The jump from early models to today's frontier systems is not just technical trivia: it translates into meaningfully better performance on the kinds of tasks authors actually care about.

That said, bigger is not always better for every situation. Most major AI providers now offer a tiered range of models designed for different purposes. Anthropic, for instance, offers Claude Sonnet 4.6 as a fast and capable everyday model, and Claude Opus 4.6 for more complex reasoning and extended tasks. OpenAI and Google follow similar logic with their own model families. For straightforward writing tasks, a mid-tier model will often respond faster and cost less, with results that are more than good enough. For complex, long-form projects that require sustained consistency and deeper reasoning, the flagship models earn their place. Understanding this range helps you choose the right tool for each stage of your writing process.

Ethical and Legal Considerations. As an author venturing into the realm of AI-assisted writing, it's imperative to address the complex landscape of ethical implications that come with this powerful technology. This encompasses a range of crucial issues that demand your attention and thoughtful consideration. First and foremost, you need to be acutely aware of potential biases lurking in AI outputs. These models, despite their sophistication, can inadvertently perpetuate societal (and other) prejudices embedded in their training data. Equally important is the thorough understanding and respect for copyright and other intellectual property rights. The line between inspiration and infringement can be blurry in the world of AI-generated content, and it's your responsibility to ensure you're on the right side of that line.

We'll address these copyright and other legal issues later in the book, providing you with a solid foundation to understand this critical aspect. Additionally, transparency about your AI use in writing is not just a courtesy, but increasingly an ethical imperative. As AI becomes more prevalent in creative fields, readers and the literary community have a right to know when and how AI has contributed to a work. These ethical considerations are fundamental aspects of responsible AI-assisted authorship. We'll explore these critical issues in greater depth as we progress, equipping you to navigate this ethical landscape confidently and responsibly.

Learning AI Tools

Forecasting the future of AI writing tools is a daunting task. It is a bit like trying to teach someone about internet search engines in the early 1990s. Any list of recommendations back then would have proudly featured Yahoo, Lycos, AltaVista, and WebCrawler. Had you been reading that guide just a few years later, Google would have already made most of it obsolete.

But here is the more useful observation: despite their differences, those search engines all shared the same basic logic from a user's perspective. Learning to use one generally prepared you to use the others. The same is true of AI writing tools today. The specific models will change, some will disappear, and new ones will emerge. What will not change is the underlying skill of knowing how to direct these tools effectively, how to give clear instructions, how to evaluate the output, and how to make it your own. That is what this book is really teaching you.

I don't possess a crystal ball, so predicting the exact trajectory of Generative AI tools is challenging. It's difficult to say whether the tools available in ten, five, or even one year will resemble those we use today. Nevertheless, I'm highly confident that while these tools will undoubtedly improve, their core functionality will remain largely unchanged. Barring a fundamental shift in AI technology, these tools will continue to generate content, including text for books. The underlying principle of inputting prompts and receiving AI-generated outputs is likely to persist, even as the quality and capabilities of these outputs advance.

Here's what makes this book different: I'm teaching you a method of working with AI, not just how to use today's hottest tools. Why? Because by the time you finish reading, some new AI wonder might have launched, and specific button-clicking tutorials would already be outdated. Instead, you'll learn principles and approaches that stay relevant no matter which AI assistant becomes next month's sensation. That said, I won't leave you floating in theory-land. I'll ground everything in practical, concrete examples using the tools I personally find most valuable right now for serious AI authors. You'll see exactly how I apply these methods in real writing projects, with step-by-step demonstrations you can follow along with. This way, you get the best of both worlds: timeless strategies plus hands-on experience with today's most effective AI writing assistants.

Let's begin with a concise overview of the AI author tools I recommend, categorized as primary and secondary. The primary tools are the cornerstone of your AI writing toolkit. These are predominantly textual tools that you'll leverage throughout your book-writing process, helping you generate the prose that will constitute the majority of your work. The secondary tools, on the other hand, will complement your writing by assisting with other elements: images, graphs, and any non-textual components that your primary tool might not provide. This dual approach ensures you're equipped to create a comprehensive, multi-faceted book that engages readers on multiple levels.

The primary tools dominating the generative AI landscape as of early 2026 include OpenAI's ChatGPT (featuring GPT-5.2 and the newer GPT-5.3 Codex for specialized tasks), Anthropic's Claude (Sonnet 4.6 and Opus 4.6), Google's Gemini (with Gemini 3.1 Pro as the current flagship), Meta's LLaMA, xAI's Grok, and DeepSeek. While numerous other tools exist, these have emerged as market leaders and are the ones I have experimented with most extensively.

It is worth noting that effectively harnessing these models for serious writing typically requires a paid subscription. Subscribing to multiple platforms simultaneously can add up quickly, and the practical benefit of experimenting broadly across many models is often marginal. For most authors, selecting one or two tools and learning to use them well is both more efficient and more cost-effective than chasing every new release.

Choosing an AI tool is not an all-or-nothing decision. Different models have different strengths, and many authors end up using more than one depending on the task. Some excel at sustained narrative writing, others at structured argumentation or research-heavy content. Some handle images natively within the same interface, as ChatGPT does with its built-in image generation, while others are purely text-based. Context window sizes also vary, which matters when you are working with long documents: some models can hold an entire manuscript in memory during a session, while others lose track of earlier content more quickly. Getting a sense of these differences will help you match the right tool to each stage of your writing process.

I have experimented with all of these tools over the course of about two years. Most often, ChatGPT proved to be the most effective for me. While it was not superior in every aspect, I found it to be the most versatile tool available. Gemini was the least impressive for a long time, and I stopped using it for a while, but it has since caught up considerably and today I use it roughly as often as ChatGPT. Claude is also an excellent tool, and for writing specifically it remains, in my view, the best of the three by a meaningful margin. I used it extensively to refine most paragraphs in this book.

I noticed subtle but significant differences in how these tools handle language. ChatGPT tends to rephrase writing into something slightly more technical, not consistently, but noticeably enough. Claude leans toward a more literary style, which I initially preferred, though I found this did not apply uniformly across all tasks. In earlier versions, Claude also had a tendency to lose track of longer documents in practice, even when its stated context window suggested otherwise. That limitation has largely disappeared in the more recent versions, which handle long-form work considerably more reliably.

Tokens are the fundamental units that AI models use to process text. Rather than whole words, tokens are often fragments of words. "ChatGPT" might be one token, while "unbelievable" could be split into three: "un", "believe", and "able". You do not need to count tokens yourself, but understanding the concept helps explain why some tools handle long documents better than others.

As of early 2026, context windows have expanded dramatically across all major platforms. Claude Opus 4.6 and Sonnet 4.6 both support a 200K context window as standard, with a 1 million token context window available in beta. Claude API Docs Opus 4.6 supports up to 128K output tokens, while Sonnet 4.6 supports up to 64K output tokens. Claude API Docs Gemini 3.1 Pro similarly offers a 1 million token context window. In practical terms, all three flagship models can now hold an entire novel-length manuscript in a single session.

Think of these token limits like the capacity of different containers. Some are large barrels that can hold a lot of text at once, while others are more like buckets. For a short story, most containers will do. For a full novel with all its chapters, character arcs, and accumulated context, you want the largest barrel available.

This is worth noting because it was not always the case. For much of the time I spent writing this book, Claude's context window was theoretically large but practically unreliable for very long sessions, while ChatGPT handled extended contexts more consistently. That gap has since closed. Today, for sustained book-length writing projects, all three major tools are broadly capable, and the choice between them comes down more to writing style and personal preference than to technical limitations.

For much of the time I spent writing this book, I used ChatGPT for lengthy, context-heavy sessions and Claude for refining specific sections. When one tool's session timed out, I would switch to the other. It was an effective but somewhat cumbersome workflow.

That has since changed. With Claude 4.6, the context window is large enough to hold an entire manuscript in a single session, which removes the main reason I was splitting work between tools. More importantly, Claude's Projects feature allows you to create dedicated workspaces for a book, upload reference materials, maintain consistent character details and plot elements across chapters, and preserve your writing style throughout the entire manuscript without losing context between sessions. For sustained, book-length work, this makes Claude a considerably more self-contained writing environment than it used to be.

You will need to discover your own optimal balance in using these tools. The AI landscape evolves quickly, and some details in this book may already have shifted by the time you read it. It is worth occasionally checking whether new models have emerged or whether token limits and features have changed. But even without that research, I can assure you that the current state of these tools is already more than sufficient for writing a book, and it is unlikely to get worse over time. As many have noted, the AI you are using today is the least capable AI you will ever use.

That said, none of this changes what writing actually requires. There is a learning curve to working effectively with AI, and the quality of what you produce will still depend heavily on your own skill, judgment, and creative voice. These tools are genuinely powerful, but they are not a substitute for authorship. AI can help you write a book you might not have been able to write entirely on your own. It cannot replace the thinking, the choices, and the craft that make that book worth reading.

If you simply ask an AI to write a paragraph from scratch, it will comply, but the result will rarely match what you could achieve by drafting a solid paragraph yourself and then using the AI to refine it. The real power lies in that collaboration: your ideas and voice, sharpened by the AI's capabilities. The most compelling results come from this partnership, not from outsourcing the writing entirely.

Now, a word about secondary tools. Books are often more than words. Depending on your project, you may need to create a cover, add illustrations, or include data visualizations. A children's book leans heavily on graphics, a scientific text requires diagrams and charts, and a travel guide benefits from maps and infographics. There is an entire chapter dedicated to these tools later in the book, but it is worth introducing them here since they are an integral part of AI authorship.

The market leaders in AI image generation currently include ChatGPT, which offers seamless text-to-image generation within the same platform you are already using for writing; Midjourney, which consistently produces some of the most visually striking results available; Google's Nano Banana, integrated within Gemini, which has become a serious contender with impressive quality and deep integration into the Google ecosystem; and Stable Diffusion, which offers the most flexibility for users who want to run models locally or customize outputs extensively. Each has its strengths and limitations, which we will explore in detail later.

Despite a few drawbacks, ChatGPT remains a valuable tool, especially if you are already subscribed, and it is the one I currently use for most of my book illustrations. One standout feature is its ability to edit and correct existing photos, something we will explore later.

Character consistency across multiple images used to be a significant limitation for AI image tools in general, but that has changed. Midjourney's V7 introduced Omni Reference, which allows you to maintain a consistent character across different scenes. Google's Nano Banana has supported character consistency since late 2025, and the recently released Nano

Banana 2 further improves this capability, maintaining the resemblance of up to five characters and the fidelity of up to 14 objects in a single workflow. This is an area that is evolving quickly, and the gap between tools is narrowing.

Midjourney still produces some of the most visually striking results available and remains a strong choice for high-quality artistic work. Its web interface has matured considerably since its Discord-only days, though some advanced features are still more fully developed there. But it requires a paid subscription and some investment in learning its interface, but for projects requiring a large number of consistent, high-quality illustrations, it remains a strong choice. That said, my personal preference for illustrations has shifted to Nano Banana, which combines impressive character consistency with the convenience of working within the same platform I already use for writing. If I were writing a children's book, that is where I would start.

Stable Diffusion deserves a brief mention. As an open-source model that can run locally on your own hardware, it was once appealing for users who wanted maximum control. Today, the quality offered by the mainstream tools has largely closed that gap without the technical overhead, and Stable Diffusion's spiritual successor, Flux by Black Forest Labs, is now considered the stronger open-source option if local generation matters to you.

Two other tools worth knowing about: Ideogram has carved out a clear niche as the best tool for generating accurate, readable text within images, making it particularly useful for book covers, posters, and any graphic that combines typography with visuals. Adobe Firefly, deeply integrated into Photoshop and other Creative Cloud apps, has become a serious option for authors already in the Adobe ecosystem, with the added advantage of being trained exclusively on licensed content, making it the safest choice for commercial use.

Beyond these, the AI image generation space moves fast, and new tools continue to appear. The ones covered here should meet the needs of most authors, but it is always worth keeping an eye on what is available.

Graphs and data visualizations are another area where AI has become genuinely useful, though the quality of results varies significantly depending on the tool and how precisely you supply the data.

The key insight here is that AI tools do not invent data. If you ask for a graph without providing specific numbers, the model will either make assumptions or produce inconsistent results. The more precise your input, the better your output. Providing the actual dataset, even as a simple table copied into the chat, makes a substantial difference.

As of 2026, Claude is arguably the strongest tool for this task. Its Artifacts feature renders interactive charts directly within the interface, allowing you to see, refine, and adjust visualizations in real time without any coding knowledge. ChatGPT also handles data visualization competently, particularly for quick prototypes and conversational iteration. Gemini is capable but has historically been less reliable for specific visualization tasks. Julius AI, a specialized tool built on top of Claude and ChatGPT, is worth trying if you work with data frequently and want a more dedicated interface.

The broader point is the same one that applies to all AI tools: expect some trial and error, provide clear instructions, and refine iteratively. Generating a usable graph rarely takes more than a few minutes.

Some books require references, not necessarily in the academic sense where every sentence needs a citation, but for non-fiction works that make substantive claims or draw on established research. Think of books like Atomic Habits: well-sourced, but readable.

By 2026, all major AI tools, including ChatGPT, Claude, and Gemini, offer web search and deep research modes as standard features. This means you can ask any of them to find and cite sources, and they will conduct multi-step searches, synthesize results, and produce referenced summaries. The differences between them are now more about quality and approach than availability. ChatGPT tends to cast a wide net quickly; Claude tends toward more authoritative sources but may be less specific about exact locations within a source; Gemini integrates well with Google's search infrastructure, which gives it an edge for finding recent material.

A word of caution that cannot be overstated: always verify any reference an AI provides before using it. Hallucination applies to citations just as much as to factual claims, and a confidently presented but fabricated source can cause real problems in a published book. The responsibility for accuracy remains yours.

For more specialized academic or heavily sourced work, dedicated reference management tools exist that integrate with word processors and automate citation formatting. That territory is beyond the scope of this book, but worth knowing about if your project requires it.

This chapter has introduced the main tools you will likely use as an AI author and offered a sense of how they fit together. As you experiment, you will develop a workflow that suits your needs and writing style. The key is knowing each tool's strengths, working with its limitations, and ensuring your own voice and judgment remain central to the process. In Chapter III, we turn to the skill that makes all of this work: prompt engineering.

Chapter III: Prompt Engineering

The term "prompt" is relatively new in the context of AI, but it plays a crucial role in how AI systems generate content. Historically, the word "prompt" has been used in various contexts, typically meaning a cue or stimulus that initiates a response or action. In AI, however, the concept of a "prompt" became prominent with the rise of advanced language models like OpenAI's GPT series, which transformed how we interact with AI.

If you are not already familiar with Generative AI tools, don't be intimidated. A prompt is simply a piece of text or a set of instructions given to an AI system to generate a response or complete a task. This input can range from a single word or phrase to a detailed description, guiding the AI on what kind of output is expected. In essence, a prompt serves as the starting point for the AI's response, shaping the direction and content of its output. Understanding how to craft effective prompts is key to getting the most out of AI tools, as the quality of the prompt directly influences the quality of the AI's response.

To write the previous two paragraphs, I used a prompt. I went to ChatGPT and wrote: "The term prompt is relatively new. A prompt is simply **[explain]**." ChatGPT understood my intention. I started by outlining the basic concept: explaining what a prompt is and how it functions. While I know how to explain a prompt myself, using AI allowed me to do it much quicker and with precision. After generating the initial text, I made a few adjustments and then fed it back into ChatGPT, asking it to add some historical context about the origin of prompts. Once satisfied with the result, I moved on to the next section. Eventually, when I reread this chapter, I fed this paragraph to Claude to refine it even further.

Crafting effective prompts in human-AI collaboration isn't always straightforward. It requires a combination of clarity, precision, and an understanding of how the AI interprets language to guide it toward the desired output. As AI becomes more integrated into our daily lives, mastering the skill of creating effective prompts is increasingly valuable. This ability to communicate efficiently with AI directly impacts the quality and relevance of the content it generates, making it essential for anyone using AI in their creative or professional work.

This skill, often referred to as prompt engineering, involves crafting clear and precise instructions, understanding the AI's capabilities and limitations, and refining prompts based on the AI's responses. In this chapter, you'll learn how to develop effective prompts tailored to your work as an AI author. While ChatGPT and Claude will be the primary examples, the principles discussed apply broadly to Generative AI, making them relevant across various AI tools.

The Purpose of a Prompt

A prompt is the instruction you give an AI to tell it what you want. It sounds simple, but the quality of your prompt has a direct and significant effect on the quality of what you get back. A vague prompt produces generic output. A precise, well-constructed prompt produces something that actually serves your purpose.

In the context of book writing, prompting is less about technical skill and more about clarity of thought. The more specifically you can articulate what you want, the better the AI can deliver it. This means thinking about tone, audience, length, structure, and purpose before you write your instruction, not after. When you prompt well, you are not just directing the AI, you are shaping the voice, depth, and direction of the content it produces.

Guiding the AI's Response

A prompt's primary role is to steer the AI's output, much like a skilled captain navigates a ship. A well-crafted prompt ensures the AI produces content that's both relevant and engaging. Take a mystery novel, for instance. A prompt like "Paint a picture of the foggy night when Detective Jane kicks off her investigation in the quiet town" will spark a scene that fits the genre and plot. On the flip side, a vague "Write something interesting" leaves the AI rudderless, likely resulting in generic or off-topic content.

Effective prompts provide crucial context and specificity, directing not just what the AI writes, but how it approaches the subject. For historical fiction set in Victorian times, you might use: "Bring to life the bustling London streets of the 1890s, highlighting the stark divide between rich and poor." This gives the AI a clear framework to create a vivid, historically accurate description. Remember, you don't need to spend hours perfecting your prompt—the AI can help refine it. It's all about mastering the art of asking the right questions. For example, if you want to write about Victorian times but know nothing about it, simply write "Victorian times" and the AI will complete the necessary details for you.

Prompts can also unlock new creative avenues by guiding the AI to explore specific themes or perspectives. In a sci-fi novel, a prompt like "Imagine a future where humans and robots coexist. Describe their daily interactions" encourages the AI to dig into the nuances of human-robot relationships. This can yield rich, imaginative content that sparks fresh ideas for your story, adding depth and intrigue to your narrative world.

What you need to understand here is that while AI has certain limitations—which I explore throughout this book, such as usage limits, copyright issues, and more—it does comply with your requests. It will always respond; you just need to know how to instruct it and guide it precisely where you want it to go. There is no right or wrong direction per se, only the direction you want it to follow. Let's examine some practical examples to help you understand how to write prompts that work best for you.

Practical Examples and Context

To better illustrate the purpose of a prompt, let's examine a few practical examples across different contexts:

Character Development:

Vague Prompt: "Describe a character." *Output*: A generic character description with little depth.

Specific Prompt: "Describe a young woman named Emily, who has a passion for painting and struggles with self-doubt after a recent failure at an art exhibition." *Output*: A detailed and nuanced character description that provides insight into Emily's personality and background.

Setting the Scene:

Vague Prompt: "Describe a city." *Output*: A broad and non-specific description of a city.

Specific Prompt: "Describe the vibrant, colorful streets of Rio de Janeiro during Carnival, focusing on the sounds, sights, and emotions of the festival." *Output*: A vivid and immersive description that transports the reader to Rio de Janeiro during Carnival.

Plot Development:

Vague Prompt: "Write a plot twist." *Output*: A generic plot twist that may not fit the story.

Specific Prompt: "Write a plot twist where the detective discovers that their trusted ally has been the mastermind behind the crimes all along." *Output*: A compelling and contextually relevant plot twist that adds depth and intrigue to the story.

Learning prompt engineering extends far beyond book writing and is crucial across various fields and applications. In business, for instance, crafting a prompt like "Analyze the current market trends for renewable energy and suggest three strategies for a startup to gain a competitive edge" can result in a detailed market analysis with actionable strategies tailored specifically for a renewable energy startup. In the field of education, a prompt such as "Create a lesson plan for teaching high school students about the causes and effects of the Industrial Revolution" can generate a structured and comprehensive lesson plan, complete with key points and interactive activities that enhance student engagement. The ability to create effective prompts is a versatile skill that can drive success in numerous professional contexts.

Crafting the perfect prompt often involves iterative refinement. This means starting with a basic prompt and gradually adding more detail or adjusting the wording based on the AI's responses. For example, if the AI's initial response to a prompt is too broad or misses the mark, you can refine the prompt by adding more specific instructions or focusing on different aspects. This iterative process helps hone the AI's output, aligning it with your expectations.

Understanding the purpose of a prompt is crucial for effectively leveraging AI in your writing and other projects. By providing clear, specific, and context-rich instructions, you guide the AI toward producing high-quality, relevant content. Whether you're developing characters, setting scenes, or crafting intricate plots, mastering the art of prompt engineering is essential for becoming a successful AI author. As we move forward, we'll dive deeper into the practical aspects of creating and refining prompts to unlock the full potential of AI in your creative endeavours.

Finding the Right Prompt for you

Mastering prompt engineering is a journey that rewards persistence and experimentation. While it's not as complex as learning a musical instrument or a new language, it does require dedication. It's more accessible than mastering a bicycle, but it still demands your time and effort. As you immerse yourself in the process, you'll develop an intuitive sense of the AI's capabilities and limitations. You'll learn to coax out the results you're after, though it may still take some finessing even after you've honed your skills. Despite the effort involved, AI assistance will help you craft your desired book more swiftly and effectively than ever before.

The ideal prompt varies depending on your specific task. Some books might call for a consistent prompt style throughout, while others demand different approaches at various stages. For a non-fiction work, you might need prompts that extract factual information, deliver clear explanations, and construct logical arguments. In contrast, a novel could require prompts that breathe life into characters, craft engaging dialogue, and paint vivid scenes.

As you progress, you'll discover that precision is key. The more specific and clear your prompts, the better the AI's performance. Vague instructions often lead to generic or off-base responses, while detailed, focused prompts yield more accurate and useful content. Developing this knack for crafting precise prompts is a vital skill that will sharpen with practice and experience.

Iterative Refinement and Experimentation

Remember, prompt engineering is a process of continuous improvement. Your initial attempt might not hit the mark, but don't let that discourage you. Many people who engage with AI for the first time or primarily use it may think it's not intelligent or capable enough because the results they get aren't satisfactory. This perception is often misguided. They might be using it incorrectly, such as treating it like a search engine, which it isn't (although it can often also search the web), or they don't know how to prompt it effectively, leading to poor results. It's crucial to understand that AI can't read minds. Its performance is only as good as the prompts it receives. The output quality directly correlates with how well you communicate your requirements to the AI.

Instead of giving up, view each response as a stepping stone. Refine your prompts based on what you receive—add more specifics, tweak the wording, or approach the task from a different angle until you achieve your desired result. This journey of refinement helps you understand how the AI interprets various inputs, enabling you to communicate your needs more effectively.

The iterative nature of prompt engineering means embracing a bit of trial and error. You might start with a broad concept and gradually narrow it down, introducing specific elements or rephrasing your prompts to guide the AI more precisely. Each iteration brings you closer to that perfect prompt that unlocks the content you envision.

This experimentation isn't just about finding what works. It's about uncovering new ways to harness AI's potential. As you explore different prompts, you'll discover creative possibilities you hadn't considered. This exploratory phase can be thrilling and eye-opening, revealing the diverse ways AI can enhance your writing process and spark fresh ideas for your book.

Examples of Prompts for AI Authors

So prompts are the way we currently instruct AI to perform tasks for us. Essentially, they are commands. If your command is short and unclear, the AI may struggle to understand your intentions, leading to poor results. This is why it's essential to learn how to craft prompts that effectively communicate what you want the AI to do. Now, let's dive into some concrete examples of prompts that I suggest using when writing books. However, it's important to note that every book requires different prompts. I'll elaborate on this later when I discuss the various types of books you can write and the specific approaches you should consider. That said, you can selectively pick from the examples provided here and tailor them to suit your specific needs.

Writing Enhancement Prompts

Writing Enhancement Prompts are designed to refine your manuscript, making it polished, engaging, and suitable for your intended audience. These are special instructions you give to AI to help make your writing better, like having a super-smart editor that can polish your work and make it more attractive for your readers. Whether you're crafting a novel, a children's book, or a textbook, these prompts help you fine-tune language, correct errors, and enhance readability. Additionally, they can assist you in adjusting your writing style to emulate admired authors, such as mimicking the character-building techniques of J.K. Rowling or the world-building of J.R.R. Tolkien. By using these prompts, you can also ensure that your writing is accessible to a general audience, making your work inclusive and appealing to a wide range of readers.

Examples:

Proofreading:

Example: "Proofread the following paragraph for grammar, spelling, and punctuation errors, and ensure it is accessible to a general audience."

Additional Example: "Check this chapter for any errors and ensure that the language is appropriate for middle-grade readers in a fantasy novel. Consider simplifying complex sentences for clarity."

Text Improvement:

Example: "Rewrite this paragraph to be more engaging and vivid, suitable for a fantasy novel aimed at young adults, drawing on the narrative style of J.K. Rowling."

Additional Example: "Enhance this informational text section to make it clearer and more concise for a general audience while maintaining an engaging tone. Consider adding examples that illustrate key points."

Style and Tone Adjustment:

Example: "Adjust the tone of this passage to be more whimsical and adventurous, reflecting the style of J.R.R. Tolkien in 'The Hobbit'."

Additional Example: "Transform this text into a more formal and academic tone, suitable for a university-level textbook. Ensure the style is consistent throughout the section."

Vocabulary Enhancement:

Example: "Replace simple words in this paragraph with more sophisticated vocabulary, but ensure the text remains accessible to a general audience."

Additional Example: "Simplify the vocabulary in this section to make it more suitable for a children's non-fiction book on space exploration. Add synonyms for complex words to enhance understanding."

Conciseness:

Example: "Condense this section of the thriller novel without losing the suspenseful atmosphere. Ensure it reads smoothly for a general audience."

Additional Example: "Shorten this textbook explanation while maintaining key information, making it clear and concise for high school students. Consider removing redundant phrases."

Structural Prompts

Structural Prompts help you organize and format your book, ensuring that it is easy to navigate and logically arranged. These prompts are like having a skilled editor who helps you plan and arrange your book's parts in the best possible way. They assist in generating titles, organizing chapters, and creating a cohesive flow throughout the book. Moreover, these prompts can help you structure your content in a way that is accessible to a general audience, ensuring that your work is inclusive and easy to understand for a wide range of readers.

Examples

Headline Generation:

Example: "Generate three potential chapter titles for a historical novel about the life of a famous explorer, ensuring they are engaging and accessible to a general audience."

Additional Example: "Suggest section titles for a textbook on environmental science, making them clear and intriguing for high school students. Consider using active verbs to make the titles more engaging."

Title and Subtitle Creation:

Example: "Propose five potential titles for a self-help book about overcoming anxiety, with matching subtitles that appeal to a broad, general audience."

Additional Example: "Create a catchy title and subtitle for a children's book about a young girl's adventures in a magical forest, inspired by the whimsical style of [whoever you want]. Ensure the title is easy to remember."

Chapter Breakdown:

Example: "Outline the first five chapters of a mystery novel, ensuring each chapter builds suspense and remains accessible to a general audience."

Additional Example: "Break down the content for an instructional book on creative writing, organizing it into logical chapters and subchapters. Use examples from popular writing guides to structure each chapter effectively. Include potential chapter summaries to guide the reader."

Subchapter Structuring:

Example: "Create a detailed subchapter outline for a science fiction novel, focusing on the protagonist's training in a futuristic academy, while keeping the narrative accessible to all readers."

Additional Example: "Develop a subchapter structure for a history textbook covering the events leading up to the American Revolution, ensuring each section is clear and informative for high school students. Consider adding bullet points for key events."

Section and Paragraph Organization:

Example: "Organize the following text into coherent sections and paragraphs for a non-fiction book on healthy eating habits, making it easy to read for a general audience."

Additional Example: "Restructure this chapter of a novel to improve pacing and ensure that each paragraph contributes to character

---

development, inspired by the pacing techniques of best-selling authors. Include transitions to maintain a smooth flow between paragraphs."

Idea and Plot Development Prompts

Idea and Plot Development Prompts are designed to stimulate creativity and help you develop and refine the core concepts of your book. These are like having a brainstorming buddy who can help you come up with cool story ideas, interesting plot twists, and memorable characters. Whether you're writing a novel, a children's book, or a non-fiction work, these prompts can help you explore different possibilities and ensure that your ideas are engaging and accessible to a wide audience. Additionally, you can instruct the AI to draw inspiration from the techniques of renowned authors, such as the character development of J.K. Rowling or the thematic depth of George Orwell.

Examples:

Plot Development:

Example: "Develop a plot twist for a dystopian novel where the protagonist discovers the true nature of their society. Ensure the twist is impactful and accessible to a general audience."

Additional Example: "Outline the main events of a children's book where the characters must work together to solve a mystery in their school. Draw inspiration from the adventure style of [whoever you want]. Include key turning points that build tension."

Character Development:

Example: "Create a detailed backstory for the antagonist in a fantasy novel, explaining their motivations and how they became the villain. Emulate the character-building techniques of J.K. Rowling."

Additional Example: "Develop a character arc for the protagonist in a romance novel, showing how they grow and change throughout the story. Make sure the character's journey is relatable and engaging for a general audience. Add emotional conflicts that drive the character's growth."

World-Building:

Example: "Describe the technological advancements in a futuristic society for a science fiction novel, focusing on how they impact daily life. Ensure that the world is immersive and accessible to readers of all backgrounds."

Additional Example: "Create the cultural traditions and folklore for a fantasy world in which a children's adventure story is set, drawing inspiration from the detailed world-building of J.R.R. Tolkien. Include elements that reflect the world's history and social structure."

Theme Exploration:

Example: "Explore the theme of resilience in a novel about a character who faces numerous challenges in their quest for justice. Make the theme relatable and meaningful for a broad audience."

Additional Example: Discuss the theme of friendship in a children's book where animals from different species work together to overcome obstacles. Ensure the message is clear and accessible to young readers."

Brainstorming Ideas:

Example: "Generate ten plot ideas for a horror novel set in an abandoned amusement park, with a focus on creating suspense and tension. Ensure that the concepts are accessible to a general audience."

Additional Example: "Brainstorm five possible endings for a mystery novel, each with a different resolution to the central conflict."

Data Completion and Integration Prompts

Data Completion and Integration Prompts assist in seamlessly incorporating factual information, statistics, and other specific data into your writing. These prompts are like having a knowledgeable research assistant who helps you find and include accurate information to support your writing. They help fill in gaps, ensure accuracy, and enhance your content with relevant data, making your work more informative and credible. Moreover, these prompts can guide you in presenting the data in a way that is clear and accessible to a general audience, ensuring that your book is both informative and easy to understand.

Examples:

Data Extraction:

Example: "Extract the key statistics from the following research paper and integrate them into a chapter about the impact of technology on education. Ensure the data is presented in a clear and accessible way for a general audience."

Additional Example: "Identify the most relevant data from this report on climate change and include it in a section of an environmental science textbook. Make sure the data is easy to understand for high school students. Add explanations for complex terms."

Fact-Checking:

Example: "Verify the historical accuracy of this passage describing the events of the Civil Rights Movement, ensuring that all information is correct and accessible to a general audience."

Additional Example: "Check the scientific claims made in this chapter about nutrition to ensure they are supported by current research. Present the facts in a way that is easy to understand for readers without a scientific background. Highlight any key findings."

Statistic Inclusion:

Example: "Find and include the latest statistics on the global increase in e-commerce over the past five years in this chapter about online business trends. Ensure the statistics are accessible to a general audience."

Additional Example: "Incorporate demographic data about literacy rates in different regions into this section of an educational policy book, making sure the information is clear and accessible. Provide additional context to help readers interpret the data."

Data Summarization:

Example: "Summarize the findings of a recent study on social media use among teenagers and include the summary in a chapter about digital communication. Ensure the summary is concise and understandable for a general audience."

Additional Example: "Condense the key points from a lengthy report on renewable energy sources into a concise summary for an environmental science textbook, making sure it is accessible to high school students."

Sentence Completion:

Example: "Tesla is currently one of the leading car companies in the world. Just in 2023, its gross revenue was [complete here]."

Additional Example: "The population of Tokyo, one of the largest cities in the world, was estimated to be [complete here] in 2023, reflecting its status as a global metropolis."

Critical Examination Prompts

Critical Examination Prompts are designed to thoroughly scrutinize your work, helping you identify potential issues and improve the overall quality of your writing. These prompts are like having a team of sharp-eyed editors and critics who can spot problems in your writing and suggest ways to make it better. They can find repetitive parts, smooth out your writing, catch mistakes, and give you feedback from different viewpoints. Whether you want gentle suggestions or more detailed critiques, these prompts help you polish your work to perfection. They're especially useful for making sure your book is top-notch, professional, and easy for most people to understand before you send it out or publish it.

Examples:

Redundancy Check:

Example: "Identify and remove any redundant phrases or sentences in this chapter of a non-fiction book about personal finance. Ensure the text is concise and accessible to a general audience."

Additional Example: "Review this dialogue in a novel for any repetitive language and suggest edits to make it more concise and engaging for a broad readership. Consider varying sentence structure for better flow."

Flow Examination:

Example: "Analyze the flow of this academic textbook chapter and suggest improvements to ensure that each section logically leads to the next. Make sure the content is accessible to a general audience."

Additional Example: "Evaluate the pacing of this action scene in a thriller novel and recommend changes to maintain reader engagement. Ensure the scene is exciting and easy to follow for a broad audience. Consider adding suspenseful transitions."

Error Detection:

Example: "Search this passage in a historical fiction novel for any factual inconsistencies or timeline errors. Ensure that the information is accurate and accessible to general readers."

Additional Example: "Examine this section of a children's science book for any incorrect information or misleading statements. Ensure that the content is accurate and understandable for young readers. Simplify complex concepts if needed."

Critique from a Perspective:

Example: "Critique this literary fiction manuscript as if you were a New York Times book reviewer, focusing on narrative style, character development, and thematic depth. Ensure that the critique considers accessibility for a general audience."

Additional Example: "Critique this bedtime story for children as if you were a parent reading it to a toddler, focusing on language simplicity and engagement. Ensure that the story is captivating and easy to understand for young listeners."

Clarity Check:

Example: "Evaluate this text for clarity and suggest revisions to make it easier to understand for a general audience. Ensure that the language is simple and straightforward."

Additional Example: "Check this section of a textbook for any complex terminology and suggest ways to explain it more clearly for students at a middle school level. Consider adding examples or analogies."

Iterative Improvement Prompts

Iterative Improvement Prompts guide the AI to go through multiple rounds of revision, critique, and enhancement, ensuring that your text is polished to perfection. These prompts are like having a tireless editor who keeps refining your work over and over, making it better each time. They're especially helpful when you want to make your writing as good as it can possibly be, making sure it's both high-quality and easy for most people to understand. By going through cycles of self-critique, revision, and improvement, these prompts help you create a manuscript that hits all your goals for quality, readability, and keeping your readers interested.

Examples:

Looped Critique and Revision:

Example: "Grade this paragraph on a scale from 0 to 100, then provide a critique. Revise the text based on the critique and repeat the process until the text achieves a grade of at least 95. Ensure the language is clear and accessible to a general audience."

Additional Example: "Evaluate this chapter for narrative flow, provide feedback, revise accordingly, and repeat until the chapter scores a 90 or higher for smooth transitions and reader engagement. Ensure that the chapter is engaging for a general audience. Add dialogue where appropriate to enhance character development."

Self-Critique and Improvement Loop:

Example: "Evaluate the following story for plot consistency, provide feedback, revise the story based on that feedback, and then reevaluate until it scores a 9 out of 10 or higher on plot consistency. Make sure the story is easy to follow for a general audience."

Additional Example: "Critique this essay for logical structure, revise based on the critique, and repeat until it scores a 95 or higher for coherence and clarity. Ensure the essay is accessible to a broad readership. Add examples to support key points."

Multiple Perspective Critique:

Example: "Critique this chapter from the perspectives of a literary scholar, a casual reader, and a book reviewer. Revise based on each critique, focusing on making the text accessible and engaging for a general audience."

Additional Example: "Evaluate this children's story from the viewpoints of a parent, an educator, and a child. Revise according to each perspective and ensure that the story is both educational and entertaining for young readers. Consider adding interactive elements like questions or prompts for discussion."

Content Personalization Prompts

Content Personalization Prompts are essential for tailoring your writing to meet the specific needs, interests, and preferences of different demographics. These prompts are like having a personal guide who knows your readers really well and can help you speak their language. Whether you're writing for teens, kids, professionals, or just about anyone, these prompts help you tweak your content so it's interesting, relevant, and easy to understand for your target readers. By using these prompts, you can make sure your writing really connects with your audience, keeps them hooked, and increases the chances that people will love your book.

Examples:

Adjusting for Age Groups:

Example: "Rewrite this chapter to make it more suitable for young adults, incorporating themes and language that resonate with teenage readers."

Additional Example: "Simplify this story to make it accessible to children aged 6-8, ensuring the language and content are appropriate. Consider adding interactive elements like questions or prompts for discussion."

Further Personalization: "Adapt this non-fiction text for a senior audience, using clear language, larger font suggestions, and relevant examples that connect with their life experiences."

Tailoring for Educational Levels:

Example: "Modify this explanation of quantum physics to be understandable for high school students, incorporating analogies that simplify complex concepts."

Additional Example: "Elevate the complexity of this chapter to suit a graduate-level audience, incorporating technical terms and in-depth analysis."

Further Personalization: "Revise this section to be more accessible to readers with no prior knowledge of the subject, ensuring that all terminology is clearly defined and examples are provided."

Cultural Relevance:

Example: "Adjust the cultural references in this novel to make it more relatable to a global audience, ensuring that readers from different backgrounds can connect with the story."

Additional Example: "Incorporate culturally diverse examples in this textbook to ensure it is inclusive and relevant to students from various ethnic backgrounds."

Further Personalization: "Rewrite this section of the story to reflect the traditions and customs of a specific culture, making the narrative more authentic and engaging for that audience."

Gender (or other) Sensitivity:

Example: "Revise this dialogue to be more gender-neutral, ensuring that it is inclusive and respectful of all readers."

Additional Example: "Adapt this character's development to avoid gender stereotypes, creating a more balanced and realistic portrayal."

Further Personalization: "Ensure that the language in this children's book is gender-inclusive, avoiding any biases and promoting equality."

Market-Specific Content:

Example: "Tailor this content for the U.S. market, incorporating references and examples that are relevant to American readers."

Additional Example: "Modify this chapter to appeal to the European market, considering cultural differences and regional interests."

Further Personalization: "Adjust this content to suit an international market, avoiding region-specific jargon and ensuring that the themes are universally relatable."

These are merely examples to spark your creativity. You can do anything you can imagine. I often use brackets (**[]**) and instruct the AI to complete the information whenever it sees them, as I showed you before. If I receive a result I'm not satisfied with, I'll adjust it with percentages, like: "**make it 10% more sarcastic**" or "**15% funnier.**" For instance, you might ask the AI to "**add 20% more detail to the description,**" "**make the tone 25% more (or less) formal,**" or "**increase the emotional intensity by 30%.**" You could also try "**adding 10% more humor to the dialogue,**" "increasing the pacing by 20%," or "making the language 10% simpler." Other options include "adding 5% more suspense to the narrative," "decreasing the level of complexity by 15%," or "making the conclusion 20% more impactful." These tweaks allow you to fine-tune the AI's responses to better match your vision.

As you gain experience, you'll develop your own method for writing and collaborating with AI. This process may vary slightly for each book you write. While creating this book, I wrote most of the text directly. Although I used AI extensively, it wasn't the primary author. While ChatGPT or Claude could technically write a book about AI-assisted writing, they wouldn't be able to convey my personal experiences and insights. My goal was to share a human perspective on writing AI-assisted books, not a computer's interpretation of the process. Still, throughout the writing process, I consistently utilized AI tools. Without them, this book would have taken at least a year to complete, and the result would have been markedly different.

The key takeaway is that I want you to focus more on how you communicate with AI and refine your requests rather than memorizing specific prompts. Your prompts will evolve over time, and you'll need to adjust them to suit your specific goals for each project. Remember, the art of writing with AI lies in the dialogue between human creativity and AI. It's about leveraging AI's capabilities to enhance your own ideas and writing style, not replacing your unique voice. As you embark on your AI-assisted writing journey, stay flexible, experiment with different approaches, and always keep your ultimate vision for your book at the forefront of your process.

In this chapter, we've explored the art of prompt engineering, emphasizing the importance of crafting clear, specific prompts to guide AI in producing content that aligns with your vision. This iterative process of refining prompts not only enhances the quality of AI-generated content but also opens up new creative possibilities, making it a vital skill for anyone working with AI. As we move forward to the next chapter, we'll dive into the writing process itself - where the real work begins. From creating that first file to tackling the challenges of writing and rewriting, this chapter will guide you through the foundational steps of bringing your book to life.

Chapter IV: Writing and Rewriting

The first step in writing a book is creating a dedicated file. While this might seem basic (and believe me, I'm an expert at stating the obvious), it's an important starting point. Open your preferred text editor—whether it's Word, Google Docs, or another—and give the file a meaningful name, like "MyBook," "BookProject," or "MyMasterpieceInProgress." If you already have a title, you can simply use that. Choose a name that inspires you, one that brings a sense of purpose and excitement every time you see it. Place the file on your desktop, where it will serve as a constant reminder of the literary journey you've begun.

Now comes the moment of truth: opening the file. While it might seem trivial, this simple action is your gateway to authorship. As you face that blank page, don't let it daunt you; instead, see it as a canvas, ready to embrace your unique voice. Begin by boldly writing your book's title at the top, and just below, type your name with pride as the author. Even if the title changes later, let it stand as a beacon before you. Each time you open this file, let these words rekindle your purpose and reignite your motivation. Trust me, there will be days when you'll need that extra spark.

Next, focus on the skeleton of your book: the chapters. The approach here will vary depending on the type of book you're writing. For a children's story or a novel, you might not need a detailed outline at this stage. However, for an informational book like this one, I found it incredibly useful to sketch out a rough chapter list. I had a clear sense of the key topics I wanted to explore, but I also understood that this structure would naturally evolve as I wrote. The value of this initial outline lies in its ability to organize your thoughts and provide a roadmap for your writing journey, all while remaining adaptable.

At this stage, you might be tempted to use AI tools to help construct your chapters, and while that can be beneficial later on, **I advise resisting that urge for now**. It's crucial to take this first creative step on your own. Relying on AI too early can box you into its suggestions, potentially steering you away from the original vision you had in mind. Embrace the opportunity to shape your book's direction before you turn to AI for further development.

You have titles for chapters? Great! Now it is time to enlist your AI assistant for further assistance. Open a fresh conversation within the chosen AI, and share everything you have so far—let it know that you're writing a book and provide details on the topic. Insert the chapter list you've created and any additional information you can offer. Then, ask the AI to evaluate your chapters: Are they well-structured? Do they cover the necessary topics comprehensively? Is there anything missing, or could the sequence be improved? You can also ask the AI for suggestions on how to enhance each chapter or to identify any gaps in the content. This will help you refine your outline and ensure that your chapters are both complete and compelling.

Don't be tempted to let the AI do all the work for you at this stage. While your AI assistant might suggest diving straight into writing, resist that urge. As I mentioned earlier, that's not the best approach when writing with AI. Instead, focus on refining the chapters. Revisit the AI's suggestions and challenge its proposals—ask it to reorganize, refine, or expand on certain aspects until the structure aligns perfectly with your vision. Keep iterating until you're confident that your chapter outline is a solid foundation.

When using two models like Claude and ChatGPT, you can compare their suggestions to see which one resonates more with your ideas. You might find that one model is better at organizing content, while the other excels in providing creative angles. You can also combine the strengths of both by merging their suggestions, refining them into a cohesive outline that works best for your project. Additionally, you can ask one model to critique or improve on what the other has proposed, giving you a more polished result.

What's most important here is the flow of the book. Ask yourself what you want to include in each chapter, and whether the next chapter naturally follows from the one before it. While you may tweak the structure later—perhaps merging chapters or adding new ones—the overall flow shouldn't change dramatically, as this could disrupt your workflow and affect the quality of your book. Take the time you need to ensure the flow is right, making sure each chapter naturally leads into the next.

Once you've finalized your chapter titles, assign each one its own page. This is where the page break function in your word processor becomes invaluable. If you're not familiar with how to use this tool, here's a quick guide for common word processors (but honestly, you can simply ask ChatGPT or Claude how to do it):

- In **Microsoft Word**: Place your cursor where you want the new page to begin. Then, go to the "Insert" tab at the top of the screen and click on "Page Break." Alternatively, you can use the keyboard shortcut: press Ctrl + Enter (on Windows) or Command + Enter (on Mac).

- In **Google Docs**: Put your cursor where you want the break. Then click "Insert" in the top menu, scroll down to "Break," and select "Page break." The keyboard shortcut is the same as in Word: Ctrl + Enter (Windows) or Command + Enter (Mac).

- In **most other text editors**, you can typically find the page break option under the "Insert" or "Format" menu. But as I said, if you have trouble locating it, don't hesitate to ask your AI assistant for guidance. A quick query should point you in the right direction.

This simple organizational trick will prove invaluable as you progress. There will be times when you feel stuck on one chapter but bursting with ideas for another. Having separate pages lets you easily jump between sections, following your inspiration wherever it leads. I used this technique while writing the very words you're reading now. When I felt lost in one lengthy chapter, I simply shifted to another where my thoughts flowed more freely.

Now that you've laid this groundwork, you're ready to begin the thrilling (and sometimes daunting) process of actual writing. Remember, the path to a finished book is rarely a straight line. It's a winding road of writing, rewriting, and yes, rewriting again. Embrace this process. Each revision is an opportunity to refine your ideas, sharpen your prose, and ultimately create a book that truly resonates with your readers.

As you embark on this journey, remember that every great author started exactly where you are now: with a blank page and a burning desire to share their story. The difference between an aspiring writer and a published author often comes down to perseverance and a willingness to refine their work. So, take a deep breath, open that file, and start pouring your thoughts onto the page. Your unique perspective deserves to be shared, and with dedication and the techniques we'll explore in this book, you have everything you need to create something extraordinary.

Now, it's important to differentiate between the various types of books you might be writing. The process of creating a children's book is vastly different from writing a novel, and both differ even more from crafting an informative book like this one. At this point, you'll need to choose the path that aligns with the type of book you wish to write. Of course, you're welcome to read through all the sections—it might even spark new ideas for your writing. However, I recommend focusing first on the category that best fits your project.

Let's break it down into more general categories:

Children's Books: If you're writing for young readers, your focus will be on crafting engaging, simple stories with vivid characters and colorful imagery. The writing process often involves thinking visually. Your chapters might be very short, or you may choose not to use traditional chapters at all, instead opting for a more fluid narrative structure that suits the attention spans and developmental stages of children.

Novels: For those venturing into fiction for older readers, you'll dive deep into character development, plot structure, and world-building. The writing process may involve extensive outlining, creating character sketches, and multiple drafts to refine your narrative arc. Chapters in novels serve both as organizational tools and as a means to build dramatic tension, often ending on cliffhangers or emotional peaks to keep readers engaged.

Short Story Anthologies: For those compiling an anthology or a collection of short stories, the writing process involves curating individual pieces that fit together thematically or stylistically. Each story should stand on its own, yet contribute to the overall narrative or thematic arc of the collection. The AI can help with maintaining thematic coherence and suggesting ways to transition between stories, but the challenge lies in balancing diversity with unity within the collection.

Informative or Non-Fiction Books: Writing an informative or non-fiction book, like this one, involves research, organizing complex information into digestible chunks, and finding ways to engage readers with potentially dry material. Your chapters will likely be structured with subheadings, bullet points, and summaries to make the content accessible and easy to follow. Subcategories in this genre might include **Self-Help**, **How-To/Instructional Guides**, and **Cookbooks**, each with its own unique demands on structure and tone. The AI can assist with organizing information and generating clear, concise content, but it's important to guide the AI with a strong understanding of your subject matter and audience.

Memoirs or Autobiographies: These personal narratives require a delicate balance of storytelling and factual recounting. The writing process might involve journaling, interviews with family and friends, and deep personal reflection. Chapters often revolve around significant life events or recurring themes, providing a coherent narrative thread through your experiences. The AI can help with organizing these narratives and refining the language, but the authenticity and emotional truth of the story are paramount and must come from you.

Comic Books. Writing a graphic novel or comic book involves a unique blend of narrative and visual storytelling. The process includes close collaboration with artists or developing your own artistic skills. Chapters, or scenes, are dictated more by the visual flow and pacing rather than traditional text structures. The AI can assist with dialogue and pacing but remember that the synergy between text and imagery is crucial in this format, requiring a more integrated approach.

Travel Books or Guides. Travel books and guides require a mix of narrative storytelling and practical advice. The writing process might involve firsthand exploration, research, and organizing content by destination, theme, or journey stages. The AI can assist in generating vivid descriptions and organizing logistical information, but the authenticity and personal insight of the travel experience are what will truly engage your readers.

Yes, this list is not exhaustive. Other forms of books, like poetry collections, also have their unique processes. However, I've chosen to focus on these particular categories because they are some of the most common and widely pursued forms of writing. Additionally, the writing processes and AI assistance strategies discussed here are highly applicable and beneficial to these types of books.

As you'll see, each type of book demands a distinct approach, and the AI tools and techniques we'll explore can be tailored to suit each one. As you continue reading, keep your specific book type in mind. When I offer examples or suggestions, think about how you can adapt them to your particular book project.

Remember, despite the differences in process, all books share a common foundation: they begin with your unique idea and voice. Whether you're crafting a whimsical tale for children or a comprehensive guide for adults, it's your personal touch that will make your book stand out. Equally important is learning how to "talk" to your AI. Once you master this skill, you won't need to constantly refer back to instructions on prompt engineering; you'll intuitively adapt your prompts to suit each new project. However, this ability could take time to develop, so be patient with yourself as you refine your approach.

In the following sections, I'll provide detailed guidance for each type of book. As I mentioned, while you can jump directly to the section that best fits your project, I encourage you to read through the entire guide on your first pass. Exploring different genres can often spark innovative approaches and fresh ideas. Perhaps the type of book you originally had in mind will be trickier than you anticipated, or maybe something else will excite you even more.

Children's Books

Writing children's books is perhaps the easiest (or quickest) type of book you can produce with AI technology. This isn't to say that children's books are simple to write or in any way inferior to other genres—far from it. Many of the children's books I loved reading to my own children hold a special place in my heart. However, using AI to create a children's book can significantly streamline the process, perhaps even more dramatically than with other types of books. Keep in mind that these books will also require illustrations, which we touched on earlier, but you can learn more about in a chapter dedicated to that topic. Here, I'll walk you through a general approach to writing children's books with AI, which you can adapt to suit your specific project.

First, you need to decide what your book will be about. This ties back to your general outline of your desired chapters which you did earlier.

You have several options. To exemplify, you can create:

- A personal children's book as a gift, which would require you to draft the stories you want to intertwine

- A book about one character or multiple characters

- A book about objects or concepts

- A book teaching a specific lesson or moral

- An adventure story set in a fantastical world

- A day-in-the-life story about a child or animal

At this point, you might feel the urge to lean on your AI assistant for direction. However, as I suggested earlier, take a moment to brainstorm on your own first. That is, unless your goal is to pump out a book quickly as a means to try making a fast buck. If speed is your priority and you're aiming to churn out content at lightning pace, then, by all means, let the AI take the reins right from the start (but be mindful of potential copyright issues; more on that later).

But let's pause for a moment to talk about that mindset. Writing solely for profit? Sure, there are authors who make a decent living, and some even strike gold. But if you're starting out with the notion that you'll whip up a children's book and get rich overnight, well, let's just say that's not exactly a winning strategy. The idea that children's books are an easy route to riches is a bit like believing you can win the lottery on your first ticket—possible, but not likely, and certainly not something to bank on. Writing, especially writing well, is a craft, not a get-rich-quick scheme.

While I may have mentioned that children's books can be relatively easier to write with AI, don't mistake that for thinking writing a successful children's book is easy. Crafting a story that truly resonates with young readers, stands out in a crowded market, and endures over time is a challenge that requires creativity, insight, and genuine effort—AI can assist, but it can't replace those essential ingredients. There are so many factors to weigh when discussing a book's success, from understanding your audience and creating engaging content to publishing. Without a strategic approach, even the most efficiently produced book can miss the mark.

Getting back to choosing what your book will be about—do you have some ideas? Great! Now you can use your AI assistant to refine them. You can experiment with different angles, ask for feedback, or even generate new ideas. And, of course, you're not limited to the categories I've offered above; feel free to explore other options and let your creativity guide you. The AI can help you brainstorm and develop your concepts, making this early stage both exciting and productive.

Once you've nailed down your concept, head back over to your preferred AI tool, like ChatGPT or Claude, and start digging into your book idea. Fire up a new chat and, if the platform allows it, give it a name that'll make it easy to find later (often by simply changing the chat name, simple as that). Now, start dumping your thoughts about your specific idea. Think of the AI as your super-smart assistant, and just let your ideas flow freely. Tell it exactly what you're after. Oh, and don't forget to mention who you're writing for—like the age group you're aiming at.

Let's say your idea is to write a book that will help children understand that each of us needs to live in a specific climate environment to thrive. Some people prefer warm places, while others like cold weather. Some enjoy humidity, while others can't stand it. But we all grow up in a specific environment that we can't change until we're adults (or if our caregivers move us somewhere). Now, let's say we want to convey this message through an analogy rather than stating it directly.

A prompt could be something like this: "I want to create an entire children's book on the concept of different flowers that need different kinds of climate. They live around the world in different climates, but they are unhappy, although their lives are good there. In the end they can only grow (be happy) in an area where the climate fits them (like cactus = sun; flowers that don't need sun = cold weather; etc.) Let's begin by outlining the main story. I want to have four different flowers." In Claude, it would look like this:

Simple enough. It took me less than a minute to write. But I started with ChatGPT on this one. In response, ChatGPT produced this:

Outline for Children's Book: "The Perfect Place for Flowers"

Main Characters:

1. **Sunny the Cactus**

   o **Climate Needed**: Hot, dry, sunny

   o **Current Location**: Rainforest

   o **Personality**: Energetic and optimistic despite feeling out of place

   o **Current Issue**: Too much moisture and lack of direct sunlight

2. **Lily the Water Lily**

   o **Climate Needed**: Warm, aquatic environments

   o **Current Location**: Desert

   o **Personality**: Calm and reflective but struggles with the heat

   o **Current Issue**: Lack of water and too much direct sunlight

3. **Rosie the Rose**

   o **Climate Needed**: Moderate climate with plenty of sunlight

   o **Current Location**: Arctic tundra

   o **Personality**: Romantic and delicate, but finds it hard to bloom

   o **Current Issue**: Extreme cold and lack of sunlight

4. **Frosty the Edelweiss**

   o **Climate Needed**: Cool, mountainous regions

   o **Current Location**: Tropical island

   o **Personality**: Strong and resilient, but wilting in the heat

- o **Current Issue**: Too warm and humid

Story Outline:

1. **Introduction**

   - o Introduce each flower in their current, unsuitable environment.

   - o Show their initial attempts to adapt to their climates and the challenges they face.

   - o Describe their daily lives and highlight their struggles despite having good lives in other aspects.

2. **The Great Adventure**

   - o Each flower learns about the climates they truly need to thrive.

   - o They decide to embark on a journey to find the perfect climate for themselves.

   - o Along the way, they meet each other and form a friendship, sharing their stories and dreams.

3. **Facing Challenges**

   - o The journey is filled with obstacles such as harsh weather, long distances, and the search for directions.

   - o Each flower's unique traits help the group overcome these challenges.

   - o They learn valuable lessons about patience, resilience, and helping one another.

4. **Finding the Perfect Place**

   - o One by one, they discover the environments best suited for them.

   - o Sunny the Cactus finds a sunny desert, Lily the Water Lily finds a calm pond, Rosie the Rose finds a beautiful garden with moderate weather, and Frosty the Edelweiss finds a cool, mountainous region.

- o They each plant themselves in their perfect spots and start to thrive.

5. **Conclusion**

   - o The flowers flourish in their new environments, becoming the best versions of themselves.

   - o They visit each other occasionally, celebrating their newfound happiness and growth.

   - o The story ends with a message about the importance of being in the right environment for personal growth and happiness.

This isn't bad, I thought to myself. But it can be much better. And here's an important point—it's almost never perfect on the first try, just like most things in life. So keep at it. Let the AI know what's not quite right and how it can improve. Don't hesitate to point out what needs work. The more specific you are with your feedback, the better the results you'll get. Remember, refining your ideas is a process, and with each adjustment, you'll get closer to what you're aiming for.

I wrote back to the AI: "You don't understand. This is an analogy of people who are living in cities with good/bad conditions; but their problem is that they either need a lot of sun or they don't."

ChatGPT refined it:

Outline for Children's Book: "The Perfect Place for Flowers"

Main Characters:

1. *Sunny the Sunflower*

   - o *Climate Needed*: Lots of sunlight, warm temperatures

   - o *Current Location*: Cloudy, rainy city

   - o *Personality*: Energetic and optimistic but feels lethargic without sunlight

   - o *Current Issue*: Lack of sufficient sunlight and warmth

2. *Lily the Shade Lily*

- o *Climate Needed*: Cool, shaded areas with minimal direct sunlight

- o *Current Location*: Hot, sunny beach town

- o *Personality*: Calm and reflective but struggles with excessive heat and light

- o *Current Issue*: Too much direct sunlight and heat

3. *Rosie the Rose*

- o *Climate Needed*: Moderate climate with a balance of sun and shade

- o *Current Location*: Harsh, desert environment

- o *Personality*: Romantic and delicate, but finds it hard to thrive in extreme conditions

- o *Current Issue*: Extreme heat and dryness

4. *Frosty the Edelweiss*

- o *Climate Needed*: Cool, mountainous regions

- o *Current Location*: Tropical, humid city

- o *Personality*: Strong and resilient, but wilting in the heat and humidity

- o *Current Issue*: Too warm and humid

Story Outline:

1. *Introduction*

- o Introduce each flower in their current, unsuitable environment.

- o Show their initial attempts to adapt to their climates and the challenges they face.

- o Describe their daily lives and highlight their struggles despite having good lives in other aspects.

---

2. *The Great Realization*

- o Each flower reflects on their discontent and realizes that their environments are not suitable for their needs.

- o They decide to seek out environments that match their climatic needs for true happiness.

3. *The Journey*

- o The flowers embark on a journey to find their perfect climates, meeting each other along the way.

- o They form a friendship, sharing their dreams and the climates they need to thrive.

- o Together, they face various challenges and help each other along the way.

4. *Finding the Perfect Place*

- o One by one, they discover the environments best suited for them.

- o Sunny the Sunflower finds a sunny, warm field; Lily the Shade Lily finds a cool, shaded forest; Rosie the Rose finds a temperate garden with balanced sun and shade; Frosty the Edelweiss finds a cool, mountainous region.

- o They each settle in their perfect spots and begin to flourish.

5. *Conclusion*

- o The flowers thrive in their new environments, becoming the best versions of themselves.

- o They visit each other occasionally, celebrating their newfound happiness and growth.

- o The story ends with a message about the importance of being in the right environment for personal happiness and well-being.

From this point, I began fine-tuning the story through an iterative process with the AI. I requested specific changes, such as including a cactus character. I also asked for title suggestions to improve the book's appeal.

Once I was satisfied with the basic concept, I instructed ChatGPT to follow the steps it had previously outlined for creating a children's book:

1. Detailed Storyboarding

2. Character Development

3. Illustrations

4. Rhymes and Pacing

5. Moral and Educational Aspects

By working through these stages with the AI, I was able to develop a more comprehensive and engaging story. My prompt to the AI was:

"Follow each of the steps closely. Begin with 1. Each time you do it - when you finish, give yourself a grade. Then, continue to remake that part until you get a 95 percent score. Then, move to the next one and do the same. Until all is done. Then reread everything, and grade the entire project."

The AI followed these instructions meticulously, working through each step and evaluating its performance. It continued refining each section until it achieved at least a 95 percent score before moving on to the next step (for now, let's set aside the philosophical and practical questions of how it grades itself and how anyone might grade such work). After completing all the steps, it reviewed and assessed the entire project to ensure it met the high standards set throughout the process.

The resulting book was decent, but not perfect. So I provided further instructions to improve specific aspects. My next prompt to the AI was:

"I want the story to be longer. I want each a page where they are in their current place (where they are unhappy), but objectively, everything is good where they are except for the weather. So, if Sunny, for example, is in a rainy place, although he is currently in a vibrant market with food and people smiles, he can't find joy because the sun is not out... Finally. I want them to realize that they need their own weather when they fly to visit each other - and then they discover how much they simple in that place (because of the weather), So redo the scenes with the entire text." After this additional instruction, we achieved the final version of the story:

Title: Bloom Where You're Planted

Cover Page:

- *Illustration:* A diverse garden with Sunny the Sunflower, Lily the Shade Lily, Rosie the Rose, and Spike the Cactus all smiling and blooming in their respective environments.

Page 1: Introduction

> *Text:* "In a world full of flowers, each one unique, four friends were searching for the perfect retreat. Sunny the Sunflower, Lily the Shade Lily, Rosie the Rose, and Spike the Cactus, silly."

> *Illustration:* The four flowers are introduced with cheerful faces, standing together in a garden, each looking distinct yet harmonious.

Page 2: Sunny the Sunflower

> *Text:* "In a city grey and cold, lived Sunny, bright and bold. He missed the sun's warm embrace, to bring a smile to his face."

> *Illustration:* Sunny the Sunflower in a gloomy, rainy city, looking out of a window with a sad expression, with small elements like a bird or butterfly trying to cheer him up. The buildings are tall and grey, with raindrops visible on the window.

Page 3: Sunny's Current Place

> *Text:* "The market was vibrant, full of food and cheer, People smiled and laughed, spreading joy and good cheer. Yet Sunny felt gloomy, his leaves hanging low, for without the sun's warmth, his happiness wouldn't grow."

> *Illustration:* A bustling market scene with colorful stalls, happy people, and Sunny looking sad despite the lively environment. There are fruits, vegetables, and flowers for sale, and people chatting and smiling, but Sunny stands in the middle, looking droopy.

Page 4: Lily the Shade Lily

Text: "In a beach town hot and bright, Lily sought the shade's delight. The sun's glare was much too strong, in the cool, she felt she belonged."

Illustration: Lily the Shade Lily under a small umbrella on a sunny beach, looking uncomfortable with the bright sun, waves, and beachgoers around. The beach is golden, with clear blue waters and people playing and sunbathing, but Lily looks wilted under her tiny umbrella.

Page 5: Lily's Current Place

Text: "The beach was stunning, with waves that danced, People played and swam, and children pranced. But Lily felt weary, her petals dry, the sun was too harsh, she longed for the sky."

Illustration: A beautiful beach scene with people enjoying the water and sand, while Lily looks wilted under the intense sunlight. There are sandcastles, surfers, and seagulls, adding to the lively atmosphere.

Page 6: Rosie the Rose

Text: "In a desert dry and wide, Rosie struggled to survive. She dreamt of gardens fair and cool, where blooming was the golden rule."

Illustration: Rosie the Rose in a harsh desert environment with dry, cracked ground, looking parched and drooping, with a mirage in the background. The sun is blazing, and there are cacti and rocks scattered around.

Page 7: Rosie's Current Place

Text: "The desert had its beauty, with dunes so grand, Adventurers explored the endless sand. But Rosie felt parched, her petals so dry, she wished for a garden where cool breezes sigh."

Illustration: A scenic desert with adventurers and camels, while Rosie struggles to stay hydrated. The sand dunes are high, and the sky is clear, emphasizing the heat.

Page 8: Spike the Cactus

Text: "In a rainforest lush and green, Spike felt out of place, unseen. He missed the desert's dry, warm days, where sunshine filled his joyful gaze."

Illustration: Spike the Cactus in a dense, humid rainforest with droplets of water on his spines, surrounded by rainforest animals like monkeys and parrots. The vegetation is thick, and the air looks humid.

Page 9: Spike's Current Place

Text: "The rainforest was vibrant, with colors so bright, Animals thrived, and trees reached great height. But Spike felt overwhelmed, with moisture all around, He missed the dry warmth of his desert ground."

Illustration: A lush rainforest with vibrant animals and plants, while Spike looks uncomfortable with the humidity. There are colorful birds, frogs, and large leaves all around.

Page 10: The Great Realization

Text: "Each flower knew they needed more, A place to thrive, a place to soar. They set out on a journey grand, to find the perfect, blooming land."

Illustration: The four flowers setting out on their journey, with a map in hand, and a bright horizon ahead. They look determined and hopeful, with a road stretching ahead of them.

Page 11: Visiting Sunny

Text: "They visited Sunny in the city grey, Saw the vibrant market where he couldn't stay. The sun was what he missed the most, in a warm field, he'd thrive and boast."

Illustration: The friends visiting Sunny in the market, seeing the lively scene but noticing Sunny's sadness without the sun. They look concerned, realizing the environment isn't right for Sunny.

Page 12: Visiting Lily

Text: "Next, they went to Lily's sunny shore, Where the heat was harsh, and she longed for more. A cool, shaded forest was where she'd bloom, away from the sun's relentless boom."

Illustration: The friends visiting Lily on the beach, enjoying the scenery but seeing Lily's discomfort in the harsh sun. They try to offer shade, understanding her need for a cooler place.

Page 13: Visiting Rosie

Text: "Then to the desert, they travelled afar, to see Rosie struggle under the sun's harsh star. A temperate garden, with sun and shade, was where Rosie's happiness could be made."

Illustration: The friends visiting Rosie in the desert, witnessing her struggle to stay hydrated and thrive. They offer water, realizing she needs a more balanced climate.

Page 14: Visiting Spike

Text: "Finally, they went to Spike's rainforest home, Where the humidity made him feel alone. A hot, dry desert was where he'd belong, where he'd grow tall and strong."

Illustration: The friends visiting Spike in the rainforest, noticing his discomfort with the moisture. They try to dry him off, understanding his need for a dry environment.

Page 15: Finding the Perfect Place

Text: "One by one, they found their spots, Places that matched their needs and thoughts. Sunny in a field so wide, with sunshine pouring from the sky."

Illustration: Sunny in a wide, sunny field, standing tall and happy with fully spread petals.

Text: "Lily in a forest cool, where shady spots made her feel full. No more harsh sun, no need to flee, In the shade, she felt so free."

Illustration: Lily in a cool, shaded forest, looking relaxed and content under the trees.

Text: "Rosie in a garden bright, With balanced sun and shade just right. She bloomed with colors rich and grand, In her perfect, temperate land."

Illustration: Rosie in a beautiful garden with balanced sunlight, blooming vibrantly among other flowers.

Text: "Spike returned to desert dry, where sunny days and warm winds lie. He stood so tall, his spines so strong, In the place where he belonged."

Illustration: Spike in a hot, dry desert, looking strong and content under the bright sun.

Page 16: Friends Reunite

Text: "The friends would visit, share their cheer, Support each other, year by year. In their perfect spots, they'd stay, Blooming brightly every day."

Illustration: The four flowers visiting each other in their perfect environments, sharing smiles and stories. They look joyous and healthy in their respective climates.

Page 17: Conclusion

Text: "So find your place, where you can grow, where happiness will surely show. With friends to help and guide your way, you'll bloom and thrive, come what may."

Illustration: All four flowers in a circle, smiling and holding hands (or leaves), with a rainbow in the background, symbolizing happiness and growth.

The next phase was illustration creation, which comes with its own set of challenges. Chief among these is maintaining character consistency throughout the book, a topic I will cover in detail in the relevant chapter. It's crucial that these characters maintain a consistent appearance from page to page, otherwise it misses out on the point a bit. To illustrate this process, let me share an example of how the first few pages of the book might look:

In a city gray and cold, lived Sunny, bright and bold.

He missed the sun's warm embrace, to bring a smile to his face

In a beach town hot and briht, Lily sought the shade's delight.

The sun's glare was much too strong, in the cool, she felt she belonged.

In a desert dry and wide, Rosie struggled to survive.

She dreamt of gardens fair and cool, where blooming was the golden ruleood day

IN A RAINFOREST LUSH AND GREEN, SPIKE FELT OUT OF PLACE, UNSEEN.

HE MISSED THE DESERT'S DRY, WARM DAYS, WHERE SUNSHINE FILLED HIS JOYFUL GAZE.

The illustration process was surprisingly straightforward. It took me just a few minutes to create the basic illustrations (more on that later). The initial results were so good that I didn't feel the need to make any changes. Afterward, I used Canva, another software, to insert the text and enhance the graphical elements, which only added a few more minutes to the process. Of course, you can use different software or apps if you prefer, and I suspect this process will become even easier as you gain experience.

The real challenge lies in maintaining character consistency throughout the book. This used to be one of the more demanding aspects of AI-assisted illustration, but the landscape has shifted considerably. Tools like Midjourney, Nano Banana, and others now offer character consistency features that were not available even a year ago. The gap between tools on this specific issue is narrowing quickly. Some trial and error is still involved, and I will cover this in more detail later, but it is a solvable problem and should not weigh heavily on your decision about whether to pursue AI illustration.

This process outlines the basic approach to writing a children's book with AI assistance. Keep in mind that this is just one example; the possibilities are almost endless. The more detailed and specific the information you provide to the AI, the more refined and tailored your results will be. I'll emphasize this throughout the book, but it's crucial to understand that AI should be viewed as an exceptionally capable assistant. In this role, it functions as:

- An extremely talented writer

- A highly skilled illustrator

- A meticulous editor

- A creative graphic designer

- An innovative brainstorming partner

All these capabilities are at your fingertips, available at minimal cost. The real skill lies in learning to collaborate effectively with these AI tools, harnessing their potential to bring your creative vision to life. For instance, you can use AI to:

1. Generate story ideas based on themes or keywords you provide.

2. Develop character descriptions and personalities.

3. Create multiple plot outlines for you to choose from.

4. Write rhyming text for poetry-style children's books.

5. Suggest age-appropriate vocabulary for your target audience.

6. Generate ideas for illustrations that match your story.

7. Edit and refine your text for clarity and engagement.

As you continue to work with AI tools, you'll develop a workflow that suits your style. You might find that you prefer to write the initial draft yourself and use AI for editing and refinement. Or you might like to start with AI-generated ideas and then shape them with your personal touch. There's no one-size-fits-all approach. The key is to experiment, learn, and most importantly, have fun with the process. After all, if you're enjoying the creation of your children's book, that joy will shine through in the final product, delighting young readers and their parents alike.

A final word about creating a children's book: As I mentioned at the beginning, these are relatively easier to produce, especially when compared to the more complex process of writing novels. However, this ease shouldn't be the main factor guiding your decision unless your primary goal is to experiment with the concept of writing with AI. In that case, starting with a children's book can be a good choice, though it will teach you little about crafting more intricate texts. Also, keep in mind that if your book includes illustrations, you may need to dive a bit deeper into the world of AI-generated imagery, which differs somewhat from AI writing. The choice is yours—just be aware of these differences from the outset.

Novels

Let's dive into the exhilarating challenge of writing a novel with AI. Unlike the more straightforward task of crafting a children's book or the structured approach of non-fiction, novel writing is a complex, immersive experience. It's a journey full of twists, turns, and deep dives into character, plot, and world-building. But fear not - your AI assistant is here to walk alongside you through every stage of this creative endeavor.

Writing a novel is a marathon, not a sprint. Even with AI, it demands time, effort, and a reservoir of creativity. But here's the beauty of it: AI can transform this arduous process into something not only manageable but also deeply rewarding. Imagine having a collaborator who's always ready to brainstorm, who never tires of refining your prose, and who can help keep your story's momentum alive. Whether you're wrestling with a tricky plot point or searching for the perfect line of dialogue, your AI assistant stands ready to help, making the entire journey of novel writing not just possible, but exhilarating. Let me first walk you through how you can use AI as your writing partner.

Brainstorming and Outlining. Gone are the days of staring at a blank page, willing inspiration to strike. Now, you can start by simply sharing your initial ideas with your AI—no matter how vague. Perhaps you envision a detective navigating the neon-lit streets of a futuristic city. Share that with your AI, and watch as it generates potential plot lines, intriguing character sketches, and fresh sci-fi concepts. These ideas aren't just suggestions; they're the sparks that can ignite your creativity, serving as the foundation upon which you'll build your unique narrative. Let the AI's input fuel your imagination, transforming a rough concept into a fully-fledged story.

Character Creation. Crafting believable, three-dimensional characters is the heart of any novel, and this is where your AI becomes an invaluable tool in your creative process. Think of it as your personal character development workshop. Start with a basic idea and let the AI help you breathe life into them. It can flesh out their backstory, uncover their quirks, reveal their deepest fears, and explore their dreams. Curious about how your artist would react when confronted with a long-lost painting that holds painful memories? Ask your AI to role-play the scene. You might be surprised at the unexpected twists and insights that emerge, sparking new ideas and deepening your character's complexity.

World-Building. For fantasy or sci-fi writers, world-building can be one of the most daunting aspects of the craft. But with your AI by your side, it becomes an exhilarating adventure. Think of your AI as a tireless research assistant and idea generator all in one. Need to flesh out the politics of your dragon-ruled kingdom or the technology driving your space opera? Your AI can help develop everything from the intricate dynamics of interstellar trade to the subtleties of a magic system. It can even conjure up the names of alien species or the lore of ancient civilizations. With the AI's help, the process of creating a rich, immersive world becomes not just manageable, but endlessly inspiring.

Drafting. This is where the rubber meets the road. As you begin writing, think of your AI as an always-available writing buddy. Stuck on a scene? Describe what you're trying to achieve, and let the AI offer suggestions to move the story forward. You can even ask it to generate a rough draft of a chapter based on your outline, giving you a solid foundation to build on. From there, you can rewrite and infuse the draft with your personal style, turning those initial ideas into something uniquely your own. The AI isn't just a tool; it's a partner in your creative process, ready to help you shape your story every step of the way.

Research on the Fly. Need to know about lock-picking techniques for your heist novel? Or the daily routines of a 12th-century monk? Your AI can quickly supply the information you need, saving you hours of digging through research. However, as mentioned, while the AI can give you a solid starting point, it's crucial to fact-check important details using reliable sources to ensure accuracy in your writing. It's also particularly useful when filling in minor details that add depth and authenticity to your story, such as the name of a specific tool used in a particular era or the typical weather patterns in a certain region during a specific month.

Editing and Revising. Once you have a draft, your AI transitions into the role of your first reader and editor. It can help identify plot holes, inconsistencies in character behavior, or pacing issues that might disrupt the flow of your story. Need more vivid descriptions for a key scene? Or perhaps you're looking to vary your sentence structure for smoother reading? Your AI can provide suggestions to elevate your writing, making the revision process more efficient and effective. It's like having a sharp-eyed editor on call, ready to help you refine your work until it shines.

Feedback and Iteration. Leverage your AI to analyze your draft for critical elements like character arcs, narrative tension, and adherence to genre conventions. Its feedback can serve as a valuable guide, highlighting areas that might need refinement. Whether it's suggesting ways to deepen a character's journey or ensuring your plot maintains the right level of suspense, the AI's insights can help you polish your novel to a professional standard, ensuring it's ready to captivate readers.

Now, imagine how AI can transform the daunting task of writing a novel into something remarkably more manageable. Let's consider a scenario: You've decided to write a story featuring four characters—two women and two men (acknowledging the binary simplification)—living in a bustling city. These characters don't know each other, but their lives intersect on one fateful day. You want the AI to help you flesh out these characters, develop their individual plots, and ultimately converge their stories.

First, you might ask the AI to create detailed backstories for each character, shaping their personalities, motivations, and the circumstances leading up to that pivotal day. Next, you'd have the AI weave together their separate plots, carefully constructing the moment when all four characters cross paths. But you don't stop there—you want the story to be told from each character's perspective, making it essentially four intertwined narratives. To add complexity, you instruct the AI to introduce subtle variations in each character's version of events, reflecting the subjective nature of their experiences while keeping the overarching plot consistent.

Finally, you'll define the length of the story and provide all the necessary details to guide the AI as it writes. What might have been a monumental task on your own becomes a collaborative effort with AI, allowing you to focus on refining the narrative's nuances while the AI handles the heavy lifting of plot development and structure.

Now that we've explored how AI can assist in each stage of the novel-writing process, let's look at how these elements come together in practice.

Imagine applying these AI-assisted techniques to a specific novel concept. This will help illustrate how AI can transform the daunting task of writing a complex narrative into a more manageable, yet still creative, process.

I turned to Claude and provided a brief description of the story I had in mind. Instead of asking for the story itself, I requested that Claude create a prompt to guide the AI in developing the narrative. Here's what he came up with:

"Create a novel with the following specifications:

1. Setting: A contemporary urban environment.

2. Characters: Develop four distinct characters:

    o   Two females and two males

    o   All living in the same city

    o   Initially strangers to each other

    o   Provide detailed backgrounds, personalities, and daily routines for each

3. Plot Structure:

    o   Craft individual storylines for each character

    o   All storylines converge on a single, pivotal day

    o   Decide on a specific moment or event where all four characters encounter each other

4. Narrative Perspective:

    o   Divide the story into four parts, one for each character

    o   Each part should tell the events of the pivotal day from that character's perspective

    o   While the core events remain consistent, include subtle variations in how each character perceives and recounts the day's events, reflecting their unique personalities and biases

5. Writing Style:

- o Adapt the writing style to suit each character's voice and personality

- o Maintain a consistent overall tone throughout the novel

6. Length and Structure:

   - o Aim for a total word count of approximately 80,000 words

   - o Divide this evenly among the four character perspectives

   - o Each character's section should have a clear beginning, middle, and end, while also fitting into the overall narrative arc

7. Themes:

   - o Explore themes of chance encounters, subjective reality, and the interconnectedness of urban life

   - o Weave these themes throughout each character's storyline

8. Consistency and Variation:

   - o Ensure that the objective events of the pivotal day remain consistent across all four accounts

   - o Include subtle differences in each character's interpretation of these events

9. Resolution:

   - o Provide a satisfying conclusion that ties together all four perspectives

   - o Show how the encounter affects each character's life moving forward

Please generate a detailed outline for this novel, including character profiles, individual plot arcs, and a description of the pivotal encounter. Then, proceed to write the first chapter from each character's perspective."

By focusing on crafting the prompt rather than jumping straight into the story, I set the stage for a more refined and tailored narrative creation process. This approach allows for greater control over the direction and details of the story, ensuring that when I'm ready for the AI to generate the full narrative, it aligns closely with my vision.

I then switched to ChatGPT, as it offered more tokens for longer outputs, and it quickly began developing the story. The outcome was quite lengthy, so I'll only share the beginning here:

Novel Outline: "Urban Convergence"

Setting

- *City:* Metropolis, a bustling contemporary urban environment characterized by skyscrapers, diverse neighborhoods, and vibrant street life.

Characters

1. *Emma Reyes*

   - *Background:* A 29-year-old graphic designer originally from a small town. Moved to Metropolis for better career opportunities.

   - *Personality:* Creative, introverted, meticulous. Values personal space but enjoys people-watching and drawing inspiration from her surroundings.

   - *Daily Routine:* Works from a co-working space, spends evenings sketching in cafes, enjoys morning runs in the park.

2. *Liam Patel*

   - *Background:* A 35-year-old corporate lawyer with a demanding job. Born and raised in Metropolis.

   - *Personality:* Ambitious, pragmatic, and somewhat aloof. Struggles with work-life balance but is deeply loyal to friends and family.

   - *Daily Routine:* Long hours at the office, frequent business lunches, and unwinds by playing squash at a local club.

3. *Olivia Chen*

   o *Background:* A 27-year-old journalist working for a local newspaper. Recently returned to Metropolis after studying abroad.

   o *Personality:* Curious, energetic, and sociable. Passionate about uncovering the truth and telling people's stories.

   o *Daily Routine:* Chases stories across the city, attends press conferences, and enjoys late-night writing sessions at home.

4. *Noah Martinez*

   o *Background:* A 31-year-old barista and aspiring musician. Grew up in a nearby suburb and moved to Metropolis to pursue his dreams.

   o *Personality:* Friendly, optimistic, and slightly scatterbrained. Balances work and his passion for music, often playing gigs at local bars.

   o *Daily Routine:* Works at a trendy coffee shop, practices guitar in the afternoons, and performs at night.

Plot Structure

Part 1: Emma's Story

- *Beginning:* Emma starts her day with a morning run in the park, feeling a sense of anticipation for a client meeting about a big project.

- *Middle:* The meeting goes well, and she spends the afternoon sketching at her favorite cafe. She notices a tense interaction between Liam and a colleague.

- *End:* While heading home, she witnesses a street performer (Noah) and feels inspired. Later, she gets caught in a sudden downpour, leading to an unexpected encounter at a coffee shop.

Part 2: Liam's Story

- *Beginning:* Liam wakes up early, preparing for a crucial court case. He feels the pressure mounting as he heads to work.

- *Middle:* He deals with a difficult client and an argument with his colleague. During lunch, he spots Olivia interviewing someone and feels a strange sense of recognition.

- *End:* After a long day, he heads to the squash club, but a sudden change of plans leads him to the same coffee shop where Emma is sheltering from the rain.

Part 3: Olivia's Story

- *Beginning:* Olivia starts her day chasing a lead on a corruption story. Her investigative work takes her across the city.

- *Middle:* She conducts interviews, including a tense one with Liam's client, and gathers evidence. She sees Emma sketching in a cafe and thinks it would make an interesting human interest piece.

- *End:* As the day concludes, she rushes to meet a source but gets caught in the rain, leading her to seek refuge in the same coffee shop where Emma and Liam are.

Part 4: Noah's Story

- *Beginning:* Noah's day begins at the coffee shop where he works. He juggles making drinks and promoting his band's gig for the night.

- *Middle:* He performs an impromptu set in the park during his break, catching Emma's attention. Later, he spots Liam during his shift and strikes up a conversation.

- *End:* After his shift, he heads to the coffee shop to meet friends but finds himself stuck there due to the rain, joining the impromptu gathering with Emma, Liam, and Olivia.

Pivotal Encounter

- *Event:* A sudden downpour forces all four characters into the same coffee shop, creating an impromptu gathering. They share their stories, realizing the interconnectedness of their lives and the city they live in.

Themes

- *Chance Encounters:* Highlighting how random meetings can significantly impact lives.

- *Subjective Reality:* Each character's unique perspective on the same events.

- *Interconnectedness:* The invisible threads that connect individuals in an urban environment.

Resolution

- *Conclusion:* The encounter leaves a lasting impact on each character. Emma gains new inspiration for her art, Liam reevaluates his work-life balance, Olivia finds a new story angle, and Noah's music reaches a wider audience.

First Chapters

Emma's Chapter

Chapter 1: Emma's Perspective

Emma tightened her laces and adjusted her earbuds, ready to lose herself in the rhythm of her morning run. The park was her sanctuary, a place where the noise of the city faded into the background. She set off, her feet pounding the familiar path, her mind already drifting to the sketches she would work on later.

The client meeting had been on her mind all week. Landing this project could mean a significant step forward in her freelance career. She arrived at the co-working space with a mix of nerves and excitement, her portfolio clutched tightly under her arm.

The meeting went better than expected. The clients were enthusiastic about her designs, and Emma left the office with a spring in her step. She decided to treat herself to a latte at her favorite cafe. Settling into her usual spot by the window, she pulled out her sketchbook and began to draw the bustling scene outside.

Her attention was drawn to a well-dressed man at a nearby table, his face tight with frustration as he argued with someone over the phone. Emma found herself sketching his profile, capturing the tension in his posture. She wondered what his story was.

The afternoon drifted by, and Emma lost herself in her work. It wasn't until the sky darkened and raindrops began to patter against the window that she realized how late it had gotten. She packed up her things and headed for the subway, but the downpour turned into a deluge.

Ducking into a nearby coffee shop, she shook the rain from her coat and looked around for a seat. The place was packed with others seeking shelter. She spotted a familiar face - the man from the cafe. He was deep in conversation with a woman holding a notepad. As she approached the counter to order a drink, she heard a guitar strum and turned to see a street performer setting up near the door.

Emma took a seat, feeling an odd sense of anticipation. The rain had brought them all here, to this moment. She pulled out her sketchbook once more, capturing the scene as it unfolded around her, unaware of how this chance encounter would weave their lives together in unexpected ways.

Liam's Chapter

Chapter 1: Liam's Perspective

Liam Patel awoke to the sound of his alarm blaring, the start of another gruelling day. He rolled out of bed, his mind already racing through the day's agenda. The court case today was critical, and the pressure weighed heavily on his shoulders.

He arrived at the office early, immersing himself in preparation. His colleague, Mark, approached with more bad news about the case. An argument ensued, escalating quickly as both men's tempers flared. Liam stormed out, needing a break from the suffocating atmosphere.

Lunch was a rushed affair at a nearby bistro. As he ate, he noticed a young woman interviewing a man at the next table. She seemed familiar, her face sparking a vague recognition. He shrugged it off, focusing on his notes for the afternoon session.

The rest of the day passed in a blur of legal jargon and courtroom drama. By the time he left the courthouse, the sky had darkened ominously. He planned to blow off steam with a game of squash, but as he reached the club, the heavens opened, and a torrential rain began to fall.

Cursing his luck, he sought refuge in the nearest coffee shop. The place was packed, but he managed to find a seat. As he sipped his coffee, he spotted the woman from lunch, now talking to a barista who was tuning a guitar.

Liam felt a strange sense of calm amidst the chaos. The rain continued to pour, but inside, the atmosphere was warm and inviting. He glanced around, catching the eye of a woman sketching in the corner. They exchanged a brief, knowing smile, as if acknowledging the serendipity of the moment.

He settled back in his chair, allowing himself to relax for the first time that day. Little did he know, this unplanned encounter would lead to connections that would challenge his tightly controlled life and open him up to new possibilities.

Olivia's Chapter

Chapter 1: Olivia's Perspective

Olivia Chen woke up with a jolt, her alarm blaring in the early morning light. She quickly dressed and grabbed her camera and notepad, ready for a day of chasing stories. Today's agenda was packed, and she thrived on the adrenaline rush.

Her first stop was a rundown neighbourhood where she was following a lead on a corruption scandal. She interviewed several residents, each story adding another layer to her article. Her next stop was a bustling cafe to meet with a source. As she sipped her coffee, she noticed a man at a nearby table, his expression a mix of frustration and exhaustion.

The interview went well, and Olivia felt a surge of excitement. This story could be big. She spent the afternoon piecing together the information, her fingers flying across the keyboard. She paused only to take note of a young artist sketching by the window. The scene struck her as poignant, a quiet moment of creativity amidst the city's chaos.

As the day wore on, Olivia realized she was running late for a meeting with another source. She dashed out of the office, only to be caught in a sudden downpour. She ducked into a nearby coffee shop, shaking off the rain and looking around for a place to sit.

The shop was crowded, but she managed to find a spot near a man she recognized from earlier in the day. He was deep in conversation with a barista who was setting up a guitar. The artist from the cafe was also there, sketching intently.

Olivia felt a sense of curiosity and anticipation. These chance encounters were the lifeblood of her work, the threads that wove her stories together. She pulled out her notepad, ready to capture whatever came next, unaware of how this rainy evening would intertwine her fate with those around her.

Noah's Chapter

Chapter 1: Noah's Perspective

Noah Martinez started his day early, the hum of the coffee shops a comforting backdrop to his morning routine. He loved his job, but his true passion was music. Between brewing lattes and serving pastries, he dreamed of making it big with his band.

During his break, he grabbed his guitar and headed to the park. The fresh air and open space inspired him, and he played a few tunes, drawing a small crowd. Among them was a woman who seemed particularly engrossed in his music. He smiled at her, feeling a spark of connection.

Back at the coffee shop, the day flew by. He served a steady stream of customers, including a harried lawyer and a journalist who seemed to be everywhere. He chatted briefly with both, enjoying the brief moments of human connection in his busy day.

As evening approached, the sky darkened, and a heavy rain began to fall. The coffee shop filled with people seeking shelter, and Noah set up his guitar near the door, ready to play a few songs to lighten the mood.

He noticed familiar faces in the crowd - the woman from the park, the lawyer, and the journalist. They all seemed drawn to the warmth of the shop, their presence creating a sense of community amidst the storm.

Noah strummed his guitar, the music weaving through the conversations and bringing a smile to his face. He felt a sense of belonging, as if the city itself had conspired to bring them all together. This rainy evening, he realized, was more than just a coincidence. It was a moment of connection, a reminder of the power of chance encounters in the vast urban landscape.

Okay, let's be clear: this is simply an example, and merely a beginning. I didn't actually write anything, and **I don't recommend doing so without significant personal input**. While AI is an incredible tool for writing, it still needs you as an author, as someone who brings forth the ideas. Remember, your AI is a tool, not a replacement for your creativity. The soul of your story—its unique voice, its emotional core—that comes from you. Use AI to enhance your writing process, to push your creativity further, but always keep your hand on the wheel.

So, don't rely solely on AI. You can use it initially to understand and learn how this process works, but not for your actual project. The result might be okay, but not great. What you need to do is first use AI as a smart assistant, one that can help you brainstorm your story. Play around with ideas. Ask it to suggest titles and subtitles. Explore potential storylines. Consider plot twists. Outline chapters.

But then, return to your file and start writing. Begin by writing freely about the aspects of the story you're most passionate about. For parts you're unsure of, refer back to the tips in the prompt engineering chapter. Ask the AI to complete or rephrase sections as needed. Remember, you can write with grammatical mistakes; it won't significantly impact the AI's understanding. The important thing is that the AI will be somewhat confined to what you actually want to write about. From there, it can flourish and help you become the AI author you aspire to be.

I would start by writing as much of the novel as I can on my own, leaving the parts where I want AI assistance for later. At the very least, you should develop a well-outlined storyline and construct your characters (with the help of AI if needed) before allowing the AI to assist with writing. Don't rely on it to draft entire chapters - it tends to struggle with that. Instead, let the AI fill in specific sections, provide examples, or enhance your text by improving the writing or articulation.

AI can be an incredible tool to elevate a poorly written story into something quite good, but only if you instruct it properly. Remember, writing a novel is more like a marathon than a sprint. It will take time, and if you aim for a quality outcome, you'll need to invest significant effort into the writing process yourself. The AI is here to assist, not to replace the essential work that only you can do.

Short Story Anthologies

Writing a short story anthology with AI assistance offers a unique blend of creativity and efficiency. Unlike the more sprawling, complex narrative of a novel, short stories provide a contained space where ideas can be explored in depth without the need for extensive development. This makes them particularly well-suited to collaboration with AI tools, which often excel at generating and refining shorter texts.

One of the first steps in creating a successful anthology is to decide on a unifying theme or concept that ties all the stories together. Whether your stories are linked by a common setting, a central theme, or recurring characters, this overarching framework will guide the creation of each individual piece. AI can be incredibly helpful at this stage, offering a range of ideas and potential themes based on your initial input. For example, if your anthology revolves around the concept of fate, you could ask the AI to generate different scenarios where chance encounters alter the course of your characters' lives. These AI-generated ideas can serve as a springboard, helping you brainstorm and flesh out the individual stories.

Character development is another crucial aspect of short story writing. Even though each story is brief, the characters still need to be fully realized and compelling. Here, AI can assist in creating rich backstories, defining personalities, and even suggesting dialogue that feels authentic. Since short stories often hinge on the depth and relatability of their characters, AI's ability to generate nuanced character details can be particularly useful. Additionally, because these are shorter texts, AI can more effectively manage character consistency and development across the anthology.

Plotting each story is where AI can really shine. Short stories often rely on a tight, well-constructed narrative arc, and AI can help you outline these arcs efficiently. Whether you're working on a twist ending, a subtle emotional journey, or a straightforward plot, AI can suggest various directions the story could take. This allows you to experiment with different ideas without getting bogged down in the process, which is particularly useful in an anthology where each story needs to stand out while also contributing to the collection's overall theme.

Short stories, by their nature, are generally easier to manage than a full novel, both for the writer and for AI tools. This is because AI is currently more adept at handling shorter texts, where it can focus on creating tight, coherent narratives without losing track of the details. As you work through your anthology, you'll find that the AI's ability to quickly generate, refine, and revise text can make the process smoother and more efficient. You can also use AI to ensure each story maintains its own distinct voice while fitting seamlessly into the larger collection.

Once your stories are drafted, the revision process begins. This is where AI can play a critical role, helping you identify and correct any inconsistencies, tighten the pacing, and enhance the overall quality of the writing. Since short stories need to be concise and impactful, the AI's feedback can be invaluable in ensuring every word serves a purpose. You might ask the AI to suggest edits that improve the flow or to point out sections where the story could be sharpened. The goal is to refine each piece until it's as strong as possible, both on its own and as part of the anthology.

Finally, as you assemble the anthology, consider the order of the stories. The sequence can significantly affect how readers experience the collection, and AI can help you explore different arrangements to find the most effective one. Whether you want to group stories by theme, tone, or narrative progression, AI can provide insights and suggestions that might not be immediately obvious.

Informative or Non-Fiction Books

When I first encountered the incredible potential of AI, I was immediately drawn to the idea of writing informative books. My mind was overflowing with concepts, and although I was eager to pen them all, I found myself particularly attracted to creating informative works on topics that captivate me. These weren't going to be the academic pieces I'd produced in the past, but rather books aimed at the general public—though not novels. I had several accomplished authors in mind as inspiration, and their influence helped shape my approach to structuring these books.

One of the most exciting aspects of writing informative or non-fiction books is the variety of formats available, including self-help books, how-to or instructional guides, and even cookbooks. Each of these formats presents unique opportunities for using AI to enhance the writing process while also ensuring the final product is engaging, informative, and tailored to its intended audience.

But what I've mainly come to believe is that AI authors have a distinct advantage when writing about subjects they thoroughly understand. Your passion for the topic doesn't just fuel your commitment to the project; it also enables you to elevate the text to new heights, adding layers of insight and nuance that might otherwise be missed. Let me share a personal example. My areas of expertise include intellectual property and copyright law, which I both teach and actively research. I've even published a book on the subject a few years ago, so I'm intimately familiar with the intricacies of these fields.

Now, consider the stark difference between an expert and a novice using AI to write an informative book, even if it's intended for a general audience. Your AI "superpowers" are significantly more potent when you're well-versed in the subject matter. It's comparable to me attempting to write about brain surgery—a field far removed from my realm of expertise. While it's true that AI might possess more raw information about both copyright law and brain surgery than either respective expert, it's crucial to remember that AI is ultimately a tool. To produce high-quality work, this tool must be wielded skillfully and judiciously.

This principle applies across various types of informative books. Whether you're writing a self-help book aimed at personal development, a how-to guide designed to teach a specific skill, or a cookbook filled with culinary delights, your knowledge and passion are what will make your book stand out. For instance, a self-help book benefits immensely from the author's authentic experiences and insights, while a cookbook thrives on the author's understanding of flavor profiles, cooking techniques, and cultural nuances.

Therefore, if you lack substantial knowledge in a particular field—be it copyright law, brain surgery, or any other specialized area—I'd strongly advise against writing about it. The final product is unlikely to meet the standards you're aiming for, and it may lack the depth and authenticity that comes from genuine expertise. Similarly, if you're writing a cookbook without a solid foundation in culinary arts, the recipes may fall flat, and the guidance might not resonate with readers who are looking for expert advice.

Instead, I recommend choosing a subject you know intimately. You don't need a Ph.D. to be an authority—your daily job, a long-term hobby, or even years of dedicated gym training can provide enough expertise to write compellingly about a topic. The key is bringing your unique perspective and knowledge to the table, using it to guide the AI effectively. Always remember, the AI won't do the heavy lifting for you—it's your insights and understanding that will truly make the book shine.

While AI is undoubtedly powerful and versatile, without personal knowledge of a subject, you'll find it challenging to verify its accuracy. As I mentioned earlier, AI can make mistakes (often referred to as hallucinations), which you need to be able to identify and correct. In my field, for instance, I can instantly spot and rectify errors in copyright law, often using AI to assist with the corrections. However, I would be at a loss trying to catch mistakes in an explanation of brain surgery procedures, or in a recipe that requires a delicate balance of ingredients.

It's also worth noting that your expertise allows you to ask the right questions and prompt the AI in ways that can lead to more insightful and nuanced content. You'll be able to challenge the AI's outputs, request clarifications on complex points, and ensure that the information presented is not just accurate but also relevant and valuable to your target audience.

Moreover, your knowledge of the field will help you structure your book in a logical and engaging way. You'll have a better understanding of what information is essential, what common misconceptions need to be addressed, and what recent developments or controversies should be included. This insider perspective is something that AI alone, no matter how advanced, cannot replicate.

Now, let's explore the practical aspects. How do we write our informative or non-fiction book, whether it's a self-help guide, an instructional manual, or a cookbook? What are the steps we need to take, from conceptualization to the final draft? In the following sections, we'll break down this process, offering tips and strategies to help you leverage your expertise and use AI tools effectively to create a compelling and informative book.

Outline the Book

This isn't just like any other book. It requires in-depth thinking and structuring. You're about to pour your knowledge into a book, and that requires preparation. As I mentioned throughout this book (sorry to repeat that), you can't just tell the AI, "Write me my book on X." It can, but as I mentioned earlier, it will be a terrible and incredibly short book. You need to use AI all along the way, from the thinking process to the structuring of the book, into the writing, and throughout the entire process.

So first, decide on your topic. You can get help from the AI if you're struggling, but I suggest you pick the topic yourself. Surely there is something you want to write about that stirs your passion and speaks to your core interests. Whether you're writing a self-help book aimed at improving mental health, a how-to guide on mastering a craft, or a cookbook showcasing your favorite recipes, start with a topic that resonates with you.

Then you can go to your AI and tell it what you want to do. Keep it simple, but also tell it not to write anything yet. Remember, it's like your highly skilled assistant that will do (almost) anything for you. Treat it like that. I remind you to tag that conversation so that you can get back to it with ease when you wish.

For example, a prompt could be: "I am beginning a book project on the future of labor in the context of AI advancements. I'd like your help to brainstorm ideas, structure the content, and develop a clear outline. Please assist me in identifying key themes, potential chapter topics, and any important questions that should be addressed. Additionally, suggest ways to organize the material to ensure it's engaging and informative for my target audience."

You can also do it shorter. As I said, if you treat it like an assistant you can ask to do things for you, then the learning curve gets much easier. For instance, you might start with something like: "I'm writing a book about AI and work. Help me brainstorm the main topics I should cover." Personally, as mentioned, I would begin by brainstorming myself, as I find the AI might box me into one direction which will limit my own creativity. But this is also a viable way if you desire it.

Remember, the goal is to start a dialogue with the AI. You can always expand and refine your requests as you go, just like you would when working with a human assistant. The key is to leverage the AI's capabilities while guiding it with your expertise and vision for the book.

For example, this is how ChatGPT responded when I used the aforementioned prompt:

Book Project: The Future of Labor in the Age of AI

Key Themes

1. **The Evolution of Labor**: A Historical perspective on how technology has transformed labor.

2. **AI and Automation**: How AI is different from previous technological advancements.

3. **The Future of Jobs**: Which jobs will thrive, evolve, or disappear?

4. **Skills and Education**: What skills will be necessary in an AI-driven world?

5. **Economic Implications**: The impact of AI on income inequality, job displacement, and economic growth.

6. **Ethics and AI in the Workplace**: Ethical considerations in AI-driven labor markets.

7. **Policy and Regulation**: Government and corporate responses to AI in the workplace.

8. **Human-AI Collaboration**: How humans and AI can work together in the future.

9. **Global Perspectives**: How AI will affect labor markets differently across the world.

10. **Case Studies**: Real-world examples of AI transforming industries.

11. **The Future of Work-Life Balance**: How AI might reshape our approach to work.

Potential Chapter Topics

1. **Introduction: The Changing Landscape of Labor**

- o   Overview of the current state of labor.

- o   Historical context: From the Industrial Revolution to the Digital Age.

- o   Introduction to AI and its potential impacts on the workforce.

2. **Chapter 1: A Historical Overview of Labor and Technology**

- o   Technological revolutions and their impacts on labor.

- o   Lessons from past transitions: Agricultural to industrial, industrial to digital.

3. **Chapter 2: Understanding AI and Automation**

- o   What is AI? Definitions and key concepts.

- o   How AI is different from previous technological advancements.

- o   Types of AI and their potential applications in the workforce.

4. **Chapter 3: The Future of Jobs**

- o   Which industries and professions are most at risk?

- o   Jobs that will emerge in the AI-driven economy.

- o   The role of creativity, empathy, and human-centric roles.

5. **Chapter 4: Education and Skills in an AI World**

- o   Skills needed for the future: STEM vs. soft skills.

- o   The future of education: Lifelong learning and continuous reskilling.

- o   How educational institutions need to evolve to meet future demands.

6. **Chapter 5: Economic Implications of AI on Labor**

- o   Job displacement vs. job creation.

o AI's impact on income inequality and wealth distribution.

o Economic growth and productivity in an AI economy.

7. **Chapter 6: Ethical Considerations in AI and Labor**

   o Ethical dilemmas in automation and AI decision-making.

   o Privacy, surveillance, and worker rights.

   o Bias in AI: Ensuring fairness and equity.

8. **Chapter 7: Policy and Regulation in an AI-driven Labor Market**

   o The role of governments in regulating AI and protecting workers.

   o Corporate responsibility and the future of employment law.

   o Universal Basic Income (UBI) and other economic safety nets.

9. **Chapter 8: Human-AI Collaboration**

   o Models of human-AI collaboration in various industries.

   o Redefining productivity and efficiency with AI.

   o The potential for AI to enhance human creativity and decision-making.

10. **Chapter 9: Global Perspectives on AI and Labor**

    o How AI will impact labor in developing vs. developed countries.

    o Cultural differences in the adoption of AI in the workplace.

    o International policies and their global implications.

11. **Chapter 10: Case Studies of AI in the Workforce**

    o AI in manufacturing, healthcare, finance, and other key sectors.

o Success stories and failures in AI-driven labor transitions.

o Lessons learned from early adopters of AI technology.

12. **Chapter 11: The Future of Work-Life Balance**

o AI's potential to reduce the working week.

o Remote work, gig economy, and the role of AI in flexible work arrangements.

o Balancing productivity with personal fulfillment in an AI-dominated world.

13. **Conclusion: The Future of Labor**

o Summarizing key insights and lessons.

o The role of individuals, businesses, and governments in shaping the future of work.

o Final thoughts on the long-term implications of AI on labor.

For me, that is too early. You might be tempted to follow this path (as I initially did to experiment) and even instruct the AI to write chapters step by step. You can specify a desired page count (though it may not adhere strictly, especially for longer works) and request adjustments. Eventually, text will appear on your screen. While it may resemble a book, I assure you it won't be a good one. It will likely contain numerous errors, redundancies, and occasionally nonsensical passages. Most parts will lack engagement.

I understand the allure of this approach, but I advise against it and I'll repeat this constantly throughout this book. Instead, first focus on outlining your chapters and ideas. At this stage, you can explore different writing strategies. For this particular book you're reading, I chose to write mostly independently. Having authored several AI-assisted books, I'm familiar with the creative process, including its dos and don'ts. AI is unlikely to offer superior suggestions on writing these types of books given my experience. It can help me consider overlooked aspects, thereby refining my methods, but I want the book's core to stem from my personal experience.

Once you've done that initial groundwork, the next step is to brainstorm your chapters. Consider what key topics each chapter will cover and roughly estimate the number of chapters and subchapters you'll need, remembering that this structure can be adjusted later. As you plan, think about your desired book length—are you aiming for a concise 100-page guide or a more comprehensive 300-page exploration? This preliminary outlining will provide a valuable roadmap for your writing process, helping you organize your thoughts and maintain a clear direction as you progress into the actual content creation.

You can modify this later. Writing, even with AI assistance, is inherently dynamic. However, a general framework will be immensely helpful. The structure you develop now will greatly facilitate proper book writing, reducing frustration (again, trust me on this). Engage with your AI tool here. Explain exactly what I've outlined—you're writing a book on X and need help conceptualizing chapters. Don't let it make decisions yet; focus on what you already know you want to write about. You can either directly state, "I'm writing this book, etc. Here are the chapters I've considered so far. What do you think? Offer suggestions for improvement/more chapters/critique my ideas/whatever you want," or ask it to prompt you for information until it believes you have sufficient chapters for your aspirations (considering length, depth, etc.).

Don't rush this crucial stage. Taking your time now will save you considerable effort later. You may feel eager to start writing, but **resist that urge**. Once you have your initial chapter outline, return to your AI assistant for further refinement. Aim for perfection, or as close to it as possible. Ask the AI to act as a critic, considering other books in the field on this topic. Your goal is to create a unique book that stands out. Alternate between Claude, ChatGPT, and other leading AI tools in the market. Repeatedly ask them to analyze your project and suggest improvements. Have them criticize and revise it. Ask them to grade themselves, and continue refining until they achieve a high score.

Here's a sample prompt:

> "Let's critically evaluate our chosen chapters. How do they compare to other books in the field? Will they make a meaningful contribution? Imagine you're a New York Times critic - what would you think when skimming these chapter headlines? What's missing from my argument? Is the flow logical and engaging? Assess the outline based on these criteria, then grade yourself. Be

rigorous in your evaluation. If your grade is below 95%, revise and try again. Provide specific advice on how to improve, then re-evaluate. Continue this process until the final grade reaches 95% or higher."

Review the outcome carefully. Don't overly rely on AI's final version as the best for you. This is why human involvement remains crucial in the process. It's YOUR book. Thoroughly examine whether these chapters align with your vision.

Next, do what I instructed at the beginning of this chapter: transfer the chapter titles into your word processor (or preferred writing tool). Format them as headlines, ensuring each chapter stands out (if you're unsure how to do this, either look at the beginning of this chapter or ask your AI assistant for guidance). Within this document, begin detailing what you want each chapter to contain. What arguments will you present? What's the main purpose of each chapter?

Repeat this process with your AI. Explain what you're doing (in the same chat, so it understands the context; no need to start from scratch). Collaborate with it to develop the subchapters you want. Ask for critical feedback again. Have it grade itself and continue refining until it deems the outcome satisfactory. Then, review it once more, making as many corrections as you feel necessary.

As mentioned, it's perfectly acceptable if some of these elements change during the writing process. You might modify some chapters and will almost certainly alter some subchapters. That's fine. However, try to maintain the general structure; significant changes could prolong the process and complicate matters unnecessarily.

At this point, you should have your chapters, subchapters, and a brief explanation of the content for each section. This forms the general outline of your book. Inform your AI assistant of this status (so it can maintain context throughout the writing process). Now, let's address the actual writing. As mentioned earlier, there are different approaches you can take. One option is to let AI write the entire book for you, with you simply reviewing and correcting the output. However, I don't recommend this approach for these types of books (or at all). While it might work for simpler genres like motivational books, these more complex works require expertise and your personal input—not just a general outline.

The second approach is more advisable. Open your word processor and start writing. Dedicate substantial time to this process, and try to write as much as you can. Avoid making this the last task of an exhausting day, especially if you've already spent time structuring the book that day. Instead, start fresh at the beginning of a day when you can sit down with your computer and simply write.

Pour all the ideas you've been wanting to include in your book onto the page. The chapter structure you've created should help organize your thoughts. If you notice something doesn't quite fit, make a note to yourself for later revision. The key now is to write.

This method allows you to infuse the book with your personal insights, experiences, and expertise. Your chapter outline serves as a guide, but don't let it constrain your creativity. If new ideas emerge as you write, capture them. You can always refine and reorganize later. Remember, this initial draft is about getting your thoughts down. Don't worry too much about perfection at this stage. The goal is to create a substantial foundation of your own content, which you can later refine and enhance with AI assistance if needed.

Begin with your introduction. This sounds like a terrible tip. And when I teach my students how to write a seminar, an academic paper or a book, I'll often tell them to write the introduction and conclusion at the end of the process. But I learned that for this process, at least for me and in this section of books, it really helps to first pour out what I want to write about. The introduction to the book is a good place to start. It'll help you organize your thoughts.

If this is your first book, it's crucial to grasp the true purpose of the introduction. The introduction is your chance to grab the reader's attention from the very first sentence. It acts as a gateway, inviting readers into the world you've created. A well-crafted introduction not only sets the tone for your entire work but also offers a compelling preview of what lies ahead. It's here that you establish your voice, demonstrate your expertise, and highlight the unique perspective you bring to the subject.

In these crucial opening pages, you're not just summarizing your book— you're making a promise to your readers. You're telling them why this book matters, why it's relevant to their lives or interests, and what they stand to gain by continuing to read. A strong introduction often begins with a hook—perhaps a provocative question, a startling statistic, or a compelling anecdote that immediately engages the reader's curiosity.

As you move deeper into your introduction, you'll want to provide context for your work. This might involve briefly exploring the current state of your field, or explaining how you came to write this book. It's your chance to connect with your readers on a personal level, sharing your journey and what drove you to put pen to paper (or fingers to keyboard).

Remember, your introduction isn't just about what you want to say - it's about what your readers need (or want) to hear. It should address their potential questions or concerns, and clearly outline the value they'll receive from your book. By the time they finish your introduction, readers should feel not only informed about what lies ahead, but excited to turn the page and dive into your first chapter.

Ok. Just to be clear, this is the type of text I would ask my AI assistant to generate for me, and then I would review it to ensure it captures the essence of what I wanted to convey. I didn't write the previous text myself; I only provided this prompt to Claude:

"If this is your first book, do understand what the purpose of the introduction is. When we write an introduction to a book, we often want to [write the purposes of an introduction and how to construct it well; rely on how introductions to bestsellers are often constructed and about your knowledge of writing]"

This approach demonstrates how AI can be a valuable tool in the writing process. It can quickly generate comprehensive content based on a brief prompt, which you can then refine and personalize. This method allows you to focus on higher-level thinking and creative input while using AI to handle the initial draft of more standard or informational sections.

By reviewing and editing the AI-generated content, you ensure that the final text aligns with your voice and vision for the book. This collaborative process between human creativity and AI efficiency can be particularly useful for sections like introductions, where there are established best practices that the AI can easily summarize.

Now, move on to the chapters. You don't have to start with the first one, although doing so can sometimes help you understand the flow of the book and the progression of your arguments. Instead, choose the chapters where you feel most comfortable, where you know the words will flow naturally. Then, begin writing. Yes, you can quickly tell the AI to "Write a paragraph on X," but remember, it will lack YOUR voice. I apologize for repeating this advice, but I understand how tempting it is to simply ask the AI to "fill it in."

What I've learned is that the current best approach is simply writing. Do it without correcting your mistakes (it doesn't matter; the AI will understand you perfectly). Just write the "story" you want to tell. Don't get too caught up with details. Just write. When you need something to be completed, add brackets (these – []) and within them indicate what you want the AI to do.

I've emphasized this final point for good reason. It encapsulates perhaps the most crucial insight I've gained throughout my writing journey. While this meticulous planning approach might appear time-consuming at first glance, it's actually quite the opposite. In reality, this method will save you considerable time and effort in the long run. More importantly, it will significantly enhance the quality of your book. The initial investment in thorough planning pays dividends, streamlining your writing process and resulting in a more cohesive, polished final product.

Consider this approach: Let's say I'm writing a book about World War II, and I need to craft a paragraph about the Nazis' rise to power in 1933. As someone knowledgeable about this history, I can later verify the AI's output for accuracy and details. Writing it myself with high accuracy would be time-consuming and demanding. Instead, I'll collaborate with the AI by starting the paragraphs and asking it to complete them. Here's an example of how this process might work:

The prompt: "This is for a book I'm writing about WWII. Help me complete the details and refine: "In the year 1933, the Nazis gained power by [complete the historical event]."

ChatGPT replied: "In the year 1933, the Nazis gained power by capitalizing on the political instability and economic hardships in Germany, leading to Adolf Hitler being appointed as Chancellor on January 30th. This pivotal event marked the beginning of the Nazi regime, as they quickly consolidated power by passing the Reichstag Fire Decree in February and the Enabling Act in March, which effectively dismantled the Weimar Republic's democratic institutions and established Hitler's dictatorship."

Claude replied: "In 1933, the Nazi Party gained power in Germany when Adolf Hitler was appointed Chancellor by President Paul von Hindenburg on January 30th. This pivotal moment, known as the Machtergreifung (seizure of power), marked the beginning of the Nazi regime and set the stage for the events that would lead to World War II."

Claude further asked me: Would you like me to expand on this event or provide more context about the political climate in Germany at that time? I answered Yes. So, it wrote this: "In the frosty dawn of January 30, 1933, a chill wind swept through the streets of Berlin, carrying with it the whispers of change. As the sun rose over the imposing government buildings, few could have imagined the dark shadow about to fall across Germany and, indeed, the entire world. On this day, Adolf Hitler, the charismatic leader of the National Socialist German Workers' Party, ascended the steps of the Reich Chancellery, summoned by the aging President Paul von Hindenburg to assume the role of Chancellor.

The appointment of Hitler was the culmination of a perfect storm that had been brewing in Germany for years. The once-proud nation, humiliated by defeat in the Great War and crippled by the harsh terms of the Treaty of Versailles, had been brought to its knees by the Great Depression. Millions of Germans found themselves unemployed, their savings rendered worthless by hyperinflation. In the cafes and beer halls of Berlin, Munich, and beyond, angry voices rose in frustration at the seeming impotence of the Weimar Republic to address the crisis."

It went on and on, but you get the point. You can guide the AI to produce text that would otherwise require significant time and effort to write. Approach your chapter-writing this way. Don't worry about going back and forth initially; instead, try to write as much as you can across all chapters. Fill in the parts you're certain about, and leave blanks for information you're unsure of or need to research further. This method allows you to maintain momentum in your writing process while leveraging AI assistance for more time-consuming portions.

When you encounter writer's block, refer back to the prompt engineering chapter. These AI tools excel at helping you overcome creative roadblocks. Need a good example, or even ten? Simply write your request in brackets, and the AI will fill them in later. If you want to discuss a topic but aren't completely confident about the details, write and explain it to the best of your knowledge, while signaling your uncertainty to the AI. It will assist in completing and clarifying these sections for you during the revision process. This approach allows you to maintain your writing flow while leveraging AI support for areas where you need additional input or verification.

The rationale behind encouraging you to write extensively at first is strategic. Once you've completed this initial draft—which will indeed be time-consuming - you can then input the entire manuscript into the AI. This comprehensive input provides the AI with a thorough context of your intended message and overall vision. Armed with this holistic understanding, the AI becomes a more effective tool for guiding you through the refinement process. It can offer more targeted suggestions for improvement, ensuring that the revisions align closely with your unique voice and the core message you aim to convey in your book.

This approach allows you to maintain control over the core content and narrative of your book while leveraging AI as a powerful tool for enhancement, fact-checking, and overcoming creative hurdles. It ensures that the final product remains authentically yours, infused with your unique insights and perspective, while benefiting from the AI's vast knowledge and ability to fill in gaps or suggest improvements.

When you feel confident that you've completed your chapters, it's time to return to the AI for assistance. Start by uploading your file to the AI and instructing it to read the content. The more you've written, the better the AI can grasp your objectives. Keep in mind that different AI models may handle this task differently; for instance, uploading an entire file might consume a significant number of tokens with some assistants (currently, ChatGPT might be more efficient than Claude for this task). Once uploaded, gradually introduce the subchapters you've written, providing clear instructions on what you want the AI to do.

It should:

1. Improve your grammar

2. Refine your phrasing

3. Offer constructive criticism

4. Complete any missing elements

Repeat this process for each chapter. Then, engage in a reflective dialogue with the AI. Upload the file again and ask it to review each completed chapter in light of the others. This helps ensure consistency and coherence across your book.

As mentioned, it's important to note that different AI tools have varying capabilities and limitations. Claude, for instance, currently depends heavily on conversation length and may reach its limit relatively quickly. As your file grows longer, you may find the conversation ending more rapidly. ChatGPT, on the other hand, generally provides more space for longer documents. However, it may "fatigue" (for lack of a better term) when dealing with extremely long documents. For example, if you upload a 300-page Word file, it might not perform as thorough a job as it would with shorter texts. Keep this in mind as you work.

If possible, break down your tasks into smaller, manageable portions - this often yields better results. Nevertheless, you can still use these tools effectively to check for redundancies and overall coherence, even with longer documents.

Remember, as your document grows longer, it becomes increasingly challenging to keep track of what you've already written and what you might have overlooked. While you'll later use AI to help with this, it's important to acknowledge that this difficulty is a natural part of the writing process and can lead to frustration. Don't let this discourage you – perseverance is key, and you will reach your goal.

For now, review your (now substantial) manuscript and focus on identifying areas that need attention:

1. Look for sections that require more refinement or elaboration.

2. Identify parts that feel incomplete or underdeveloped.

3. Note any areas where you feel you could add more depth or clarity.

4. Pay attention to transitions between chapters and sections, ensuring smooth flow.

Finished with a first draft? Congratulations! I'll devote an entire chapter on what to do after that. But here is a preview: Turn to Claude or ChatGPT (or any AI as long as it is good enough and it supports long context windows) and enlist its help to polish your manuscript. Recall the prompt engineering techniques we discussed earlier. Instruct the AI to act as various types of critics and to grade itself. When it's done, have it repeat the process until it achieves a satisfactory grade (I often use 95% as a benchmark).

Remember, the entire book might be too lengthy for the AI to process at once. After it has read the whole book, work through it chapter by chapter to make adjustments. Always remind the AI to consider the entire book to reduce redundancy and improve overall flow.

Once you've completed this AI-assisted revision, it's time for you to read the book yourself, without AI assistance. I recommend printing it out at least once. Be critical as you read through it. Identify what doesn't work, what repeats unnecessarily (don't over-rely on the AI's previous feedback), and what needs more development. Mark these areas yourself, then return to the AI to refine those specific parts.

Now, read it one last time. This time, try not to be overly critical. Reflect on whether this aligns with your vision. Even if the final version differs from your initial dream, resist the urge to start over from scratch. I can assure you that you'll love many parts and be amazed that you wrote them. You may dislike other sections and feel you could have written them differently or better. But remember, this is just one book. You want to complete it at some point, and you can always write another (which will be easier now that you have this experience).

Memoirs or Autobiographies

Writing memoirs or autobiographies is a deeply personal endeavor, one that doesn't naturally align with AI authorship—at least not in the traditional sense. These works are rooted in your lived experiences, your memories, and your unique perspective. The AI can't create those for you (well, it could fabricate them, but that would entirely defeat the purpose, wouldn't it?). The true essence of a memoir or autobiography lies in the authenticity of your story and the distinct voice through which you tell it.

That said, AI tools can still play a significant role in helping you craft your memoir or autobiography. While they can't live your life for you, they can assist in various aspects of the writing process. Whether it's structuring the narrative, deciding what to include or leave out, organizing chapters, or refining your writing style, AI can be a valuable partner in bringing your story to life.

Here's how AI can help:

1. *Outlining and Structure*: AI can help you organize your thoughts and memories into a coherent structure. It can suggest different ways to arrange your life events for maximum impact.

2. *Writing Assistance*: Think of AI as an almost perfect editor and proofreader. It can offer suggestions for better wording, more engaging ways to tell your stories, and help maintain a consistent tone throughout your book.

3. *Memory Jogging*: By inputting key events or periods of your life, AI can generate questions or prompts that might jog your memory about related events or details you may have forgotten.

4. *Research Support*: For contextualizing your personal experiences within broader historical events, AI can quickly provide relevant information and fact-checking.

5. *Emotional Analysis*: Some AI tools can analyze the emotional tone of your writing, helping you ensure that you're conveying the intended feelings in each section of your memoir.

6. *Language Enhancement*: AI can suggest more vivid descriptions or metaphors to bring your experiences to life on the page.

7. *Consistency Checking*: It can help you maintain consistent character descriptions and timelines throughout your narrative.

8. *Audience Consideration*: AI can offer insights on how different passages might be perceived by readers, helping you tailor your writing to your intended audience.

9. *Ethical Considerations*: AI can flag potentially sensitive content and suggest ways to approach difficult topics tactfully.

And of course, the other stages of book production are similar to other genres—you can use AI to create visuals, assist with the publishing process, generate marketing materials, and so on.

Here's a sample prompt for someone looking to write a memoir with AI assistance:

"I want to write a memoir about my life, focusing on key experiences that have shaped who I am today. Please help me structure my thoughts and begin this process. Here are some details to work with:

1. I was born in [year] in [location].

2. A defining moment from my childhood was [brief description of event].

3. My career has been in [field], with a significant achievement being [achievement].

4. A major personal challenge I've overcome is [challenge].

5. An important relationship in my life has been with [person/role], because [reason].

Based on this information:

1. Suggest a possible structure for my memoir, including potential chapter titles.

2. Provide a list of 10 thought-provoking questions that will help me dive deeper into these experiences and their impact on my life.

3. Draft an engaging opening paragraph for my memoir that captures the essence of my journey.

4. Recommend three different writing styles or tones I could consider for my memoir, explaining how each might affect the reader's experience.

5. Suggest ways I can weave broader historical or cultural contexts into my personal narrative to give readers a fuller picture of the times I've lived through.

6. Provide tips on how to approach writing about sensitive topics or difficult memories in a thoughtful and constructive way.

7. Offer ideas for incorporating other elements like family recipes, song lyrics, or photographs into my memoir to enrich the narrative.

Please note that your role is to assist and inspire. I'll be providing the actual content and personal reflections. I'm looking for guidance on structure, style, and ways to make my memoir as engaging and meaningful as possible."

You can also take a different approach. Try instructing the AI to interview you, asking all the questions it needs to gather the information for your book. Once you've provided your answers, either by typing or recording them—whichever is more comfortable for you—the AI can then start drafting the content. This method can be especially convenient, as it allows you to focus on speaking your thoughts aloud, making the process more natural and potentially more fluid for some.

Here's a prompt you could use for such a task: "I want to write a memoir about my life, but I'd like you to guide me through the process by asking me questions. Please follow these instructions:

1. Ask me a series of questions about my life, covering various aspects such as childhood, education, career, relationships, major life events, challenges, and achievements. Start with broad questions and then ask follow-up questions based on my responses.

2. After each question, wait for my response before moving to the next question.

3. Adapt your questions based on the information I provide, delving deeper into areas that seem significant or emotionally impactful.

4. Include questions about the historical and cultural context of different periods in my life.

5. Ask about any objects, photos, or documents that might be important to my story.

6. Inquire about the people who have had the most influence on my life.

7. Ask about my personal growth, changes in perspective, and lessons learned throughout my life.

8. Once you feel you have gathered enough information, inform me that you're ready to start outlining the memoir.

9. Present a proposed outline for the memoir based on the information gathered.

10. Ask if there are any areas I'd like to expand on or any parts I'd prefer to keep private.

11. Finally, begin drafting the memoir, starting with an engaging introduction. Pause after the introduction for my approval before continuing with the rest of the book.

Remember, your role is to guide and assist. The content and personal reflections will come from me. Please help me structure my thoughts and experiences into a compelling narrative."

This approach allows for a more conversational and potentially more comprehensive gathering of information, which can then be structured into a memoir with the AI's assistance. I've inserted it into ChatGPT, and this is how it would begin:

ChatGPT 4o ⌄   ⬆ EL

🌐 **Starting the Memoir Journey**

1. Childhood

Let's start from the beginning. Can you tell me about your earliest memories of childhood?

> My first memory was when I was three years old. We went to Austria and we hiked through the mountains. I think I fell in love with this kind of nature since then.

🌐 That sounds like a beautiful and formative experience.

2. Early Childhood Environment

↓

Can you describe the environment you grew up in? What was your home and

 Message ChatGPT

ChatGPT can make mistakes. Check important info.

I didn't have any plans to write a memoir, but I decided to test this method out by instructing the AI to "Make up answers to these questions." Unsurprisingly, it did just that. The process took some time because there were quite a few questions, but it managed to create a full fictional memoir. While I won't share the entire fictional memoir here, if you're curious and would like to read the outcome, it's freely available here:

Remember, while AI is a powerful tool, the core of your memoir or autobiography should always reflect your authentic voice and personal experiences. Use AI to enhance and refine your writing, but never to replace the unique perspective and truth only you can offer. You can choose the approach that works best for you, whether it's having the AI ask you questions or taking a more hands-on role in the writing process. I also recommend experimenting with different tools, as each one can provide a distinct voice, which is especially important in memoir writing. For example, you might start with ChatGPT for the first draft and then refine it further with Claude, allowing each tool to contribute its strengths to your final manuscript.

Scripts

Writing scripts for television or movies is also becoming a much easier task. Writers no longer need to worry about consistency or formatting issues. AI can help maintain character voices throughout the script, ensure proper scene transitions, and even suggest dialogue that fits each character's unique personality. It can assist with pacing, making sure the story hits all the right beats at the right times. Writers can focus more on the creative aspects of storytelling, while AI handles the technical details like proper script formatting and scene numbering.

Moreover, AI can help generate ideas for plot twists, character arcs, and even entire storylines based on initial premises. It can quickly provide research on specific topics or settings, saving writers countless hours of background work. For TV series, AI can help track complex character relationships and story arcs across multiple episodes or seasons, reducing continuity errors.

However, it's crucial to remember that while AI can significantly streamline the scriptwriting process, the core creative vision should still come from the human writer. AI is a powerful tool, but it shouldn't replace the unique perspective and emotional depth that a skilled writer brings to a script. Use AI to enhance your writing process, but always maintain your creative control and distinctive voice.

Let's consider an example. I've always been a huge fan of the TV show *Seinfeld*. I thought (and still think) that Larry David and Jerry Seinfeld were absolute geniuses. However, after watching countless episodes, you start to notice a pattern. The show's success isn't solely rooted in its brilliant writing—although that's certainly a key factor—but also in the depth and consistency of its well-developed characters. Each character is so distinctly crafted that their interactions and the humor arising from those interactions feel incredibly natural, yet meticulously planned. This character-driven approach is what makes *Seinfeld* not just a series of funny moments, but a timeless exploration of human quirks and relationships.

So, how would I go about creating a script for a *Seinfeld* episode using AI? (Let's set aside copyright issues for now.) If I simply prompt ChatGPT with "Create a new *Seinfeld* episode," it will generate one right away, and the result isn't half bad—I've tried it myself several times. However, the outcome can be significantly better if you put a bit more thought into it and guide the AI with more specific instructions.

Here's an example of how I approached it. This is what I wrote to ChatGPT (version 3.5; a while ago). Note that the mistakes are intentional (in the sense that I didn't bother to waste time correcting them, as these AI tools understand exactly what I mean even with many errors):

Write a scene in Seinfeld. Kremer borrows Jerry's car for his "job" (which he does not say what it is (he is an uber driver), but he implies that it is something which could be interpreted in many ways. Jerry agrees, mainly because he was talking to George and Kraemer asked quickly while they were doing something else. Then, an hour later Jerry gets a call to go on a TV show, but he has to go now (a famous show host calls him, saying that someone famous canceled on him). He then remembers that Kraemer took his car (Saying: Kraemer! to himself), so he calls up an uber. He goes down to see that Kraemer picks him up. Then they talk about it in the cab (in the traditional Seinfeld way... Jerry saying something like: "You didn't say my car is needed for the job..." Kraemer saying something like: "It's only a tool, I'm the one doing all the job". Then he drops him off, after charging him, saying, no tip? - Someone is getting one star...).

This is what ChatGPT produced (try reading it in their voices):

INT. JERRY'S APARTMENT - DAY

Jerry and George are in the middle of an animated discussion about whether Superman would need to wear a seatbelt. Kramer bursts through the door, full of his usual energy.

KRAMER: Jerry, buddy, can I borrow your car for a job? It's urgent!

Jerry, distracted by the debate, doesn't give it much thought.

JERRY: Yeah, sure, take the keys. But what kind of job?

KRAMER: It's...a people job. Gotta move people, Jerry!

Kramer grabs the keys and exits swiftly. jerry and George continue their debate.

CUT TO:

int. Jerry's apartment - an hour later

Jerry's phone rings. he answers and immediately his face lights up with excitement.

JERRY: (into phone) Hello?...Yes, this is Jerry Seinfeld...Really? Tonight? I'll be there!

He hangs up and turns to George.

JERRY: That was Bryon Allen! I'm going on "Comics Unleashed" tonight because Kevin Hart cancelled!

GEORGE: That's huge, Jerry!

JERRY: Yeah, I gotta get downtown now. Where are my keys? ...Kramer!

Realizing his situation, Jerry frantically uses his phone to book an Uber.

CUT TO:

EXT. JERRY'S APARTMENT - A FEW MINUTES LATER

Jerry goes downstairs. A car pulls up, and to his surprise, it's Kramer behind the wheel.

JERRY: Kramer? You're my Uber driver?

KRAMER: Surprise, buddy! It's all part of the gig economy. I'm giggin', Jerry!

JERRY: You didn't mention that my car was "the job!"

KRAMER: Jerry, the car's just a tool, I'm the artist. The conduit for the metropolitan transit desires!

Jerry, annoyed but in a hurry, gets into the car.

CUT TO:

INT. JERRY'S CAR - CONTINUOUS

The car ride is awkward. Kramer is overly enthusiastic about his new job, while jerry is visibly irritated.

JERRY: So, you use my car to drive people around and then charge me for the ride?

KRAMER: Well, you gotta pay for the service, Jerry. It's the way of the road!

they arrive at the tv studio. jerry reaches for his wallet and hands Kramer some cash.

KRAMER: No tip?

JERRY: You're driving my car!

KRAMER: (sighing) Someone's getting one star...

Jerry rolls his eyes, exits the car, and heads into the studio.

KRAMER: (calling out) Break a leg, Jerry! If you need a ride home, you know who to call!

JERRY: (muttering to himself as he walks away) I think I'll walk...

FADE OUT.

I would have loved to see that scene come to life (and with the rapid advancement of AI tools, we might soon have that capability—but that's a topic for another book). I would have changed it a bit and further instructed the AI to make subtle changes and amendments and suggest how to make it funnier as well (like Kramer asking Jerry if he wants a half empty bottle of water that Jerry forgot in the car; while Jerry replying: "That's my water!"). But you can see where it goes.

This concept isn't far-fetched; it reminds me of one of the first AI-generated phenomena we saw online, the so-called "Nothing, FOREVER," an endless Seinfeld episode created entirely by AI. It wasn't bad, but the parts I saw were not even close to being as funny or witty as the one I made.

At this point, it is important to note that creating such scripts and bringing them to life could be problematic from a copyright perspective, which I'll cover later—here, I'm only using it to make a point (an educational one). I'm not really planning to create a Seinfeld episode. But more importantly, this goes back again to creativity. The key is to input your creativity, which you can also use AI to help generate, but do this before it starts producing your actual material. Engage with the AI for creative brainstorming and idea generation in the preliminary stages, not while it's already crafting your script.

I must point out here that I'm not sure what the future of screenwriting will be like. Unlike most of the other types of writing I explored here, scripts could become much quicker and easier to produce with AI. I'm not suggesting we won't need creative ideas—we'll still need people to generate and develop concepts for scripts (although their jobs might change as well). However, those who actually write the scripts may be less needed, or at least we might need fewer of them.

Let's take a brief detour into this topic. This raises significant questions about the future of the industry, especially considering the recent Writers Guild of America (WGA) strike in 2023. The strike centered on fair pay, job security, and concerns about AI's impact on writing. Writers feared that as AI tools improved, their roles might shrink, with studios potentially using AI to produce content more cheaply and quickly.

When the strike ended, the writers secured a deal with better pay and specific guidelines regarding AI use in their work. The agreement stipulated that AI couldn't replace writers but acknowledged that AI might be used as a tool in the creative process. This delicate balance highlights the challenges of integrating new technology while safeguarding human creativity in storytelling.

This situation underscores the need to rethink how the industry operates. Unlike writing full books, which still requires a significant amount of human creativity, scriptwriting could be more easily automated. We must carefully consider how to incorporate AI into the industry while still valuing and protecting the roles of human writers.

This topic extends beyond the scope of this book and is explored more thoroughly in my upcoming work, "The Day Everyone Lost Their Jobs," which I aim to complete very soon. Nevertheless, I wanted to highlight this issue because, unlike writing full books, these tasks could potentially be automated quite rapidly, prompting a reevaluation of the entire industry. Consider this: AI presents script writers (for movies, TV shows, theater, etc.) with unprecedented opportunities to overcome the repetitive, Sisyphean aspects of their work. This allows them to focus more intensely on the creative elements, now with the assistance of highly capable AI tools. As a result, the barrier to entry for artistic creation in these fields has significantly lowered, potentially allowing almost anyone to join this group of artists.

Before AI, if you wanted to write a script, where would you begin? How would you set a scene and write it effectively? The technicalities of script formatting, the intricacies of scene description, and the art of crafting compelling dialogue could be daunting for newcomers. But with AI as your writing partner, these barriers to entry are significantly lowered. It can guide you through the process, offer formatting suggestions, and even help brainstorm creative scene setups, allowing aspiring writers to focus more on their stories and less on the technical aspects of scriptwriting.

Comic Books

Creating comic books with the assistance of AI presents a unique set of challenges, even for those already familiar with the medium. While the process might seem straightforward at first—after all, it combines both writing and visual art—it requires careful attention to several distinct elements that are crucial for success. Among these, character creation and consistency stand out as particularly important, and mastering these aspects will be essential to producing a coherent and engaging comic book.

The first step in creating a comic book is developing your concept. What story do you want to tell, and how do you want to tell it? Start by outlining your plot, deciding on the main narrative arc, and identifying the key moments driving your story forward. At this stage, it's crucial to have a clear idea of your target audience, as this will influence both the tone of your writing and the style of your illustrations.

Once your concept is solidified, the next step is to create your characters. This is where the process becomes particularly intricate, as comic book characters must be visually distinctive and narratively compelling. Your characters will drive the story, and their design should reflect their personalities, motivations, and roles within the narrative. It's not just about how they look, but also about how they move, express emotions, and interact with the world around them. This is where AI tools can offer valuable assistance, especially for those who may not have extensive experience in character design.

In the next chapter, I will explore how to use creative tools like Midjourney to assist in creating and refining your characters. This tool can help you visualize your characters in different poses, outfits, and settings, ensuring they remain consistent throughout your comic. However, it's important to remember that while these tools can generate stunning visuals, the heart of your characters—their backstory, motivations, and development—must come from you.

With your characters in place, you can begin scripting your comic. This involves writing dialogue, setting up scenes, and planning out how the story will unfold across the pages. AI tools like ChatGPT can assist with generating dialogue, suggesting scene descriptions, or even offering ideas for plot twists. However, as with any AI-generated content, it's crucial to review and refine these suggestions to ensure they align with your vision and maintain the unique voice of your comic.

Next comes the layout stage, where you decide how each page will be structured. Comic book layout is an art in itself, requiring a balance between text and images, pacing, and the flow of action from panel to panel. At this point, it's essential to consider how your story will be visually communicated. Each panel should serve a purpose, whether it's to advance the plot, develop a character, or create a dramatic effect.

After finalizing your layout, it's time to produce the actual illustrations. This can be done using a combination of AI tools and your artistic skills. While tools like Midjourney can generate character designs and backgrounds, you might still need to adjust these elements to ensure they fit seamlessly into your comic's overall aesthetic. The key is to blend the AI-generated art with your personal touch, creating a cohesive and visually appealing product.

Finally, the lettering process brings your comic to life. This involves placing the dialogue, sound effects, and any other text within the panels. It might seem like a small detail, but good lettering can significantly impact the readability and overall feel of your comic. AI tools can assist here as well, helping you choose fonts, sizes, and placements that enhance your story without overwhelming the artwork.

Creating a comic book with AI is a multi-step process that requires careful planning, creativity, and attention to detail. While AI can provide invaluable assistance at every stage, from character design to dialogue writing, it's your vision that will ultimately shape the final product. In the next chapter, we'll take a closer look at how to use Midjourney to create consistent and compelling characters for your comic.

Travel Books or Guides

Writing travel books or guides is an exciting yet challenging endeavor, especially when utilizing AI tools to assist in the process. While AI can provide valuable support, it's crucial to approach this type of book with a great deal of caution. Travel guides must be grounded in real experiences or thoroughly researched information, and relying too heavily on AI without proper verification can lead to significant inaccuracies, as I discussed earlier with the concept of AI "hallucinations."

When developing a travel book, it's essential to ensure that the places, events, and experiences you describe actually exist and are accurately portrayed. This is especially true for lesser-known locations, unique experiences, or local traditions that may not be well-documented online. Here's a step-by-step approach to writing a travel book or guide with AI assistance, while ensuring accuracy and reliability:

1. **Start with Your Own Experiences**: Begin by outlining the places you've visited and the experiences you've had. If you're writing about a destination you've personally explored, draw from your own knowledge and observations. Use AI tools to help you structure your content, but be cautious about letting them generate details without your input.

2. **Research Thoroughly**: If you're writing about places you haven't visited, conduct thorough research using reputable sources. Guidebooks, travel blogs, official tourism websites, and personal testimonials can provide reliable information. You can then use AI to help organize and present this information, but always cross-reference the AI's output with your research.

3. **Verify Every Detail**: Whether you're using AI to fill in information or generate descriptions, make it a habit to verify everything. Use multiple sources to confirm facts, and never rely solely on AI-generated content for critical details like locations, directions, or recommendations.

4. **Be Specific in Your Prompts**: When asking AI for information, be as specific as possible. For example, instead of asking for general recommendations, specify the type of experience you're looking for, the target audience of your book, and the unique aspects you want to highlight. This can help reduce the risk of AI generating irrelevant or inaccurate content.

5. **Use AI for Organizational Help**: AI can be incredibly helpful in structuring your travel book, suggesting chapter layouts, and helping you think of topics to include. For example, you can ask the AI to assist in organizing sections on accommodation, dining, local attractions, and travel tips. Just ensure that the content it helps you generate is fact-checked and aligns with your personal experiences or verified research.

6. **Consider Including Personal Anecdotes**: Travel books resonate more with readers when they include personal stories and unique perspectives. Use AI to help you weave your anecdotes into the broader narrative, but ensure these stories remain authentic and true to your experiences.

7. **Test the AI's Recommendations**: Before including AI-generated recommendations in your book, test them out. For instance, if the AI suggests a restaurant or hotel, check its current status online, read recent reviews, and if possible, get feedback from locals or recent travelers.

8. **Stay Updated**: Travel information can quickly become outdated. If you're using AI to help update an existing travel guide or to write a new one, make sure to regularly verify that the information remains current. This includes checking for changes in business operations, travel restrictions, and local regulations.

By following these steps, you can create a reliable and engaging travel guide with the assistance of AI, while ensuring that the content remains accurate and trustworthy. The key to a successful travel book is the authenticity of your narrative and the reliability of the information you provide. AI can be a powerful tool in your writing process, but it should always be used thoughtfully and carefully, especially when accuracy is paramount.

*

These are all merely examples, of course. As I mentioned, I've had experience with many of these types of books over the past year, some more than others. I can offer advice, but I can't predict exactly what your journey will be like. Each writer's path is unique. What I can surmise is that if you engage in sufficient trial and error, resist the temptation to let the AI do all the work for you, and truly dedicate yourself to the process, you'll reach your goal, eventually.

Writing is a journey of continuous refinement, with each draft bringing you closer to your ultimate vision. As you progress, remember that the process of writing, revising, and rewriting is crucial to crafting a compelling narrative. With your chapters outlined and ideas taking shape, you're well-positioned to continue molding your book into something truly impactful. Now that your text is forming, it's time to consider how visuals can enhance your book. Whether through images, graphs, or illustrations, these elements can bring your content to life and engage your readers more deeply. In the next chapter, we'll explore how to effectively integrate visuals into your work, adding another layer of richness to your storytelling.

Chapter V: Making Visuals

Welcome to the magical realm of making pictures with words, and no, I'm not talking about your flowery prose. We're diving into the world of visuals, where generative AI has thrown open the doors to anyone with an idea and a keyboard. Even if you're crafting the next literary masterpiece, you'll need at least one picture: that attention-grabbing book cover. But why stop there when AI can whip up visuals faster than you can say "writer's block"?

As you might have guessed from the tone, I asked the AI to inject a bit of humor into this chapter when I rewrote it. This ties back to the writing process: you can make the AI do whatever you want, tonally speaking. So don't be shy. Experiment with different styles until you find the voice that fits your project. Now, back to visuals.

Here's the thing: with generative AI, suddenly everyone's a Picasso. Or at least a very efficient clip art generator. Writing a children's book? AI can conjure up illustrations that would make Dr. Seuss do a double-take. Penning a business tome? Prepare for charts and graphs so sleek they'll make Excel weep with envy. Crafting a travel guide? AI can create postcard-perfect scenes of places you've never been, just don't blame me when the real thing doesn't quite measure up. And for the cookbook authors among you, AI food photography is so mouthwatering it should come with a drool warning.

Creating visuals used to be a whole different beast from writing, like being asked to paint the Sistine Chapel when you've just mastered stick figures. With AI, it's more like playing an advanced version of Pictionary. You describe it, AI draws it. It's not necessarily easier than writing, but it's considerably faster than learning to draw realistic hands, which, ask any artist, are the stuff of nightmares.

In this chapter, we're diving into AI-assisted visual creation: generating images realistic enough to make you question reality, illustrations that would take a human artist weeks, and data visualizations that actually make sense. Some of this will be as easy as chatting with a very enthusiastic, slightly robotic art student. Other parts might require you to flex creative muscles you didn't know you had. But here's the beauty of it: with AI, you're no longer constrained by your artistic skills. You're limited only by your imagination and your ability to craft a clear prompt.

Now that we've established the importance of visuals, let's tour the art gallery of book elements you might create. First up: book covers, the supermodels of the book world. They need to be eye-catching enough to make people judge your book by its cover, but in a good way, as in "I must read this immediately" rather than "Did a kindergartener design this?"

Moving inside, we find illustrations ranging from simple doodles to complex scenes that make your words dance off the page. Then there are photographs, either AI-generated (because who needs to leave the house?) or stock photos, for when you need a slice of reality in your literary pie.

For the number crunchers, there are graphs and charts to make data look dapper, and infographics for when you need to explain rocket science in three easy pictures. Maps guide your readers through real or imaginary lands, while diagrams help you explain complex ideas without writing a textbook within your book.

Don't forget icons and symbols, the shorthand of the visual world, perfect for when a picture really is worth a thousand words. Character designs keep your cast consistent, preventing your hero from suddenly sprouting a third eye or changing hair color every chapter. And let's not overlook page decorations, because sometimes your words deserve to be framed on every page, like the literary masterpieces they are.

In the coming sections, we'll cover what works like a charm, what might make your AI art generator throw a digital tantrum, and how to coax the best results from your silicon-based artist. We'll focus on three main categories: images and illustrations, data visualization, and layout and design. Whether you're sprinkling a few images throughout your opus or creating a visual extravaganza, the goal is the same: enhance your story, clarify your ideas, and make your readers' eyes as happy as their minds.

Whether you're aiming to sprinkle a few images throughout your opus or create a visual extravaganza that rivals a Hollywood production, we've got you covered. Remember, the goal here isn't just to make your book pretty—it's to enhance your story, clarify your ideas, and make your readers' eyes as happy as their minds. By the time we're done, your book will be so visually stunning, it'll make coffee table books burn with envy. So roll up your sleeves, fire up your AI, and let's turn your book into a visual masterpiece.

Images and Illustrations: Where Words Meet Pixels

Welcome to the wild world of AI-generated images and illustrations, where your imagination is the limit and occasionally, so is the AI's interpretation of your imagination. This is likely where you'll spend most of your time playing visual artist for your book. No actual artistic talent required, just a knack for describing what you want and a dash of patience.

By 2026, the landscape has consolidated around a handful of genuinely excellent tools. My personal go-to is Nano Banana, Google's image generation model integrated directly into Gemini. It combines strong visual quality, character consistency, and the convenience of working within the same platform I already use for writing. ChatGPT remains a solid option, particularly for quick iterations and seamless integration into your writing workflow. Midjourney continues to produce some of the most aesthetically striking results available, and is worth considering for projects where visual quality is paramount. Each has its strengths, and many authors end up using more than one depending on the task.

As for cost, using all of them simultaneously is like subscribing to every streaming service at once. Sure, you'll never run out of options, but your bank account might start sending you passive-aggressive notifications. If you're already paying for ChatGPT and Claude, which I recommend, adding more subscriptions requires some thought. Start with what you have, experiment, and only add tools when you have a specific reason to.

Now, before we dive into the tools themselves, let's talk about the secret sauce that applies to all of them: prompts.

Just like with text generation, it all comes down to how you ask. You're essentially playing a game of digital Pictionary with an AI that's eerily good at guessing but occasionally hilariously off-base. The key to winning this game? Be specific. Really specific.

Instead of asking for "a red apple," try something like: "A Honeycrisp apple with a single drop of dew on its surface, sitting on a rustic wooden table, with a soft-focus background of a sun-dappled orchard." The difference in output is remarkable.

Here's a quick checklist of what to include in your visual prompts:

1. The subject (e.g., "a majestic lion with a flowing mane")

2. The style (e.g., "in the style of a vintage travel poster")

3. The mood (e.g., "exuding an aura of mystery and intrigue")

4. The lighting (e.g., "bathed in the warm glow of a sunset")

5. The angle (e.g., "viewed from a bird's-eye perspective")

6. The supporting elements (e.g., "surrounded by a lush jungle teeming with exotic flowers")

The more detail you provide, the closer you'll get to the image in your mind's eye. That said, AI, like that one friend who never quite gets your jokes, will sometimes interpret your prompts in unexpected ways. Embrace the happy accidents. Sometimes they're better than what you had in mind.

One more thing worth noting: the same prompt can produce meaningfully different results across different tools. If one tool isn't delivering what you want, try another before assuming the idea doesn't work. You might be surprised.

ChatGPT

ChatGPT is an image generation tool built directly into the platform you're probably already using for writing. No extra tools, tabs, or installations required. You simply describe what you want, and it creates an image to match.

It works just like chatting. Say "show me a dog playing football," and you'll get an AI-generated image in seconds. Sometimes it's spot-on. Sometimes it's creative in ways you didn't ask for. You might get a dachshund balancing a football on its nose or a bulldog treating it as a chew toy.

The trick is in the prompt. Compare these two:

Basic: "A dog playing football."

Detailed: "A realistic digital painting of a Golden Retriever catching a football in mid-air, leaping in a sunny park, vibrant colors, dynamic composition."

The second prompt gives ChatGPT what it needs to deliver something much closer to your vision. It's like the difference between asking for "a sandwich" and describing your perfect BLT.

Best of all, you never have to leave your writing workflow. While you're working on your book, ChatGPT is right there in the chat, ready to illustrate your scenes as you go. Getting the perfect image often involves some back-and-forth, tweaking your prompts based on what ChatGPT produces. Think of it as creative dialogue rather than a one-shot request.

Now, two main challenges worth understanding.

The first is character consistency. ChatGPT has improved substantially here, and the current model maintains facial likeness and visual continuity across edits within the same conversation. You can also upload a reference image to anchor a character's appearance across multiple generations. That said, it is not flawless, and working across separate conversations still requires some effort.

One effective approach is to build a detailed character first, then use that image as a reference for subsequent scenes. Here is an example prompt:

"Create a cute cartoon-style character named Poto the Potato. Poto has a soft, round, light-brown body with a few small freckles like a real potato. He has big, kind eyes, a gentle smile, short stubby legs, and tiny arms. Poto wears a green leaf as a hat and carries a little backpack made of burlap. His look is childlike and friendly, perfect for a children's book. Use soft, warm colors and place him in a cozy vegetable garden setting."

Once ChatGPT has generated Poto, you can continue in the same conversation: "Now make Poto the Potato surf a wave."

The result will not always be identical, but it will be close enough to work with. A few prompt tweaks usually do the trick.

The second challenge involves content restrictions. ChatGPT operates within OpenAI's content guidelines, which prohibit explicit violence, deepfakes, and content promoting hate or discrimination. On copyright, the behavior is less predictable. Sometimes ChatGPT will refuse to generate an image involving a recognizable copyrighted character or style, and sometimes it will comply without hesitation. The same prompt can produce different responses on different occasions. Do not rely on ChatGPT as your copyright compliance system. That responsibility remains yours, and we will cover it in more detail later.

Midjourney

Midjourney remains one of the leading AI image generation platforms, particularly valued for its artistic quality and visual richness. It excels at creating complex scenes, fantastical landscapes, and hyper-realistic portraits, and consistently produces results that feel closer to professional-grade artwork than most competitors. For projects requiring a strong, distinctive visual identity—illustrated children's books, comics, branding materials—it remains a serious contender.

Accessing Midjourney. Midjourney is accessible in two ways: through its full website at midjourney.com, or through Discord. The website now offers a complete, user-friendly interface, and most users will find it the more comfortable option. Discord remains available for those who prefer the community environment or want early access to experimental features, but it is no longer the primary way to use the platform.

In both cases, the basic workflow is the same: you type a description of the image you want, and Midjourney generates several variations for you to choose from. For example: a dog playing football in a sunny park, full of energy and joy.

Creating Consistent Characters. One of Midjourney's most important capabilities for authors is maintaining visual consistency across a series of images. In V7 (the current default model), the main tool for this is Omni Reference: you provide an existing image of your character, and Midjourney uses it as a visual anchor when generating new scenes. On the website, you drag your reference image into the prompt bar. On Discord, you use the --oref parameter followed by the image URL.

You can control how strictly Midjourney adheres to the reference using the --ow (omni-weight) parameter. The default is 100; higher values (up to 1000) keep the character's appearance more faithful to the original, while lower values give the model more creative freedom. It's worth experimenting, since different projects benefit from different settings.

For maintaining a consistent style across images—rather than a specific character—Midjourney also offers Style Reference (--sref), which captures the mood, colors, and textures of a reference image without copying specific people or objects.

Versioning. Midjourney allows switching between model versions using the --v parameter. V7 is the current default, offering better prompt understanding, improved image coherence, and the Omni Reference feature. If you need a different aesthetic or are working with an older project, you can switch back to V6.1 through the settings. Niji 7, launched in January 2026, is a specialized model for anime and Eastern illustration styles, offering a major boost in visual coherence for that aesthetic. Midjourney

Challenges. Midjourney is a powerful tool, but it comes with a learning curve. Mastering the various parameters and understanding how they interact takes time and experimentation. The platform also requires a paid subscription starting at $10 per month, which is worth factoring in before committing—especially if your project doesn't demand the level of artistic quality that justifies it over free or cheaper alternatives.

Google Gemini / Nano Banana

Google entered the image generation space more quietly than its competitors, but has moved fast. The current default model for image generation across Google's ecosystem is Nano Banana 2 (technically Gemini 3.1 Flash Image), released in late February 2026. It replaces the original Nano Banana and brings together the speed of the Flash model with much of the quality previously reserved for the higher-end tier.

Nano Banana 2 can maintain character consistency for up to five characters and fidelity of up to 14 objects in a single workflow—which makes it genuinely useful for illustrated storytelling, not just one-off image generation. The model also draws on Gemini's real-world knowledge base and real-time web search to more accurately render specific subjects, generate infographics, and turn notes into diagrams.

For those who need even higher quality, Nano Banana Pro (Gemini 3 Pro Image) remains available on paid tiers. It supports consistent resemblance for up to five individuals, integrates up to six high-fidelity reference shots, and can blend as many as fourteen standard references—making it the more powerful option for complex, multi-character projects.

The main advantage of Gemini's image generation is its integration. If you're already working in the Gemini ecosystem—using it for writing, research, or editing—image creation happens in the same conversation, without switching platforms. The results are solid, improving rapidly, and for many authors, more than sufficient.

Using Traditional Methods (instead)

AI isn't the only way to bring your book's visuals to life — and that's a good thing. Traditional tools and professional designers still have a lot to offer. If you're working with a publisher (more on that later), they may provide access to skilled cover designers who understand your genre, your audience, and the visual cues that help books stand out in crowded markets. That experience matters, especially when aiming for strong positioning in bookstores and online platforms.

If you're designing the visuals yourself, traditional software remains a powerful option. It gives you granular control over every element — and for some creators, that hands-on process is part of the creative joy. Yes, it can be more time-consuming than prompting an AI, but it's also an opportunity to fully shape your aesthetic from the ground up.

That said, focusing only on convenience vs. craftsmanship misses the bigger picture. The real shift AI brings isn't just speed — it's access. The ability to generate professional-grade images, even with no design background, fundamentally expands who can create and publish. This isn't just a new tool — it's a new phase in creative independence.

In the end, there's no one "right" method. Whether you use AI, traditional tools, a publisher's design team, or some hybrid of all three, what matters is that the result serves your book. Choose the tools that align with your vision — not because they're newer or older, but because they help your story look like it belongs in the world.

Stock Photo Websites

When you're in need of a quick and efficient visual solution, stock photo websites can be your go-to option. Platforms like Shutterstock, Adobe Stock, Unsplash, and Getty Images offer extensive libraries of high-quality images. These professionally shot and edited photographs can be perfect for book covers, promotional materials, or any other visual needs you might have in your project.

The cost structure of these platforms typically revolves around subscription models. You can opt for monthly or annual plans that grant access to a set number of images per period. For those with more sporadic needs, there's usually a pay-per-download option, though this can add up quickly if you require multiple images. It's worth noting that licensing costs may come into play depending on your intended use. Commercial purposes or high-circulation books, for instance, might necessitate additional fees for extended licenses.

While stock photo websites offer convenience and quality, they do come with certain drawbacks. One of the main concerns is the potential lack of uniqueness. Since these images are available to anyone with a subscription, you might find your chosen visual being used elsewhere. This can somewhat dilute the distinct identity you're trying to create for your book or project.

Another limitation of stock photos lies in customization. While you can edit these images to some extent, there's only so much modification you can do before it becomes challenging to align the image perfectly with your vision. You might find yourself compromising between what's available and what you had initially imagined.

Despite these drawbacks, stock photo websites remain a valuable resource in the visual creation toolkit. They offer a balance of quality, convenience, and cost-effectiveness that can be particularly useful when time or budget constraints are pressing. As with any tool, the key is to understand both its strengths and limitations, using it strategically to enhance your project's visual appeal.

Digital Illustration Software

For those who crave complete creative control and possess a flair for design, digital illustration software offers a world of possibilities. Programs like Adobe Photoshop, Adobe Illustrator, and Procreate provide powerful tools that allow you to create custom visuals from the ground up. These platforms are the digital equivalents of a fully stocked art studio, giving you the freedom to bring your exact vision to life.

When it comes to costs, it's important to consider both the financial and time investments. Adobe products, for instance, operate on a subscription model that can be quite expensive, especially if you need access to the full Creative Cloud suite. Procreate offers a more wallet-friendly option with a one-time purchase, but it's exclusively available on iPad. Beyond the monetary aspect, there's also a significant investment of time required to master these tools. If you're new to digital illustration, you might find yourself needing to invest in tutorials or courses to fully harness the software's capabilities.

While the creative freedom is exhilarating, it's worth noting some drawbacks. Creating high-quality visuals from scratch can be a time-intensive process, particularly if you're not already proficient with the software. This can pose challenges if you're working under tight deadlines. Unlike AI tools that can generate images based on simple text prompts, digital illustration software demands a certain level of artistic and technical skill. For newcomers, the learning curve can be steep and potentially frustrating.

Hardware considerations also come into play. To achieve optimal results, you'll need a robust computer or tablet equipped with a good graphics card and a high-resolution display. This is especially crucial when working with large tiles or intricate designs. The need for specialized equipment can add to the overall cost and complexity of this approach.

Despite these challenges, digital illustration software remains a powerful tool for those who want to create truly unique, customized visuals. It offers a level of control and potential for originality that's hard to match with other methods. For those willing to invest the time and resources, the results can be truly spectacular, allowing you to create visuals that are perfectly tailored to your book's needs and your creative vision.

Benefits and Drawbacks of Traditional Methods

When it comes to creating visuals for your book, traditional methods are like that old flip phone in your drawer - they still work, but they're not exactly cutting-edge. Personally, I'd only go this route if I absolutely had to. In the age of AI, using traditional methods when you can craft your dream image in seconds seems like trying to win a drag race with a horse and buggy. Sure, there's the copyright issue, which we'll dive into later, that might appeal to some creators or publishers. But let's be real - we're living in the future, and AI is the jetpack to traditional methods' bicycle.

Still, for the sake of completeness, let's take a quick tour through the world of old-school visual creation. On the plus side, traditional methods can produce high-quality results. A skilled photographer or illustrator can create stunning visuals that make your readers' jaws drop. And you get granular control over every aspect of the image - assuming you have the technical skills and patience of a saint.

But here's where the shine starts to wear off. Traditional methods are often more expensive than a first-class ticket to Mars. Stock photos, software subscriptions, hiring professionals - your wallet will be begging for mercy. And time? Forget about it. You could write an entire sequel in the time it takes to master Photoshop. Then there's the "stock photo syndrome." Nothing says "generic" quite like seeing the same smiling model on your book cover and a teeth whitening ad.

In the end, while traditional methods have their place, they're like choosing to write your novel on a typewriter when you've got a state-of-the-art laptop at your fingertips. AI tools offer speed, affordability, and limitless creativity without the steep learning curve. They're democratizing visual creation, allowing authors to bring their visions to life without needing a degree in graphic design or a fortune in their bank account.

Sure, traditional methods might appeal to some for legal certainty or nostalgia. But in my view, embracing AI tools is like upgrading from a horse-drawn carriage to a Tesla - why wouldn't you want to zoom into the future?

Data Visualization

In the world of book writing, sometimes you need to present complex data in a way that doesn't make your readers' eyes glaze over. Whether you're crafting a business book, a scientific paper, or a non-fiction narrative that relies on statistics, good data visualization can make your content more engaging and easier to understand.

AI-Powered Tools. The major AI writing tools have all developed solid data visualization capabilities, each with a slightly different approach.

Claude remains the strongest option here. Through its Artifacts feature, it can generate interactive, rendered charts and graphs directly in the conversation window — not just code, but actual visual output you can see, adjust, and iterate on in real time. If you're working with data and want to see results immediately, this is the most seamless experience.

ChatGPT is competent for quick visualizations and handles the back-and-forth of iterative requests well. It can generate charts and the underlying code within the conversation, making it a practical choice if you're already working in ChatGPT for other parts of your writing.

Gemini has improved significantly and integrates naturally with Google's ecosystem — useful if your data lives in Google Sheets or you need visualizations tied to real-time information.

For users who want a dedicated tool rather than a general-purpose AI, Julius AI (julius.ai) specializes in data visualization from natural language descriptions. You describe the chart you want, and it builds it — a good option for non-technical users who need more control than a general AI provides.

Whichever tool you use, persistence pays off. If the first result isn't what you wanted, rephrase the request or ask for specific changes. A few iterations usually gets you where you need to be.

Specialized Software. For more complex or professionally customized visualizations, dedicated software still has a place. Tableau handles large datasets and interactive dashboards at a professional level. Excel and Google Sheets remain reliable for standard charts — especially if your data is already there and you just need a clean output without switching platforms.

Choosing the Right Tool

When selecting a data visualization tool for your project, consider a range of factors to ensure the best fit. Evaluate the complexity of your data; complex datasets might require advanced tools like Tableau, while simpler visualizations could be handled by AI tools or spreadsheet software. Assess your technical skills, as AI tools can provide a good starting point for those less comfortable with traditional software. Consider your interactivity needs, especially for digital books, where tools like Tableau or advanced Excel charts might be necessary. Factor in your time and budget constraints; AI tools often offer quick, cost-effective solutions, while specialized software may require more investment in learning and licensing. Lastly, consider how well the tool integrates with your existing data collection and analysis workflow.

By weighing these aspects – data complexity, your technical proficiency, interactivity requirements, resource limitations, and workflow integration – you can choose a visualization tool that best serves your specific needs and enhances your book's content effectively. Remember, the goal of data visualization is to make your information more understandable and engaging for your readers. Whether you use cutting-edge AI or tried-and-true spreadsheet software, choose the tool that helps you tell your data's story most effectively.

Layout and Design

They say you can't judge a book by its cover, but let's be honest - we all do. The layout and design of your book, from its cover to its internal pages, play a crucial role in attracting readers and enhancing their experience. Let's explore some tools that can help you create a visually appealing book, both inside and out.

Book Covers: Making a First Impression

Your book cover is your first chance to grab a potential reader's attention. It needs to be eye-catching, relevant to your content, and professional-looking. In my experience, AI image generators like ChatGPT, Midjourney, or Gemini can be powerful tools for creating book covers. By following the prompting tips we discussed earlier, you can craft unique and compelling cover designs that align with your book's theme and genre.

These AI tools offer a level of creativity and customization that can rival professional designs. You could even experiment with uploading your entire manuscript draft to see what kind of cover the AI might generate based on your content. This approach can lead to unexpected and intriguing results that capture the essence of your book.

Personally, I strongly recommend using AI tools like Gemini or Midjourney for creating book covers, as I did for this book. These AI-powered solutions offer unparalleled speed and flexibility, allowing you to craft the perfect cover in just a few minutes. You can easily tweak and refine your designs until you achieve exactly what you're looking for, all without the need for extensive design skills or expensive software.

However, if you're interested in exploring tools specifically designed for book cover creation, there are options available. While these may not harness the full power of AI, they do offer templates and features tailored for book covers. Here are a few to consider:

Professional Design Software (e.g., Adobe InDesign): For those who want full control over their cover design, professional software like Adobe InDesign is the way to go. InDesign offers a comprehensive suite of tools for layout and design, allowing you to create complex, multi-layered designs with precise control over every element. It's the industry standard for a reason, but it does come with a steeper learning curve and a higher price point. If you're comfortable with design principles and willing to invest the time to learn the software, InDesign can help you create truly unique and professional-looking covers.

Page Layout and Infographics: Enhancing the Reading Experience

The interior of your book deserves as much attention as the cover. A well-thought-out layout and carefully designed infographics can significantly enhance readability and effectively convey complex information, especially if you're writing a children's book. While conventional tools often suffice, here are some additional tools worth considering:

Canva (with AI features): Canva has expanded significantly into what it calls a "Creative Operating System," with AI now woven throughout the platform rather than offered as an add-on. You can generate complete layouts, infographics, and visual elements from a text prompt, and the AI tools — grouped under the Magic Studio umbrella — handle everything from image generation to text editing to background removal. It remains particularly useful for authors creating infographics, chapter title pages, and decorative visual elements, and is still one of the friendliest options for children's book design. The learning curve remains low.

Adobe InDesign: We mentioned InDesign for cover design, but it truly shines when it comes to page layout. It offers precise control over typography, spacing, and image placement, allowing you to create professional-looking page layouts for both print and digital books. InDesign also excels at creating master pages and styles, ensuring consistency throughout your book. If you're planning a visually complex book or a series with a consistent look, InDesign is hard to beat.

Microsoft PowerPoint: Don't dismiss PowerPoint as just a presentation tool. It can be surprisingly effective for creating page layouts and infographics, especially if you're already familiar with it. PowerPoint's shape tools, SmartArt features, and slide master capabilities can be repurposed to create consistent layouts and attractive graphics. While it may not offer the precision of InDesign, it's an accessible option for creating simple layouts and infographics, particularly if you're on a budget.

Choosing Your Design Tools

When selecting design tools for your book's layout, several factors come into play. Consider your existing design skills and how much time you're willing to invest in learning new software. Evaluate your budget constraints for both time and financial resources. Assess the complexity of your book's layout requirements, as some projects may need more advanced features than others. Determine whether you're creating for print, digital formats, or both, as this will influence your tool selection. Finally, reflect on the level of customization you desire for your book's design. These considerations will guide you towards the most suitable tools for your specific project, balancing functionality, ease of use, and cost-effectiveness.

Remember, the goal is to create a book that's not only pleasing to the eye but also enhances the reader's experience of your content. Whether you opt for AI-assisted tools or professional design software, choose the option that best helps you present your ideas clearly and attractively.

Other Unique Visual Elements

AI opens up possibilities for creating unique and interactive visual elements beyond traditional images, illustrations, and graphs. These unconventional options can significantly enhance your book's engagement and functionality. Throughout this book, you've seen how AI can generate standard visuals, but now we're venturing into more experimental territory.

The "other" category includes elements that blur the line between visual and interactive content. These are not just things to look at, but components readers can engage with, decode, or use to access additional content. They transform your book from a static text into a dynamic, multi-layered experience.

Some of these elements, like QR codes, you've encountered throughout this book. They've allowed you to access up-to-date information, supplementary resources, and interactive content that couldn't be contained within the pages. But QR codes are just the beginning. There are color-based scannable codes, encrypted visual puzzles, and even augmented reality markers that can bring your pages to life.

These elements serve various purposes: they can provide real-time updates to your content, offer interactive challenges to reinforce learning, or simply add an element of fun and discovery to the reading experience. They're particularly useful in fields like AI, where information evolves rapidly and the ability to link to current resources is invaluable.

QR Codes: Bridging the Physical and Digital Realms

QR codes are powerful tools for extending your content beyond the page. These square barcodes, easily generated with AI, connect your physical book to online resources. In the rapidly evolving field of AI, QR codes are particularly useful for linking to regularly updated information. They allow readers to access the most current tools, techniques, and insights long after your book's publication.

QR codes can direct readers to supplementary videos, interactive web pages, downloadable resources, or social media platforms where discussions about your book's topics continue. This dynamic link ensures your book remains relevant, constantly evolving alongside changes in the AI field.

Example AI prompt: "Create a QR code that links directly to the Amazon review page for my book. Ensure the code is optimized for print—scannable in black and white, with no dense design elements that might affect readability. Optionally, embed a small book icon at the center without compromising scan reliability."

You can see the output here—this QR code leads straight to the review page on Amazon:

And yes, if you've enjoyed the book so far, I'd truly appreciate it if you **left a quick review**. It helps enormously—not just with visibility on Amazon's algorithm, but also by letting others know the book is worth their time. Even a sentence or two goes a long way.

Enhancing Aesthetics: Color-Based Scannable Codes

Color-based scannable codes, inspired by platforms like Spotify, offer a more visually pleasing alternative to traditional QR codes. AI can create these unique color-based identifiers for your book, linking to audio content, video supplements, or exclusive online resources.

These color codes can be designed to complement your book cover, match chapter themes, or evolve throughout the book, creating a visually cohesive journey for readers. Their eye-catching nature may encourage more engagement with your supplementary digital content.

Example AI prompt: "Design a Spotify-inspired scannable color code for **www.mybook-audioguide.com**. Use a color palette complementing my book cover design, focusing on shades of blue and green. Ensure the code is distinct enough to be easily scanned by smartphone cameras."

Encrypted Visual Puzzles and Ciphers

AI can assist in creating visually appealing encrypted puzzles or ciphers. These elements add an interactive layer to your book, challenging readers to decipher hidden messages or unlock additional content. Such puzzles can range from simple substitution ciphers to complex visual enigmas, depending on your target audience and the book's theme.

Example AI prompt: "Design a visually appealing substitution cipher puzzle using symbols instead of letters. The hidden message should be 'AI transforms writing'. Include a subtle hint within the design to help readers get started."

Interactive Elements for E-books

For digital publications, AI can generate a wide array of interactive visual elements. These may include clickable diagrams, zoomable images with hidden details, or animated illustrations that respond to user input. Such features transform passive reading into an engaging, exploratory experience.

Example AI prompt: "Create an interactive diagram of the AI writing process for an e-book. Include clickable elements that reveal more detailed information about each step when tapped."

All of these are mere examples. If you can imagine it, there will likely be an AI that could do it for you. The key is to think creatively about how visual elements can enhance your content and engage your readers in new ways. Remember that your book might be in both digital and physical forms, so adapt to each. The digital realm has fewer constraints than the physical one, so you can do things there you can't in the physical one (and vice versa).

Whether it's interactive 3D models in digital books, textured patterns in physical copies, or augmented reality features that bridge both worlds, AI can help create unique visual experiences. The goal is to enhance the reader's engagement with your content, transforming your book into an immersive, multi-sensory experience. As AI technology evolves, so will the possibilities for book design and interactivity. The only real limit is your imagination and your understanding of your audience's needs.

*

In this chapter, we explored the transformative potential of AI in creating visuals for your book. From designing eye-catching covers to crafting intricate illustrations, AI tools like ChatGPT, Midjourney, and Stable Diffusion have opened up new possibilities for authors. These tools can turn your descriptions into vivid images, making even the most complex visual ideas accessible, regardless of your artistic skill level. Traditional methods of visual creation, while still valuable, often require more time, skill, and financial resources, but they offer unparalleled control and customization. The focus was on selecting the right tools for your project, whether you're creating data visualizations, infographics, or full-page illustrations. Ultimately, the goal is to enhance your book's appeal and convey your ideas in a visually compelling way.

As exciting as AI tools are, they come with their own set of challenges. In the next chapter, we'll shift our focus to the barriers you might encounter when writing with AI. From ethical considerations and copyright issues to the limitations of AI-generated content, we'll explore the obstacles that can arise and how to navigate them. Understanding these challenges is crucial to making the most of AI's potential while avoiding pitfalls that could derail your project. So, let's dive into the complexities of writing with AI and learn how to overcome them.

Chapter VI: The Barriers

After diving into the previous chapters, you might be thinking, "Writing with AI? Piece of cake!" But hold your horses – it's not all smooth sailing. Don't panic, though. We're not talking about the actual writing part. That does get easier with practice and is definitely less hair-pulling than writing without AI. The process itself isn't rocket science. You'll be the idea maestro, and the AI will be your tireless assistant, doing much of the heavy lifting. Even the brain-wracking part isn't as daunting as you might fear. AI can be your personal creativity gym, pumping up your thoughts and flexing your imaginative muscles. Who knows? It might even start spotting you on those big idea lifts. But remember, you're still the one calling the shots in this literary workout.

While AI is an incredible writing partner, it's not without its quirks. As you embark on this journey together, you'll encounter a few speed bumps along the way. These range from the AI's occasional digital hiccups to some trickier questions about rights and ethics. Don't sweat it, though – these aren't brick walls, just hurdles you can learn to clear. Some might seem higher than others, and a few you might not even need to jump. I'm laying out this obstacle course not to scare you off, but to give you a heads-up. Think of it as a map of the terrain ahead. This way, when you're deep in your writing adventure or gearing up to share your masterpiece with the world, you'll be ready for whatever comes your way.

To help you overcome these challenges, I've organized potential roadblocks into distinct categories. We'll explore physical barriers like content restrictions and usage limits; legal issues including intellectual property rights; technical obstacles such as the learning curve; quality concerns in achieving human-like creativity; ethical considerations around transparency; financial aspects of using AI tools; hurdles in the publishing industry; and psychological barriers you might encounter. This breakdown will give you a clear picture of what to expect and how to prepare as you embark on your AI-assisted writing journey.

By understanding these challenges from the outset, you'll be better equipped to master the world of AI writing. This is one reason I recommend reading this book before starting your own AI-assisted writing project. Consider these obstacles as speed bumps rather than walls—with practice and determination, you can learn to maneuver around them effectively. In the following sections, we'll examine each type of challenge in detail and explore strategies to overcome them.

It's important to remember that not all of these barriers are tangible. Some are concrete, like usage limits or subscription costs. Others are less tangible, like ethical dilemmas or psychological challenges. Each type of barrier requires a different approach to overcome. By recognizing these challenges and preparing for them, you're taking the first step toward becoming proficient in AI-assisted writing. The goal isn't to make these barriers disappear completely. Instead, it's about learning how to work around them and use them to enhance your writing process.

As we explore each type of barrier, keep in mind that every writer's experience with AI will be unique. Some challenges might feel significant to you, while others might barely register. The key is to stay open-minded and flexible, applying these insights in a way that fits your own writing journey. With patience and practice, you'll find that many of these initial hurdles actually become steppingstones to a smoother, more creative writing process.

Let's dive into each category of barriers, starting with the physical limitations you'll encounter when using AI writing tools. By understanding these challenges, you'll be better equipped to harness the power of AI while maintaining your unique voice and vision as an author.

The Physical Barriers

As you start experimenting with AI writing tools, you'll encounter what I call "physical barriers." Despite their name, these aren't tangible obstacles, but rather inherent limitations built into the AI tools and platforms you'll be using. It's important to understand that these barriers can vary significantly across different AI models and platforms.

What constitutes a restriction on one platform might be perfectly acceptable on another. For example, one AI might implement strict content filters that prohibit certain types of writing, while another might offer more flexibility. Some platforms might impose stringent usage limits, while others provide more generous allowances. Even the underlying algorithms that different models use to process and generate text can create unique limitations or opportunities.

These variations mean that your experience with AI writing tools can differ dramatically based on your chosen platform. A tool that works seamlessly for one project might prove frustratingly limited for another. As we explore these barriers in detail, keep in mind that they're not universal across all AI writing tools.

It's important to distinguish between these physical barriers and potential legal issues. Even if you find ways to overcome technical limitations, you must remain aware of legal considerations. For instance, bypassing a restriction to create copyrighted content might be technically feasible but could result in legal complications. We'll examine these legal aspects more thoroughly later in this chapter.

Don't let these challenges deter you. With effort and creativity, you can either overcome these barriers or learn to work around them effectively. Some might appear more complex than others, and some may not even apply to your specific project. I'm highlighting these barriers to provide you with a comprehensive view of the landscape, enabling you to make informed decisions both when you begin writing and later as you prepare to publish.

In the following sections, we'll break down these physical barriers into more specific categories and examine how they might manifest across different AI platforms. Understanding these nuances is key to selecting the right tool for your specific needs and working effectively within its constraints.

Content Restrictions

When writing a book with AI assistance, you may encounter various content restrictions. These are like invisible boundaries that the AI won't cross, and they can surface at different stages of your writing process. In essence, some AI tools will simply not generate the content you've requested, and it's important to understand why and how this happens.

Let's start with the most common hurdle: image creation. If you're working on an illustrated book, or just want some visuals to spark imagination, you'll quickly notice that AI image generators have some strict rules. They often refuse to create images of recognizable people, especially celebrities or public figures. Try asking for a picture of Elvis Presley or Barack Obama, and you'll likely hit a wall. The same goes for well-known fictional characters. Want an image of TinTin for inspiration? The AI will probably say no.

These image restrictions may encompass trademarked logos, distinctive art styles of renowned artists, and even certain landmarks. For instance, you might be surprised to learn that the Eiffel Tower at night is off-limits due to copyright on its illumination (yes, you read that correctly). You'll also find that requests for explicit or violent imagery are swiftly rejected. This extends to content that could be considered controversial or sensitive. These constraints aren't just arbitrary rules – they're implemented to prevent copyright infringement and promote ethical AI use, ensuring that these powerful tools aren't misused or inadvertently stepping on legal toes.

It's worth noting that different AI platforms handle these restrictions slightly differently. For instance, ChatGPT tends to be more stringent, often refusing to generate anything that might infringe on IP rights like copyright (and I will explain more about copyright later on). Midjourney, while still cautious, sometimes interprets prompts more loosely, occasionally resulting in outputs that come closer to IP boundaries. Stable Diffusion, on the other hand, offers more flexibility, allowing users to create a wider range of content, but with that flexibility comes a greater responsibility to ensure that the outputs don't violate IP rights or ethical guidelines.

But content restrictions aren't just about images. Even in the text realm, where restrictions are generally less stringent, you might encounter some barriers. For example, if you're writing a book that involves real people or events, the AI might hesitate to generate content that could be considered defamatory or invasive of privacy. It might also refuse to produce text that's overtly discriminatory or hate speech.

When you're in the brainstorming phase, thinking with the AI, you might hit some unexpected snags. Let's say you want to write a fantasy novel inspired by Harry Potter. You might ask the AI to help you create a magical school setting similar to Hogwarts. While the AI can certainly help with general ideas about magical education, it might refuse to directly mimic specific elements from J.K. Rowling's work. This is to avoid potential copyright issues.

Similarly, if you're writing a thriller and ask the AI to help plot a detailed crime, you might find it reluctant to provide specifics about illegal activities. This is part of the ethical (and legal) guidelines built into many AI systems to prevent generating potentially harmful content. For non-fiction writers, content restrictions might come into play when dealing with sensitive topics. The AI might be cautious about generating content related to certain political issues, ongoing conflicts, or controversial scientific theories.

When it comes to intellectual property (IP) issues, both ChatGPT and Claude are (currently) designed to avoid directly copying copyrighted text. In simple terms, copyrighted text is any original written work that's legally protected, like books, articles, or even social media posts. However, ChatGPT and Claude handle this challenge a bit differently. ChatGPT might sometimes produce content that sounds very similar to existing works if you give it prompts that point in that direction. It's like asking a human to write in the style of a famous author – they might unintentionally echo some phrases. Claude, on the other hand, tends to err on the side of caution. It's like that friend who's always worried about accidentally plagiarizing, sometimes to the point of being overly careful.

To overcome these restrictions, there are a few strategies you can employ. First, recognize that these limitations can vary significantly between different AI platforms. What's forbidden on one might be allowed on another. Some open-source AI models, for instance, have fewer restrictions but may require more careful use to ensure ethical and legal compliance.

You can switch to an AI model that doesn't have the specific restriction that's currently holding you back. If you need a drawing that ChatGPT is unwilling to create, you might try Stable Diffusion. If ChatGPT doesn't allow you to create a crime scene for your book, you could use GPT-J or GPT-NeoX, open-source models that generally have fewer content restrictions for text generation.

Another strategy is rephrasing your request. Let's say you're trying to write a crime story using ChatGPT, but the AI hesitates due to ethical concerns. In this case, clarify that you're crafting a book plot, not planning real criminal activities. If the AI still balks, try a different angle. You could describe your project as a "fictional mystery scenario" or a "hypothetical detective case study." Alternatively, consider breaking down the scene into less explicit components. Instead of focusing on violent details, emphasize the setting or the characters' emotions. These approaches can help you navigate around content restrictions while still achieving your creative goals.

This approach isn't just for text – it works for image generation too. Say you're trying to create a picture of a famous person but the AI is being stubborn. Instead of asking for them by name, try describing their looks. For example, rather than requesting "a portrait of Elvis Presley," you could say "a man with dark pompadour hair, sideburns, and a white jumpsuit." The same goes for trademarked characters. Instead of asking for "Mickey Mouse," try describing "a cartoon mouse with large round ears and red shorts." By focusing on specific features or characteristics without using names, you can often sidestep the AI's restrictions while still getting the image you want. It's like playing a game of visual charades with the AI - you're giving it all the clues without saying the actual name.

Keep in mind, that while these clever workarounds can be helpful, it's important to respect the reasons behind these restrictions. Always make sure you're using AI-generated content ethically and legally, and stick to the rules laid out by the platform you're using. By understanding these limitations and learning to navigate them creatively, you can make the most of AI's help in your writing process. It's about finding that sweet spot between unleashing your creativity and staying on the right side of content generation ethics and legal boundaries. Think of it as a dance - you're working with the AI, not against it, to create something amazing while still playing by the rules.

Usage Limits

As you explore AI-assisted writing more deeply, you'll soon discover that your AI tools aren't an unlimited resource. Many AI platforms come with usage limits that can significantly impact your writing process. These restrictions vary widely between different AI services, so it's crucial to understand what you're working with.

Time-based limits are a common type of restriction. Some AI writing assistants might cap how long you can use them in a single session or limit you to a certain number of messages per hour. Others might impose daily or monthly usage caps. For book writers, this could mean carefully planning your AI-assisted writing sessions to maximize your allotted time.

Example (from Claude):

⚠ You are out of messages until 7 PM

Token limits are another critical factor to consider. As discussed earlier, a 'token' is a unit of text processing. Many AI platforms restrict how many tokens you can use per day or per request. This is particularly relevant when working on longer pieces of writing. You might find that your AI assistant can only handle a chapter at a time, rather than an entire manuscript, leading some writers to break their work into smaller chunks to accommodate these limits.

To remind you, when it comes to usage limits, ChatGPT and Claude used to have notable differences. ChatGPT generally allows for longer continuous interactions. You can often work with larger chunks of text, which can be beneficial when you're writing or editing entire chapters. This makes ChatGPT particularly useful for tasks that require maintaining context over a longer conversation, such as developing a complex plot or conducting an in-depth analysis.

Claude, however, tends to have stricter limits on conversation length. It's more likely to cut off a conversation after a certain amount of back-and-forth, requiring you to start fresh or carefully manage the information you're feeding it. This limitation means you might need to be more strategic in how you use Claude, breaking your work into smaller, more focused sessions. However, this has lately changed, meaning that Claude now offers much longer conversations, especially if you work within a project.

Output length limitations can also pose challenges. Some AI tools restrict how much text they can generate in a single go. While brainstorming ideas or generating draft content, you might need to make multiple requests to get a substantial amount of material. For book authors, this could require more back-and-forth with your AI assistant than initially expected.

Rate limiting is another form of usage restriction you might encounter. This is when an AI platform slows down your requests if you're using it too frequently. Designed to prevent overuse and ensure fair access for all users, rate limiting might require you to pace yourself and plan for potential slowdowns if you're rapidly firing off questions or requests to your AI tool.

For image generation, ChatGPT and Midjourney also have different usage limits (and IP considerations). ChatGPT typically allows a certain number of image generations per day/month, with paid tiers offering more. Midjourney operates on a subscription model with different tiers allowing for varying numbers of "fast" generations per month.

It's important to note that the limitations often differ between free and paid tiers of AI services. Free versions typically impose stricter usage limits, while paid versions offer more generous allowances, though even these have their caps. As you dive deeper into AI-assisted writing, you might find yourself weighing the costs and benefits of upgrading to a paid service. As I mentioned earlier, when it comes to generating quality text, you often don't have a choice; investing in at least one paid service is essential to achieve the best results.

These usage limits can significantly influence your writing process. They might affect how you structure your writing sessions, how you break down your book into manageable sections for AI assistance, and even how you approach the revision process. For instance, you might start your day using your AI tool to brainstorm ideas or outline a chapter, mindful of your token usage. Then, you could switch to writing independently, saving some of your AI usage for later when you need help with editing or refining your prose.

Understanding these differences in usage limits and IP approaches can help you choose the right tool for different stages of your writing process. For instance, you might use GPT for initial drafting where you need to work with larger chunks of text, then switch to Claude for more focused editing sessions. Similarly, you might use ChatGPT for concept art that needs to be clearly distinct from existing IP, while turning to Midjourney for more abstract, mood-setting images.

Keep in mind that these limits aren't uniform across all platforms. What's restrictive on one service might be more lenient on another. As you gain experience with AI-assisted writing, you'll likely develop strategies for working within these limits or choose tools that best fit your writing style and needs. Some writers even use multiple AI tools strategically, leveraging the strengths and limitations of each to maximize their productivity.

Understanding these usage limits is key to effectively planning your AI-assisted book writing journey. By knowing what to expect, you can structure your work to make the most of your AI tools without encountering unexpected roadblocks. While these limits can sometimes feel frustrating, they can also encourage more focused and efficient use of AI in your writing process, ultimately helping you to develop a more balanced and productive approach to AI-assisted authorship.

The Legal Barriers

Venturing into AI authorship isn't always a smooth ride, especially when it comes to legal matters. You might be unfamiliar with IP laws or even the fine print in your agreement with the AI company (yes, those terms of use are a contract). It's easy to think, "I created this book - the ideas, the text, the images – it's all mine, even if AI helped." But the reality is more complex. There are several legal questions you need to consider, and they're not just theoretical—they could significantly impact your rights as an author. Understanding these issues is crucial as you navigate the exciting, yet sometimes murky, waters of AI-assisted creation.

Legal challenges often emerge when you're ready to publish your AI-assisted work, or more problematically, after you've already released it – especially if you've self-published. It's crucial to be aware of these issues because publishers will inevitably ask questions, and you'll likely need to sign waivers or agreements addressing them. While these concerns shouldn't deter you from writing, they may influence your choice of AI tools or subscription plans. You might also need to reconsider some of the images you create or make compromises in your creative process. Being prepared for these legal nuances can help you navigate the publishing landscape more smoothly and protect your work in the long run.

The legal landscape for AI-assisted writing is intricate and rapidly evolving. It primarily revolves around IP rights, which mainly include copyright and trademarks, and contractual obligations with AI companies. Within this realm, we'll explore various aspects such as ownership of AI-generated content, potential infringement issues, and the implications of using AI tools with different terms of service. As this field continues to develop, understanding these legal nuances becomes crucial for authors seeking to protect their work and navigate the complexities of AI-assisted creation.

Mastering the legal landscape of AI-assisted writing requires an informed and cautious approach. These considerations shouldn't stifle your creativity, but rather guide your choices in tool selection and usage. The aim is to leverage AI's capabilities while adhering to legal boundaries. This involves carefully reviewing the terms of service for each AI tool, understanding your rights to the generated content, and recognizing any commercial use restrictions.

Let's be honest – poring over lengthy legal documents isn't exactly a thrilling pastime. But here's a handy workaround: put your AI assistant to work analyzing those terms of service and boiling down the essential points for you. Ask it to break things down in everyday language. While this approach isn't a replacement for professional legal advice, it can give you a clear snapshot of your rights and responsibilities. By using this method, you can navigate the intricacies of AI-assisted writing more efficiently, staying informed without getting lost in a sea of legal terminology. It's like having a knowledgeable friend explain the fine print to you - making the whole process less daunting and more manageable.

Before we dive deeper, let's get something crystal clear: What you're about to read isn't legal advice. I'll say it again: **This is not legal advice.** As someone who specializes in IP law, I know that giving solid legal guidance for a book project requires a deep dive into all the nitty-gritty details. Plus, the legal world of AI and IP is changing faster than a chameleon on a disco floor, and it's different depending on where you are in the world. What I'm about to share is more like a bird's eye view of the current legal landscape. It's a good place to start, but it's not the whole story, and it's definitely not set in stone.

The world of AI and copyright law is changing faster than you can say "artificial intelligence." That's why it's crucial to keep your finger on the pulse of the latest developments. If you find yourself scratching your head over legal puzzles or complex questions, it's a smart move to chat with a legal pro. They can give you advice that's tailor-made for your unique situation and location. Think of this chapter as your trusty compass, pointing you in the right general direction, rather than a turn-by-turn GPS. It'll give you a feel for the terrain, but when it comes to the nitty-gritty details, a legal expert is your best bet.

The key message is this: Be mindful of potential legal considerations, but don't let them stifle your creative ambitions. Instead, use this awareness to make informed decisions about your AI tools and writing processes. By staying informed and choosing resources wisely, you can harness AI's power to enhance your work while safeguarding your rights and respecting those of others.

As I see it we're amid a seismic shift in copyright law. As AI reshapes our creative landscape, legal frameworks will likely evolve to accommodate these changes. While you might encounter hesitation from publishers wary of potential liability in the short term, it's reasonable to expect the legal terrain will become clearer and more navigable in the coming years. This period of uncertainty may give way to a more defined, AI-friendly legal environment, opening new possibilities for writers and creators.

Let's explore the legal landscape through two primary lenses: *Rights Granted* and *Avoiding Infringements*. The first theme centers on selecting a platform that bestows appropriate rights to your work. This decision is crucial, as some AI tools may not offer exclusive rights to your outputs, or may do so only under specific subscription tiers. It's essential to be aware of these nuances.

The second theme—avoiding infringements—addresses potential legal risks inherent in AI-assisted writing. Regardless of your ownership status, it's vital to be vigilant about possible infringements in your book to sidestep liability. Remember, even when an AI tool generates content, you, as the author, could still be held accountable for any infringement within that material.

Understanding these legal considerations is paramount for any AI author. It's not merely about shielding yourself from potential legal entanglements; it's about ensuring your creative work truly belongs to you and that you possess the necessary rights to publish and profit from it. In the following sections, we'll examine each theme in depth, equipping you with knowledge to navigate the intricate legal terrain of AI-assisted writing.

Rights Granted by AI Platforms for Authors

As an AI author, understanding the rights you have to the content you create with AI assistance is crucial. Different AI platforms offer varying levels of rights, and in some cases, these rights can change based on your subscription tier or whether you're using consumer or commercial plans. It's important to note that while most major platforms now assign ownership of outputs to users, the legal question of whether AI-generated content is copyrightable at all remains unresolved — and this is arguably a more fundamental concern than the contractual terms themselves. Let's examine the landscape of rights granted by popular AI writing and image generation tools, focusing on what's most relevant for authors.

As of now, ChatGPT allows users to own the content they generate, whether using the free or Plus subscription. OpenAI goes further than simply not claiming ownership — its terms explicitly assign to users all of OpenAI's right, title, and interest in the output, to the extent permitted by applicable law. OpenAI may use user inputs and outputs to improve its models unless you opt out in your settings. This means you can use the text you generate for your book without OpenAI retaining rights over it. While this arrangement is generally sufficient for most authors, it's worth reviewing OpenAI's terms and considering how it may impact negotiations with publishers. Note also that outputs may not be unique — other users could receive similar content from the same model, and OpenAI's assignment does not extend to those other users' outputs.

Claude, Anthropic's AI assistant, grants users ownership of the content they generate. Under Anthropic's commercial terms (which apply to API, Team, and Enterprise plan users), Anthropic explicitly assigns to the customer its right, title, and interest in outputs, and will not use commercial customer content to train its models. Anthropic also provides legal indemnification against copyright infringement claims for authorized commercial uses of its outputs — meaning Anthropic will defend its commercial customers and pay for approved settlements or judgments. For consumer users (Free, Pro, and Max plans), Anthropic similarly assigns rights in the output, but the indemnification protections do not apply. Additionally, since late 2025, consumer users can choose whether their conversations are used for model improvement — those who opt in are subject to a five-year data retention period, while those who opt out retain the standard 30-day retention. These training and privacy updates do not apply to commercial plans, where data is never used for training by default. The broader legal landscape regarding AI-generated content remains uncertain, as copyright protection generally requires human authorship. Authors should review Anthropic's terms and consider publisher requirements to ensure compliance with evolving copyright laws.

Google's Gemini follows a comparable model. Google states it will not claim ownership of generated content, and you can use it in your books or other projects. However, Google's terms are spread across multiple documents and vary significantly depending on whether you're using the free consumer version, a paid business plan, or the API. With free and unpaid tiers, Google may use your content to improve its services and machine learning technologies, including training models. With paid and enterprise tiers, data handling terms are more protective. As with the other text-based AI tools, Google doesn't claim ownership of your content but also doesn't grant you exclusive rights — and you acknowledge that Google may generate the same or similar content for other users. Authors should be aware of these nuances and consider which tier they're using, especially if working on sensitive or commercially valuable content.

When we move to image generation AI, the rights landscape becomes more varied. ChatGPT now includes native image generation capabilities, granting users full usage rights to the images they generate, including for commercial purposes. This is particularly beneficial for authors looking to create unique illustrations for their books. You can use, modify, and sell these images as part of your work. For Enterprise customers, OpenAI also offers IP indemnification for output. While OpenAI may use your prompts and generated images to improve their models (unless you opt out), they don't claim any rights to the images themselves. This approach aligns more closely with what publishers typically expect.

MidJourney's rights structure is more nuanced than many authors realize, and it's important to understand what actually varies by subscription level. All paid subscribers — across Basic, Standard, Pro, and Mega plans — own the assets they create and can use them commercially. The key distinction between tiers is not ownership but privacy: images generated on Basic and Standard plans are public by default and can be viewed and remixed by other MidJourney users. Only the Pro and Mega plans include "Stealth Mode," which keeps your images private — a critical feature for authors needing confidentiality for book illustrations or branding. Free trial users, on the other hand, receive no commercial rights at all; their images are licensed under Creative Commons Attribution-NonCommercial 4.0 (CC BY-NC 4.0).

There is one important revenue-based restriction: if you or your company earns more than $1,000,000 in annual gross revenue, you must subscribe to a Pro ($60/month) or Mega ($120/month) plan to retain full ownership and commercial rights — even if you personally have a Basic or Standard subscription. MidJourney does not offer a separate "Enterprise" plan; the Pro and Mega plans serve that function.

Additionally, by using MidJourney, you grant the platform a broad, perpetual license to use, distribute, and create derivative works from your content. Content generated in public settings is publicly viewable and can be remixed by others unless you use Stealth Mode. It is also worth noting that unlike Anthropic and Microsoft, MidJourney does not offer IP indemnification — if your generated image infringes on a third party's work, you bear the legal risk.

Stable Diffusion, developed by Stability AI, potentially offers some of the most flexible rights, but the situation is more complex than simply "open source." Earlier versions of Stable Diffusion (such as SDXL 1.0 and earlier) were released under a permissive OpenRAIL license that allowed broad use with minimal restrictions. However, newer versions — including Stable Diffusion 3.5 — use the Stability AI Community License, which introduces a revenue-based threshold: commercial use is free for individuals and businesses with annual revenues under $1,000,000, with no restrictions on the number of images created. But if you or your company exceeds that revenue threshold, you must obtain an enterprise license from Stability AI to continue using the models commercially.

If you run Stable Diffusion locally on your own hardware, you do have full control over the images you generate — your prompts and outputs never leave your system, and there is no platform retaining data or training on your content. However, the license terms still apply to the model weights themselves. If you're using a hosted version of Stable Diffusion through a third-party service, you'll need to check the specific terms of that service provider, as they may impose additional restrictions.

For authors, the key takeaway is this: with most text-based AI tools (ChatGPT, Claude, Gemini), you are assigned ownership of the content you generate. All three major platforms now actively assign their rights in outputs to users, rather than merely declining to claim ownership. While this is generally sufficient for writing and personal use, it's important to consider that your rights are only as strong as the underlying law allows — and under current copyright doctrine, purely AI-generated content without sufficient human authorship may not be copyrightable at all. This means the contractual assignment of rights, while important, does not guarantee that you hold enforceable copyright over the output. You may need to be prepared to address this issue in your negotiations with publishers, who often expect exclusive rights and clear copyright status. Consider how to make your work more uniquely yours beyond the AI-generated content.

With image generation tools, the situation is more nuanced. ChatGPT's integrated image generation offers perhaps the most straightforward and author-friendly terms, granting you full usage rights. MidJourney grants commercial rights and ownership to all paid subscribers, but privacy varies by tier — only Pro and Mega plans keep your images private, which is essential for authors needing confidentiality. Stable Diffusion, when used locally, offers the most control and privacy, but the latest model versions have revenue-based licensing restrictions, and running it locally requires technical expertise.

It's crucial to note that all these platforms have terms that allow them to change their services or terms at any time. This means the rights you agree to today might change in the future. Staying informed about these changes is vital for maintaining control over your work and understanding your position when approaching publishers.

In terms of privacy — a key concern for many authors — most AI platforms have broadly similar policies, though important distinctions exist between consumer and commercial tiers. For consumer plans, platforms generally reserve the right to use your content to improve their models, though most now offer opt-out mechanisms. OpenAI allows users to opt out of data training in their settings. Anthropic, since its 2025 consumer terms update, gives users the explicit choice to allow or disallow model training on their conversations, with those who opt in subject to longer data retention. Google may use free-tier content for model improvement.

For commercial and enterprise plans across all major platforms, the terms are typically more protective — data is generally not used for model training by default.

This means that while your work won't be published or reused directly, fragments of your input — unique phrases, styles, or structural patterns — may inform future model generations in diluted or abstracted forms if you're on a consumer plan that uses data for training. It's highly unlikely that any substantial portion of your work would be reproduced verbatim, but traces of your creative input could theoretically influence the model's outputs elsewhere.

For image generation, the situation is similar. Your prompts and resulting images may be used to refine the system's generative capabilities on consumer tiers, though again, it's unlikely that any image would be duplicated as-is. Elements such as composition, color schemes, or stylistic features might subtly influence future generations.

Importantly, even when user data is used, it is typically anonymized and aggregated. This means it's stripped of personal identifiers and processed in bulk, making it extremely difficult to trace any output back to a specific individual. Still, if you're working on highly sensitive or confidential material, this level of anonymization may not be sufficient.

For those needing stronger guarantees of privacy, there are more secure options. ChatGPT Enterprise ensures that none of your data is used for training purposes by default. Anthropic's commercial plans (Team, Enterprise, and API) similarly guarantee that data is not used for model training. For image generation, you can use open-source models like Stable Diffusion locally, ensuring that your prompts and outputs never leave your own system. These approaches offer the highest level of control over your data, though they typically require more technical knowledge or financial investment.

In conclusion, as an AI author, you should carefully consider which tools you use based on the rights you need for your specific project and how these rights might affect your publishing prospects. For most book writing, the ownership rights assigned by text-based AI tools are sufficient for the writing process, but you should be aware that the copyrightability of AI-generated content remains an open legal question — one that may affect your ability to enforce exclusive rights. For illustrations or other visual elements, you may need to be more selective, opting for plans that offer both commercial rights and privacy (such as MidJourney's Pro or Mega plans), or tools that grant more comprehensive control (such as running Stable Diffusion locally). Always read the current terms of service for any AI tool you use, and when in doubt, especially for significant projects, don't hesitate to seek legal advice. By being informed about your rights and their implications, you can confidently use AI to enhance your writing while protecting your creative work and navigating the publishing landscape effectively.

Personally, I believe that in this new age of AI-assisted creativity, traditional concerns about absolute rights exclusivity need to be reframed, not discarded. If some parts of your project — like an illustration generated through an AI platform — are created under non-exclusive terms or could theoretically resemble other outputs, that doesn't eliminate your copyright over the final, compiled book. You still hold rights in the overall expression and structure of your work.

That said, exclusivity still matters, especially if you plan to license your book, adapt it for other media, or publish through traditional channels. What's more, the legal landscape around AI-generated content is still evolving, and rights questions aren't only about ownership — they're also about infringement. In my view, the more urgent legal risk for most authors is unintentional infringement: generating something that too closely resembles protected content, characters, or visual styles. That's where authors need to stay sharp.

This is also why I strongly believe that AI authors should write the core of their books themselves, and use AI to enhance — not replace — their writing. If you're the one generating the ideas, shaping the prose, and guiding the creative direction, you maintain not just creative control but legal safety. The more original your input, the lower your risk of accidentally reproducing someone else's protected work. Let me now explain about infringements.

Copyright and Trademark Infringement Risks

As an author using AI, it's crucial to understand the terrain of copyright and trademark law. While AI tools can supercharge your writing process, they also introduce new legal risks that shouldn't be ignored. The major concern is inadvertently creating content that's too similar to existing copyrighted works. Different AI models handle this risk in different ways, and understanding those differences helps you steer clear of legal pitfalls. Think of it as having a map of a minefield: the more you understand where the dangers lie, the more confidently you can move forward.

Copyright protects original creative works. It applies to books, music, visual art, films, software, and more. It gives the creator exclusive rights to use, reproduce, and profit from their work. If you write a novel, copyright law prevents others from copying or selling it without your permission. It's basically a legal "hands off" sign for your creative expression (not your ideas themselves, since copyright does not protect ideas, only the way you express them). Common copyright violations include copying someone else's work without permission, distributing copyrighted material unlawfully, or assuming that something is free to use just because it's online. For instance, you can't paste entire paragraphs from Harry Potter into your own book and expect to get away with it. That's a textbook copyright violation.

Despite their sophistication, AI tools can occasionally generate content that resembles existing protected works. This might result from the AI's training data or from the way user prompts guide the generation. As the author, you bear full responsibility for making sure your final output doesn't infringe on someone else's intellectual property. Take ChatGPT, for example. It's trained on a broad and undisclosed mix of licensed, publicly available, and web-sourced text. While it's designed to produce new, non-verbatim content, there is always a risk, especially if you prompt it to imitate specific authors, styles, or works, that the result might be too close to something that already exists. OpenAI includes filters to minimize this risk, but they are not infallible. Claude, known for its more cautious ethical alignment, is more likely to reject prompts that might generate infringing or closely derivative content. Gemini, too, is trained to produce original work, but it still draws on large volumes of web data, so the potential for unintended overlap remains.

When it comes to image generation, the risks can be even more pronounced. ChatGPT's image generation is trained to avoid reproducing copyrighted characters or artworks, but vague or overly descriptive prompts (like "draw Mickey Mouse in a forest") can sometimes yield outputs that resemble protected images. MidJourney, while known for producing stunning art, has been flagged for outputs that closely echo real-world artist styles, particularly when prompts mimic a recognizable aesthetic. This concern is not unique to MidJourney; it applies across image generation models more broadly. The Getty Images v. Stability AI lawsuit in the UK, which reached a first-instance judgment in November 2025, illustrates how these issues are now reaching the courts. Stable Diffusion, especially when run through open-source forks, varies widely depending on the dataset and implementation, and some versions may produce outputs more prone to resemblance or reuse.

Another underappreciated risk comes not from training data, but from the sameness of prompts. For instance, if you ask ChatGPT to "Write me a children's book with a fun character," it might suggest Milo the Mushroom. Seems innocent enough, until you realize that dozens of other authors received the same suggestion. Many of them, just like you, thought their AI would do all the creative work. Now you've got a character and concept that's not only unoriginal but potentially mirrored across dozens of near-identical books. This isn't necessarily a legal problem in the copyright sense (nobody owns the name "Milo the Mushroom"), but it can result in work that feels derivative or indistinguishable from others, and could expose you to reputational or commercial issues. The lesson here is simple: if you want unique, original, and safe content, you need to be the one driving the creativity. The more specific and original your input, the more distinctive and legally secure your output will be. AI is powerful, but if you let it autopilot your project, it may take you somewhere you didn't want to go, and that someone else already got to first.

It's also important to be aware of fair use, a legal doctrine in the United States that allows limited use of copyrighted material without permission from the rights holder. This can apply to quoting a few lines from a book in a review, using a film clip for educational purposes, or including part of a song in a parody. Fair use aims to balance the rights of creators with the broader public interest in free expression. That said, fair use is not a blanket permission. It's assessed on a case-by-case basis, using four key factors: the purpose and character of the use (e.g., commercial or transformative), the nature of the copyrighted work, the amount and substantiality of what was used, and the effect of the use on the market for the original. If your book is commercial, fair use is much harder to defend. And remember: fair use is a legal defense, not a right. It only protects you after you've been challenged, which may already mean expensive legal trouble.

The question of whether using copyrighted works to train AI models constitutes fair use is itself a major unresolved legal issue. In May 2025, the U.S. Copyright Office released Part 3 of its Copyright and Artificial Intelligence Report, which addressed generative AI training specifically. The Office concluded that it is not possible to prejudge litigation outcomes and that some uses of copyrighted works for AI training will qualify as fair use and some will not. Notably, the Office identified the fourth factor, the effect on the market, as likely the most significant consideration. It highlighted three areas of market harm: lost licensing revenue (since a voluntary licensing market between publishers and AI labs is already emerging), market dilution from the aggregate impact of AI-generated content, and lost sales where AI outputs effectively substitute for purchases of the original work. For authors, this means the legal environment around AI-generated content is still actively being shaped, and relying on fair use as a blanket justification is risky.

Also, fair use is mainly a U.S. concept. The EU, for example, doesn't have a general fair use doctrine. Instead, it relies on a limited set of specific exceptions that are far narrower and less flexible. However, the EU does have a text and data mining (TDM) exception under the Digital Single Market Directive (Articles 3 and 4), which is directly relevant to AI. Article 3 permits TDM for scientific research purposes, while Article 4 allows broader TDM but gives rightsholders the ability to opt out and reserve their rights. Other countries vary widely, making fair use a risky foundation for AI-assisted work aimed at international audiences. Personally, I recommend not relying on fair use at all when writing with AI. If your image looks too much like Donald Duck, don't wait to see if Disney's lawyers agree. Just change it. The only exception might be when you're directly critiquing something and need to reference a protected work. Even then, you're assuming a legal risk.

The copyrightability of AI-generated content is a subject of growing debate, with significant legal developments occurring across multiple jurisdictions. In the United States, the Copyright Office has been increasingly specific about where the line falls. In January 2025, it published Part 2 of its Copyright and Artificial Intelligence Report, which provided detailed guidance on the human authorship requirement. The Report reaffirmed that human authorship remains a bedrock requirement of copyrightability and that works entirely generated by AI are not copyrightable. Crucially, the Office stated that prompts alone, even highly detailed ones, generally do not provide sufficient human control over the expressive elements of the output to make the user an author. However, the Report also clarified that human authors are entitled to copyright protection for their works of authorship that are perceptible in AI-generated outputs, as well as for the creative selection, coordination, or arrangement of material in those outputs, or creative modifications of the outputs. In other words, the more you shape, edit, arrange, and transform the AI's output with your own creative judgment, the stronger your copyright claim.

This position was reinforced by the courts. In Thaler v. Perlmutter, the D.C. District Court held in 2023 that copyright requires human authorship, and in 2025 the D.C. Circuit affirmed, describing human authorship as a "bedrock requirement." The court also denied a petition for en banc rehearing in May 2025, solidifying this as the strongest judicial precedent on the issue. While AI-generated content itself does not qualify for protection, the combination of AI assistance with meaningful human creativity can produce copyrightable works, depending on the specific facts of each case.

The method presented in this book is consistent with that framework, positioning AI as a tool rather than a substitute for human authorship. By structuring your workflow so that AI assists rather than autonomously generates content, you retain the necessary level of human creativity that supports copyright protection. AI may help refine ideas, generate suggestions, or improve structure, but the writing itself remains guided and shaped by the author. Under this approach, your work is well positioned to meet the Copyright Office's requirements, though it's important to understand that copyrightability is always assessed on a case-by-case basis. The more substantial your creative contribution, the more confident you can be in your copyright claim.

Different jurisdictions are evolving in different directions. The United Kingdom is actively grappling with AI and copyright, but the situation is far more unsettled than many assume. In late 2024 and early 2025, the UK government ran a public consultation on potential changes to UK copyright law related to AI training. The government's initially preferred option was a text and data mining exception that would allow AI developers to use copyrighted material unless rightsholders opted out. However, creative industries pushed back strongly, and the Data (Use and Access) Act 2025, which received Royal Assent in June 2025, was passed without the controversial AI copyright provisions. Instead, the Act requires the government to publish a report on the use of copyright works in AI development, along with an economic impact assessment, by March 18, 2026. As of early 2026, the government has acknowledged that workable solutions for transparency and opt-out mechanisms have yet to be found, and the debate remains very much open. The outcome of the appeal in Getty Images v. Stability AI, expected later in 2026, may also shape the UK's approach significantly. For authors, this means the UK landscape is in flux, and no new exceptions allowing AI training without permission have actually been enacted.

Japan has historically adopted a more permissive approach. Its 2019 Copyright Act amendments, particularly Article 30-4, allow the use of copyrighted works for information analysis purposes, including AI training, as long as the use is not aimed at "enjoyment" of the creative expression itself. This legal framework has been welcomed by technology firms. However, the picture is becoming more nuanced. In 2025, a major lawsuit (Yomiuri Shimbun v. Perplexity AI) challenged Article 30-4's scope, particularly regarding AI outputs that effectively substitute for original content consumption. Japan's Agency of Cultural Affairs also published a "Checklist & Guidance on AI and Copyright" in July 2025, which clarified that training on a small group of a specific creator's works for the purpose of generating outputs containing their creative expressions may fall outside Article 30-4's protection. So while Japan remains more AI-friendly than many jurisdictions, it is not a blanket safe harbor.

These jurisdictional differences highlight just how fragmented and unstable the current legal landscape is. What's permissible in one country could expose you to infringement claims in another. For authors working internationally, or even just publishing to a global audience, understanding these distinctions is crucial.

For all of these reasons, you should always carefully review any AI-generated content and be ready to make substantial edits to ensure originality. Keep records of your writing process, including prompts used and edits made. This kind of documentation can serve as evidence of your human creative contribution if questions about copyrightability ever arise. If you're using AI to generate images, try reverse image searching them to check whether they closely resemble existing content. And while no one expects you to become a copyright lawyer overnight, staying generally informed about legal developments in your target markets is a smart way to protect your work.

In conclusion, while AI tools offer tremendous potential for authors, they also introduce meaningful risks, especially around copyright and trademarks. I've focused mostly on copyright here, but don't forget the importance of trademarks too. You should avoid using any recognizable logos, mascots, or symbols. That means skipping things like the Nike swoosh or the McDonald's arches in your book illustrations, even if the AI "suggests" them. By understanding these risks, reviewing your content critically, and staying informed, you can harness the power of AI while minimizing legal exposure. The goal isn't to scare you off from using these tools. It's to help you use them wisely. AI should enhance your creativity, not replace your voice or judgment. That's how you make something truly original, and keep it yours.

The Technical Barriers

As you dive deeper into the realm of AI authorship, you'll bump into a few technical and financial hurdles that might throw a wrench in your creative gears. While AI has the power to supercharge your writing, it's important to be ready for the challenges that come with it. The three main speed bumps you'll encounter are: getting the hang of AI tools (it's like learning to ride a bike, but the bike keeps changing shape), dealing with AI's occasional mood swings when it comes to output quality, and managing the costs associated with AI services and supporting technology. Let's take a closer look at these obstacles and how to navigate them.

Learning Curve

Becoming proficient with AI writing tools is akin to learning to ride different types of bicycles. You might start with a user-friendly model like ChatGPT, which is relatively easy to get rolling with. However, as you explore more specialized tools or advanced features, you'll find yourself adjusting to new "terrains" and "handling" characteristics.

The time investment required to master these tools can be substantial. Each AI model has its own quirks and preferences. A prompting strategy that works brilliantly with one might fall flat with another. For instance, you might discover that Claude responds better to detailed, specific prompts, while ChatGPT can sometimes produce interesting results with more open-ended queries.

As you navigate this learning curve, you'll likely experience moments of frustration. Your prompts might not yield the results you're looking for, or you might find yourself frequently adjusting your approach. This is all part of the process. With practice, you'll develop an intuition for crafting effective prompts across different models.

Moreover, the AI landscape is constantly evolving. New models are released, existing ones are updated, and capabilities change. This means your learning journey is ongoing. You'll need to stay adaptable, ready to adjust your techniques as the tools themselves evolve.

The good news is that, like riding a bike, the process does get easier with practice. Over time, you'll develop a feel for which tool is best suited for specific writing tasks. You might prefer one AI for brainstorming creative fiction, another for drafting formal documents, and yet another for research and fact-checking.

Remember, everyone's learning curve is different. Some authors might click with AI writing tools almost immediately, while others might take more time to find their rhythm. Be patient with yourself and persistent in your practice.

Inconsistency in Outputs

Even as you gain proficiency with AI writing tools, you'll still face the challenge of inconsistent outputs. This inconsistency typically presents itself in two main forms: hallucinations and difficulties in maintaining uniformity across multiple generations.

Hallucinations are a persistent challenge in the AI writing process. Even with carefully crafted prompts, these errors can subtly slip through, often blending seamlessly with accurate information. The real danger lies in their plausibility, making them difficult to detect without vigilant fact-checking. This issue is especially problematic in projects demanding high factual accuracy, such as historical fiction or non-fiction. You may find yourself spending considerable time verifying details provided by the AI, which can slow down your writing process. If these hallucinations make it into your final draft, they could seriously undermine your credibility as an author. Different AI models are prone to different types of hallucinations, so part of your ongoing learning process will involve identifying which models are more reliable for specific types of information and when extra caution is necessary

The second major inconsistency challenge is maintaining coherence across multiple generations of content. This becomes particularly evident in longer projects like novels or comprehensive non-fiction books. The AI's lack of persistent memory means that details established in one session might be contradicted in another, leading to inconsistencies in plot, character traits, or factual information throughout your work.

This lack of continuity can manifest in various ways, such as character motivations shifting unexpectedly, established world-building rules being broken, or previously stated facts being contradicted. These inconsistencies can disrupt the flow of your narrative and require significant editing to correct. Additionally, inconsistencies may arise when using different AI platforms; for instance, if you used ChatGPT for one section and Claude for another, you might notice differences in style and tone, further complicating the editing process.

Maintaining consistency also extends to tone, style, and narrative voice. You might find that the AI suggests content that doesn't align with the established mood or style of your work, requiring you to constantly adjust and refine its outputs to maintain a cohesive voice throughout your project.

Strategies for Success

To navigate these technical barriers effectively, consider the following strategies:

1. **Systematic Learning**: Approach each AI tool methodically. Experiment with different prompting techniques and keep notes on what works best for each model and task.

2. **Create Reference Documents**: Develop detailed "bibles" for your projects, including character traits, plot points, and important facts. Reference these in your prompts to maintain consistency.

3. **Fact-Checking Routine**: Establish a rigorous fact-checking process, especially for critical plot points or factual claims in your writing.

4. **Combine AI Tools**: Use different AI models for different tasks based on their strengths. This can help mitigate individual weaknesses.

5. **Continuous Editing**: View AI-generated content as a first draft. Be prepared to substantially edit and refine the output to ensure consistency and accuracy.

6. **Stay Informed**: Keep up with developments in AI writing technology. New features or models might offer solutions to current challenges.

7. **Balance AI and Human Input**: Remember that your judgment, creativity, and oversight are crucial. Use AI as a tool to enhance your writing, not replace your authorial voice.

In conclusion, while these technical barriers present real challenges, they're not insurmountable. With patience, practice, and a strategic approach, you can harness the power of AI to enhance your writing while navigating its limitations.

Financial Barriers

Integrating AI tools into your writing process can greatly enhance productivity and creativity, but it also introduces financial considerations that need careful management. These financial barriers mainly arise from subscription costs for AI services and investments in supporting technology.

Subscription costs for AI writing tools can add up quickly, especially as multiple services are often needed for comprehensive coverage. With new software emerging daily, it's tempting to try out different tools, which can further increase expenses. To be effective, you might need several subscriptions. At a minimum, I recommend subscribing to both ChatGPT and Claude, with Midjourney also worth considering depending on your visual needs.

For example, ChatGPT Plus and Claude Pro each cost $20 per month, offering expanded usage and access to advanced features. Specialized tools like Jasper AI are more expensive, with the Creator plan starting at $49 per month. Image generation adds another layer of expense: Midjourney offers tiered pricing, with plans ranging from $10 to $60 per month depending on your needs, and a Mega plan at $120 for high-volume users. As you explore more advanced or niche tools, these costs can add up quickly. A typical setup might include subscriptions to both ChatGPT and Claude, totaling $40 per month, plus an entry-level Midjourney plan at $10, and perhaps Jasper AI at $49. Altogether, your monthly expenses could easily reach $100 or more, depending on the tools and tiers you choose.

While these costs may seem substantial, especially for those starting out or working with limited budgets, it's important to keep them in context. Tools like ChatGPT and Claude are becoming integral parts of many people's productivity toolkits, far beyond just book writing. Their broad utility can help justify the expense as they support a wide range of tasks, from research to creative brainstorming.

Beyond AI subscriptions, you might also need to invest in supporting technology. While almost any computer will suffice for basic tasks, having a faster computer can enhance your experience with AI tools. Other helpful investments include an additional monitor for improved workflow and specialized software for tasks like word processing and book formatting.

Overall, the costs for a well-rounded AI assisted writing setup - including AI subscriptions, necessary technology, and potentially additional tools - could reach around $150 per month or $1,800 per year.

To manage these financial barriers effectively, start by prioritizing your most pressing needs and invest in tools that address those first. Make use of free trials to assess how each tool fits into your workflow before committing to a subscription. Consider starting with a minimalist setup and gradually expanding your toolkit as your needs evolve and your budget allows. Also, stay informed about emerging AI tools and open-source projects that might offer similar capabilities at lower costs, potentially reducing your financial burden over time.

By thoughtfully implementing these strategies, you can create a sustainable AI-assisted writing environment that enhances your craft without placing undue strain on your finances. The goal is to leverage AI to improve your writing process and output, finding the right balance between investment and return to ensure long-term success.

Publishing Industry Barriers

As AI-assisted writing becomes more prevalent, authors face a new set of challenges within the publishing industry. These barriers primarily revolve around the acceptance of AI-assisted works and the increasing market saturation due to the accessibility of AI tools.

Although I'm not directly involved in the publishing industry, I assume that the acceptance of AI-assisted works in traditional publishing is still evolving. Authors may encounter resistance from some publishers due to concerns about the originality of AI-generated content, the perceived value of such work, and the potential legal implications that remain unclear in the rapidly changing landscape of AI and copyright law.

Some publishers are approaching AI-assisted works with caution, unsure of how to evaluate or market such content. They may worry about public perception, fearing that readers might view AI-assisted books as less authentic or valuable than entirely human-authored works. This concern can lead to reluctance in taking on AI-assisted projects, potentially limiting publishing opportunities for authors who heavily rely on AI tools.

In response to these concerns, many publishers are implementing disclosure requirements for AI usage. Authors may be asked to provide detailed information about the extent of AI involvement in their work, specifying which parts were AI-generated and which were human-written. This transparency is aimed at addressing ethical concerns and potential legal issues, but it also puts additional responsibility on authors to meticulously document their writing process.

These disclosure requirements can vary widely between publishers. Some may require a simple acknowledgment of AI usage, while others might ask for a breakdown of the AI tools used and their specific contributions to the work. Authors should be prepared to have open discussions with potential publishers about their use of AI and to provide any required documentation.

The evolving nature of these acceptance and disclosure practices means that authors need to stay informed about current industry standards and be ready to adapt their approach based on the requirements of their target publishers. It's also worth noting that some forward-thinking publishers are embracing AI-assisted works, seeing them as innovative and potentially opening new creative avenues. Authors might find more receptive audiences with these publishers or with digital-first publishing platforms that are often more open to technological advancements in writing.

Beyond acceptance issues, AI-assisted writing is contributing to increased market saturation, presenting another significant barrier for authors. The accessibility and efficiency of AI writing tools have lowered the barriers to entry for aspiring authors, leading to a surge in the number of books being produced and published, especially in the self-publishing sector.

This flood of new content makes it increasingly challenging for individual works to stand out. Readers are faced with an overwhelming number of choices, making it harder for any single book to capture attention. For authors, this means that simply producing a well-written book is no longer enough – the ability to market effectively and create a distinctive brand becomes crucial.

Distinguishing your work in an AI-saturated market requires a multi-faceted approach. First and foremost, focus on developing a unique voice and perspective that AI alone cannot replicate. Your personal experiences, insights, and creative vision are what will set your work apart. This aligns with my advice to use AI as an assistant, not as a replacement for your writing. Leverage AI as a tool to enhance these unique qualities, rather than relying on it to generate the core content of your work.

Emphasize the human elements of your writing process in your marketing efforts. Readers are often interested in the story behind the story – share your inspiration, your research process, and how you've used AI to augment (rather than replace) your creative efforts. This transparency can help build trust with your audience and differentiate your work from more AI-heavy productions.

Consider targeting niche markets or exploring unique genres where the saturation might be less intense. AI tools are often trained on general data, making them less effective in highly specialized areas. Your expertise in a particular field, combined with judicious use of AI, could help you create content that stands out for its depth and authenticity.

Building a strong author platform becomes even more critical in a saturated market. Engage with your readers through social media, author websites, and email newsletters. Create content that complements your books, such as blog posts, podcasts, or videos, to establish your authority and build a loyal following. This direct connection with your audience can help your work rise above the noise of an overcrowded market.

Collaboration with other authors or industry professionals can also help distinguish your work. Consider co-authoring projects, seeking endorsements from established authors, or participating in anthologies. These collaborations can bring fresh perspectives to your work and help you tap into existing reader bases.

While the challenges of market saturation are significant, they also present opportunities for innovation. Explore new formats or hybrid forms of storytelling that leverage the strengths of both human creativity and AI capabilities. This could lead to groundbreaking works that capture readers' imaginations and set new trends in the publishing world.

As the publishing industry continues to grapple with the implications of AI-assisted writing, authors need to remain adaptable and proactive. Stay informed about industry trends, be transparent about your use of AI, and focus on creating works that showcase your unique voice and vision. By navigating these barriers thoughtfully, you can position yourself for success in the evolving landscape of AI-assisted publishing.

Psychological Barriers

Let's talk about something we've all felt at one point or another – that nagging voice in the back of our minds whispering, "You're not good enough. Someone's going to find out you're a fraud." Sound familiar? Welcome to the club of imposter syndrome, where even the most accomplished among us sometimes feel like we're just pretending to be writers.

Now, imagine adding AI to this already complex emotional cocktail. Suddenly, that voice gets a new script: "If AI helped you write this, are you even a real author?" It's enough to make you want to slam your laptop shut and take up knitting instead. But hold on to your keyboards, fellow wordsmiths, because we're all in this together, and there's a way through this AI-enhanced maze of self-doubt.

We've all been there. You pour your heart into a piece, craft each sentence with care, and then, just as you're about to hit 'send' or 'publish', that familiar dread creeps in. "Is this actually any good? What if everyone hates it? What if they find out I'm not a 'real' writer?" Now, throw AI into the mix, and it's like adding jet fuel to that fire of self-doubt.

When you use AI in your writing process, those feelings can intensify. You might find yourself wondering, "Did I write this, or did the AI? Do I deserve credit for this work?" It's as if the line between your creativity and the AI's capabilities has blurred, leaving you unsure of where you stand.

But here's the thing – using AI doesn't make you any less of a writer than using a thesaurus or spell-checker does. In fact, skillfully wielding AI tools is an art in itself. Think about it: you're not just writing anymore; you're orchestrating a symphony of human creativity and AI. That's not impostor syndrome; that's next-level authorship. The future.

So, how do we quiet that voice that says we're frauds for using AI? First, let's reframe how we think about AI authorship. Instead of seeing it as a crutch, think of it as a superpower. You're not cheating; you're evolving. You're like Iron Man with his suit – the power comes from how you use the tool, not just the tool itself.

Remember, AI can generate text, but it can't replicate your unique experiences, your emotional depth, or your understanding of the human condition. It can't capture the essence of that heartbreak you experienced in high school or the joy of your first publication. That's all you, and it's what makes your writing uniquely yours, AI assistance or not.

Try keeping a "creativity journal" where you document your writing process, including how you use AI. This isn't just for posterity; it's a tangible reminder of your creative decisions. When that imposter voice pipes up, flip through this journal. You'll see that while AI might have suggested a phrase or helped with research, the heart and soul of the work – the creative vision – that's all you. I know I mentioned this all the time, but it is crucial.

Now, let's talk about the flip side of this AI coin – the siren song of overreliance. It's tempting, isn't it? With AI, writer's block seems like a thing of the past. Got a plot hole? Ask the AI. Need a snappy dialogue? The AI's got your back. But beware, intrepid author, for here lies a trap that can snare the unwary.

Overreliance on AI is like overreliance on GPS. Sure, it'll get you to your destination, but you might miss out on the scenic routes, the unexpected detours that lead to hidden gems. In writing terms, you risk losing those quirky metaphors, those unique turns of phrase that make your writing distinctly yours.

Don't forget to unplug regularly. Have AI-free writing sessions where it's just you, your thoughts, and a blank page. It might feel scary at first, like taking off your training wheels, but it's crucial for maintaining and developing your innate creativity.

Remember, at the end of the day, it's your name on the cover of that book, your voice telling that story. AI is a tool in your writing toolkit – a powerful one, yes, but a tool nonetheless. You're the artisan wielding that tool, shaping your narrative with a blend of silicon smarts and human heart. So the next time you find yourself doubting your abilities or tempted to let AI take the wheel, take a deep breath. Remind yourself that you're not an imposter – you're a pioneer, navigating the new frontier of AI-assisted creativity. And pioneers, my friend, are anything but frauds. They're the ones who shape the future.

Now, go forth and write. Use AI as your secret weapon, not your crutch. Embrace the doubt, wrestle with the temptation of overreliance, and emerge as the author you're meant to be – one who harnesses the power of AI while remaining unequivocally, undeniably human.

*

I hope I haven't discouraged you from becoming an AI author. This book would have been terribly incomplete without these warnings. There are many things we must all be aware of before beginning our journey, as these issues will surface when you write. I want you to approach this not with fear, but with awareness. Keep these challenges in the back of your mind, but remember that you can overcome them. Without AI, the barriers to writing were much higher. This is the revolution I'm referring to - anyone can write now. Not every work will be of similar quality, but by following the toolkit I'm giving you, you can write well, very well. Perhaps even better than your favorite author. Don't be afraid of it; just jump in. When you do, you'll have a first draft in a matter of weeks.

Chapter VII: First Draft

Every AI-assisted book is a unique creation, much like the author who brings it to life. The journey from concept to completed manuscript is as varied as the individuals who embark upon it. The time it takes to write your book can fluctuate dramatically, influenced by a myriad of factors that are both personal and technical in nature.

Some of these factors are directly related to your own skills and experiences. How quickly do your fingers dance across the keyboard? Are you a hunt-and-peck typist or a touch-typing virtuoso? Your familiarity with technology plays a crucial role too. Are you comfortable navigating word processors and online platforms, or does the prospect of a new software interface make you break out in a cold sweat? When it comes to AI technology specifically, are you an early adopter who's been experimenting with chatbots and language models since their inception, or is this your first foray into the world of AI?

Other factors are more closely tied to your relationship with the book itself. How intimately do you know your subject matter? Are you writing about a topic you've studied for decades, or are you exploring new intellectual territory? Your ability to articulate ideas clearly is another critical element. Some authors have a gift for translating complex concepts into accessible prose, while others may struggle to convey their thoughts on paper. The complexity of the book you're writing also plays a significant role. A straightforward how-to guide will likely come together more quickly than a densely researched historical novel or a comprehensive academic text.

But here's the encouraging news: if you persist, if you refuse to let setbacks derail you, and if you faithfully apply the guidance provided in this book, you will eventually reach a significant milestone. You will complete your first draft. It's a moment of triumph that every author, whether novice or veteran, cherishes.

Picture it: your word processor – be it Microsoft Word, Google Docs, Scrivener, or any other program – will be brimming with pages of your own creation. You'll have fully developed chapters, each one a testament to your creativity and hard work. For many authors, the word count at this stage is already impressive, often surprising even the writer themselves. This is the point where your project truly begins to resemble a real book, a tangible manifestation of your ideas and efforts.

When you reach this pivotal moment, pause. Take a deep breath. Allow yourself to bask in the glow of accomplishment. Completing the first draft is widely recognized as one of the most challenging aspects of writing a book. It requires discipline, creativity, and perseverance. Many aspiring authors never make it this far, so you've already achieved something remarkable.

Now, let's be clear: this version isn't likely to be ready for publication just yet. But – and this is where the magic of AI-assisted writing comes into play – if you've diligently followed the tips on effectively collaborating with AI that we've explored in earlier chapters, your first draft may be considerably closer to the final version than you might expect. This is not to say you've allowed the AI to do all the heavy lifting. On the contrary, you've used it as a tool to enhance your own creativity and productivity, resulting in a draft that's more refined than it might otherwise have been at this stage.

This advantage of AI-assisted writing becomes particularly apparent when we consider the typical state of a first draft. Traditionally, the initial version of any written work – whether it's a novel, a law review paper, or a non-fiction book – is often rough around the edges. It's entirely normal, and even expected, for this draft to be riddled with mistakes, typos, and redundancies. Clarity often takes a backseat to the sheer act of getting ideas onto the page. In essence, the first draft is typically a messy, unpolished version of your thoughts. And that's okay - writing is, after all, a process of refinement and improvement.

When you eventually sit down to reread your work, you're likely to encounter a range of issues. The flow of your narrative or argument might feel disjointed in places, and you may notice inconsistencies in your arguments or characterizations. Ideas that seemed brilliant during a late-night writing session might not hold up as well under the scrutiny of a fresh perspective. This is all part of the process and is where the real craft of writing often begins. You may also stumble upon embarrassing remnants, like brackets ([]) that you used to prompt the AI to complete certain sections but overlooked during editing.

However, this is also where the advantages of AI authorship become even more apparent. If you've followed the steps and techniques outlined in this book, leveraging AI as a collaborative tool rather than a crutch, your draft will likely be more polished than a typical first draft. While it's important to remember that it won't be perfect - it will still require work, refinement, and perhaps even significant revisions – it's probably in much better shape than it would have been without AI assistance.

The AI tools you've employed throughout your writing process can help in numerous ways. They can assist in maintaining consistency in tone and style across your manuscript. They can flag potential redundancies or contradictions that might have slipped past your notice. They can even help in structuring your arguments or narrative more coherently. The result is often a cleaner, more coherent first draft that provides a stronger foundation for your subsequent revisions.

Of course, the key here is that you've been diligent in applying the AI collaboration techniques we've discussed earlier. You've used AI as a tool to augment your own creativity and skills, not as a replacement for them. You've maintained your unique voice and vision while leveraging AI to enhance your productivity and overcome common writing hurdles.

In this chapter, we'll explore the next crucial steps in your writing journey: the process of revising and improving your first draft. We'll cover a range of topics designed to help you transform your initial manuscript into a polished, publishable work. We'll discuss the importance of taking a break before diving into revisions, allowing you to approach your work with fresh eyes. We'll explore techniques for reading and evaluating your own work objectively, a skill that's crucial for effective self-editing.

We'll also look at how to leverage AI tools for in-depth analysis of your manuscript, using their capabilities to identify areas for improvement that you might have missed. We'll dive into strategies for addressing common first-draft issues like plot holes, pacing problems, or weak arguments, providing you with practical approaches to strengthen your work.

The role of beta readers will be another important topic. We'll discuss how to choose effective beta readers, what kind of feedback to ask for, and how to incorporate their insights into your revision process. We'll also cover techniques for fine-tuning your prose, helping you to polish your language and maximize its impact on the reader.

Finally, we'll walk through the final checks and preparations you should make before submitting your manuscript, ensuring that your work is as polished and professional as possible. You'll need to recheck that your work is original and does not infringe upon others' copyright.

By the end of this chapter, you'll have a comprehensive toolkit for refining your first draft, bringing you one step closer to your goal of a published book. Remember, the journey doesn't end with the first draft—in many ways, it's just beginning. But with the right approach and the innovative use of AI tools, you're well-equipped to navigate the revision process successfully. Let's begin this exciting next phase of your writing journey.

Reading and Revising Your First Draft

You've reached an important milestone by completing your first draft. Now comes a crucial step that might seem obvious but is often overlooked or rushed: reading your draft from start to finish. This isn't just a casual skim; it's a focused, intentional read that demands your full attention and concentration.

The importance of this step cannot be overstated. While it might be tempting to immediately turn to your AI assistant for help, resist that urge. For this initial read-through, you need to engage with your work directly, without any AI intermediation. Why? Because this first, unassisted read will give you the clearest picture of your work as a whole.

As you read, you'll start to notice patterns and issues that weren't apparent when you were in the thick of writing. You'll spot repetitive phrases or ideas that seemed fresh when you wrote them but now stand out as redundant. You'll identify sections that need more development or explanation. Perhaps most importantly, you'll get a sense of the overall flow and structure of your book. Does the narrative or argument progress logically? Are there gaps in your reasoning or story? Do some parts feel out of place or unnecessary?

This read-through will also highlight areas where your writing could be stronger. You might notice awkward sentences, unclear explanations, or weak transitions between sections. Pay attention to these, but don't get bogged down in trying to fix everything immediately. For now, your goal is to get a comprehensive overview of your work.

To make this process as effective as possible, I recommend doing two separate read-throughs: one digital and one non-digital. Yes, I know printing out an entire manuscript isn't the most environmentally friendly option, and if that's a significant concern for you, by all means, stick to digital. However, in my experience, reading a printed version often reveals things that I miss when reading on a screen, and vice versa.

There's something about the tactile experience of holding physical pages, the ability to easily flip back and forth, and the change in how your eyes interact with the text that can bring fresh insights. When I read a printed version, I often catch subtle issues with pacing or spot connections between different parts of the book that I hadn't noticed before. On the other hand, reading digitally allows for easier searching and can help you spot consistency issues with names, dates, or terminology.

If you do decide to print your manuscript, I suggest waiting a few days after you've written the last word before you start reading. This brief pause can help you approach your work with fresher eyes. Even a short break can make a significant difference, allowing you to come back to your writing with a bit more objectivity. You might be surprised at how differently you perceive your work after just a few days away from it. That said, the optimal length of this break can vary depending on your personal preferences and the type of book you're writing. For a technical manual or a timely non-fiction work, you might want to dive back in sooner. For a novel or a more reflective piece, a longer break could be beneficial. Trust your instincts on this.

When you're ready to begin your read-through, create an environment conducive to focus and comfort. Find a quiet place where you won't be disturbed. I often prefer to lay on a comfortable couch or settle into a cozy armchair. The key is to choose a spot where you can maintain concentration for extended periods. Have a pen (or digital annotation tool) at the ready – you'll want to make notes as you go.

Now, here's where our AI-assisted approach diverges from traditional writing advice. As you're reading and making comments, keep in mind the capabilities of your AI assistant. Your notes shouldn't just be about improvements you want to make; they should also reflect what you know the AI can do to help refine your draft.

For instance, if you notice a section that feels repetitive, don't just mark it for deletion or revision. Instead, make a note to ask the AI to search for similar repetitive patterns throughout the book. If you come across a particularly well-written paragraph, note that you want the AI to analyze its style and apply similar techniques to other sections.

This approach extends to all aspects of your review. If you spot inconsistencies in character development (for fiction) or argument structure (for non-fiction), note how you might use the AI to check for and resolve these issues throughout the manuscript. If you find a section

179

that needs more research or elaboration, jot down specific questions or prompts you can later pose to your AI assistant.

Remember, you're not just reading as an author at this point; you're reading as an AI-augmented editor. Your notes are not just for you; they're the beginning of a dialogue with your AI collaborator. This mindset can help you maximize the benefits of AI assistance in your revision process.

As you read, don't hesitate to write down anything that comes to mind. If something doesn't feel right, make a note, even if you're not sure why it bothers you. These instinctive reactions can often point to underlying issues that become clearer upon further reflection or discussion with your AI assistant.

Once you've completed your thorough read-through of the printed version (if you chose to print), it's time to transfer your notes and insights to the digital version. If you only read digitally, you should do this on the go. This is where you can start making some of the smaller, more straightforward changes. Use your AI tool of choice for tasks like rewriting awkward sentences or fleshing out underdeveloped paragraphs. However, resist the temptation to run your entire manuscript through the AI just yet. We're still in the phase of identifying issues and making targeted improvements.

After incorporating these initial changes, it's time for your digital read-through (or your second read-through). Follow a similar process of noting issues and areas for improvement, but now you have the advantage of being able to make changes on the fly with AI assistance. Just remember to maintain the discipline of reading your work in order. Don't skip around, even if you're tempted to jump to sections you know need work. Reading in sequence helps you maintain a sense of the overall flow and structure of your book.

Now, a word about the psychological aspect of this process: reading your first draft can be a challenging experience. It's not uncommon to feel disappointed or discouraged when you notice the gap between what you envisioned and what you've actually produced. Remember imposter syndrome? It's likely to resurface at this stage. This is completely normal, and it's crucial not to let these feelings derail you.

At this point, you might also find yourself feeling somewhat exhausted. The draft is lengthy, and the passionate enthusiasm you felt while writing just a few days ago might have waned. The initial spark that drove you to pour words onto the page may have dimmed in the face of the daunting task of revision.

Remember, this temporary dip in motivation is a natural part of the creative process. Many writers experience this emotional rollercoaster when faced with their first draft. The key is to push through these feelings, recognizing them as a common hurdle rather than a reflection of your work's quality or your abilities as a writer. Take a deep breath, step back if needed, and approach your draft with fresh eyes. Your current state of mind doesn't diminish the value of what you've accomplished. This draft, imperfect as it may seem, is a significant milestone on your journey to creating a polished, published work.

This is just the first draft. The purpose of this read-through isn't to judge your work, but to identify areas for improvement. Every book goes through multiple rounds of revision before it reaches its final form. What you're doing now is laying the groundwork for those revisions. In the coming days and weeks, you'll refine and polish your work until it meets your goals.

Moreover, you'll likely benefit from external input later in the process. Beta readers, editors, and even your AI assistant will provide fresh perspectives that will help improve the quality of your work. For now, take pride in the fact that you've completed a first draft – a feat that many aspiring authors never achieve. You're well on your way to realizing your goal of writing the book you've always wanted to create.

In the next section, we'll explore how to leverage AI tools to address the issues and opportunities you've identified in your read-through, taking your manuscript to the next level of refinement.

Reworking Your Draft with AI Assistance

After reading your draft twice and making initial corrections, your book should take shape nicely. Now it's time to elevate your revision process by harnessing the power of AI for analysis and improvement. The AI that has been your faithful writing companion throughout this journey can now become an equally powerful ally in evaluating and refining your work. The methods you'll use here build upon the prompt engineering techniques you've already learned and applied during the writing process. However, the focus now shifts to analysis and improvement of your existing draft, requiring a slightly different approach that we'll explore in detail.

Before we dive into the specifics of using AI for revision, it's crucial to revisit the current limitations of the technology. As you know, different AI models have varying capabilities when it comes to handling text. The concepts of context window and tokens that we discussed earlier play a significant role in this process stage, particularly when working with longer manuscripts. For most books, especially those that aren't short children's stories, the length of the manuscript will exceed the context window of current AI models. This limitation means that the AI can't examine your entire book in one go. While this may change in the future as technology advances, it's the reality we must work with for now.

At the time of writing, I find ChatGPT to be one of the best tools for examining lengthy documents, as it can maintain a longer conversation within its contextual window. This capability is particularly important for the kind of in-depth analysis we're aiming for in this revision stage. However, the field of AI is rapidly evolving, so by the time you're reading this, there may be other tools that are equally capable or even superior. Always be open to exploring new options as they become available.

It's important to note that even AI tools capable of handling longer conversations may sometimes "slack" in their work. This is part of the limitations I discussed earlier. Due to the financial (or other) considerations involved in running these complex models, they are relatively limited in their capacity to truly engage with a lengthy document like a 200-page book. This limitation means that if you ask for an analysis of your entire book, the AI might only do a mediocre job, potentially not examining the entire manuscript as thoroughly as you requested. While this is currently a drawback of the technology, there's no need to be alarmed. The AI will still be immensely helpful in examining most parts of your book and will provide valuable ideas and corrections. You can't rely on it to catch every error or instance of repetitiveness, but you can use it as a powerful tool to supplement your own careful review. Remember, you're likely to catch things the AI didn't, and even if you don't, the combined effort of your review and the AI's analysis will yield far better results than working without AI assistance.

I'm optimistic that these limitations will continue to be addressed as the technology evolves. In the future, we may see more companies offering AI models with larger contextual windows specifically designed for analyzing books. It's not far-fetched to imagine dedicated book-writing software with integrated AI capabilities tailored for this purpose.

Now, let's talk about the actual process of using AI for revision through prompt engineering. Just as you used various prompts to assist you in writing the book, you can now craft prompts to aid in examining and improving it. The beauty of this approach is its flexibility — you can shape your prompts to suit the specific needs of your book, regardless of its genre or subject matter. Consider focusing on individual chapters rather than trying to analyze the entire book at once. You might prompt the AI to analyze a specific chapter's structure, pacing, and how well it connects to the overall narrative. For fiction works, you could ask the AI to review the dialogue and actions of a particular character throughout the book, identifying any inconsistencies in their personality or behavior. If you're writing non-fiction, you might ask the AI to examine the main argument presented in a chapter, assessing its logical flow and the strength of the evidence provided.

Let's explore some specific examples of how you can use AI to analyze and improve different types of books. For fiction books, character consistency and development are crucial. You might use a prompt like this: "Analyze the character of [Character Name] throughout the book. Identify any inconsistencies in their personality, speech patterns, or behavior. Also, track their character arc and suggest ways to make their development more compelling." This type of analysis can help ensure that your characters remain true to themselves while also growing throughout the story.

Plot structure and pacing are other critical elements in fiction. You could ask the AI: "Examine the plot structure of my novel. Identify the key plot points (inciting incident, rising action, climax, falling action, resolution). Are they well-placed for maximum impact? Suggest improvements to the pacing, especially in chapters [X, Y, Z] where the action seems to lag." This kind of analysis can help you ensure that your story maintains a gripping pace and satisfying structure.

For genres like fantasy or science fiction, world-building is paramount. You might prompt: "Review the world-building elements in my [fantasy/sci-fi] novel. How consistent and believable is the created world? Are there any logical inconsistencies or areas that need more development? Suggest ways to make the world more immersive and engaging." This can help you create a rich, believable setting for your story.

Dialogue is another area where AI can provide valuable insights. Try a prompt like: "Analyze the dialogue in Chapter [X]. Does each character have a distinct voice? Is the dialogue natural and effective in revealing character and advancing the plot? Provide suggestions for improving weak dialogue exchanges." This can help ensure that your characters' conversations feel authentic and serve the story effectively.

For non-fiction books, the focus shifts to elements like argument coherence and technical accuracy. You might ask the AI: "Examine the main argument presented in Chapter [X]. Assess its logical flow and the strength of the evidence provided. Are there any logical fallacies or weak points in the argumentation? Suggest ways to strengthen the argument and make it more compelling." This type of analysis can help ensure that your non-fiction work presents a strong, well-supported case.

Technical accuracy is crucial for specialized subjects. Consider a prompt like: "Review Chapter [X] for technical accuracy in the field of [subject area]. Identify any outdated information, potential inaccuracies, or areas where more current research could be incorporated. Suggest updates or areas that might need fact-checking." This can help ensure that your work remains current and authoritative.

Accessibility and clarity are important for all non-fiction works, but especially those aimed at a general audience. You might prompt: "Read Chapter [X] as if you were a layperson with no background in [subject area]. Identify any jargon, complex concepts, or assumptions that might be unclear to a general reader. Suggest ways to make the content more accessible without oversimplifying." This can help you strike the right balance between depth and accessibility.

For business or self-help books, case studies often play a crucial role. You could ask: "Analyze the case study in Chapter [X]. How effectively does it illustrate the main points of the chapter? Is it relatable and applicable to a wide audience? Suggest ways to enhance the case study or propose an alternative that might be more impactful." This can help ensure that your practical examples resonate with your readers and effectively illustrate your points.

For memoirs or autobiographies, maintaining a consistent and authentic narrative voice is crucial. You could prompt: "Examine the narrative voice throughout the book. Is it consistent and authentic? Identify any sections where the voice seems to shift or where it could be strengthened to better convey your unique perspective and experiences." This can help ensure that your personal story is told in a compelling and genuine way.

Emotional impact is also key in personal narratives. Try a prompt like: "Analyze Chapter [X], focusing on its emotional impact. Are the described experiences and feelings conveyed effectively? Suggest ways to deepen the emotional resonance without oversentimentalizing." This can help you strike the right emotional tone in your memoir.

For memoirs that intersect with historical events, balancing personal narrative with broader context is important. Consider: "Review how historical context is integrated into Chapter [X]. Is there a good balance between personal narrative and broader historical events? Suggest ways to enhance the interplay between personal experiences and the historical backdrop." This can help your personal story resonate within its larger historical context.

Regardless of the type of book you're writing, certain elements are universally important. The opening and closing of your book are crucial. You might ask: "Analyze the opening chapter and the concluding chapter of the book. How effectively do they hook the reader and provide a satisfying conclusion, respectively? Suggest ways to make the opening more compelling and the conclusion more impactful." This can help ensure that your book starts strong and ends memorably.

Thematic consistency is another universal concern. Try a prompt like: "Identify the main themes of the book. Analyze how consistently these themes are developed throughout the narrative. Suggest ways to reinforce key themes, especially in chapters where they seem underdeveloped." This can help ensure that your book's central ideas are effectively woven throughout the narrative.

Finally, the flow between chapters is crucial for maintaining reader engagement. You could ask: "Examine the transitions between chapters throughout the book. How smooth and logical are they? Identify any abrupt shifts or disconnects, and suggest ways to improve the flow between chapters." This can help ensure that your book maintains a smooth, coherent progression from start to finish.

Remember, these prompts are starting points. Feel free to modify them to better suit your specific needs and the unique aspects of your book. The key is to be specific in your requests and to focus on areas where you feel AI analysis can provide the most value. As you work through these analyses, don't forget to trust your own instincts as well. The AI is a tool to enhance your revision process, not to replace your authorial judgment.

Use its insights to spark your own creativity and critical thinking, leading to a final product that's polished, engaging, and true to your vision.

I know you're feeling exhausted by now, but this is a crucial moment as you're just steps away from sending your manuscript to a publisher or directly to print (if you're self-publishing; more on that soon). Once you've completed this AI-assisted revision process, take the time to read through your entire manuscript one last time. This final read-through is your opportunity to assess how well the AI-suggested changes have integrated with your original text and to catch any issues that both you and the AI might have missed in earlier rounds. As you read, continue to make improvements on the go. Pay close attention to the overall flow of your narrative or argument. Does each chapter lead logically to the next? Are key points or plot developments introduced at the right moments? This is your chance to fine-tune the structure and pacing of your book.

Also, take note of how your book feels as a cohesive whole. Sometimes, in focusing on improving individual sections, we can lose sight of the bigger picture. Does your book still convey the main message or story you intended? Are there themes or ideas that could be developed further to tie everything together more effectively? This final review is your opportunity to ensure that your book is not just well-written on a technical level, but also impactful and meaningful as a complete work.

Incorporating Feedback from Beta Readers

After you've completed your AI-assisted revisions, it's time to consider bringing in a crucial element of the traditional writing process: beta readers. These individuals can provide an invaluable external perspective on your work, offering insights that neither you nor your AI assistant can provide. In this section, we'll explore how to choose beta readers, what questions to ask them, and how to effectively incorporate their feedback alongside your AI-assisted revisions.

However, I want to stress from the outset: **THIS IS NOT MANDATORY**. Part of the AI revolution is the fact that we don't necessarily need other humans anymore for these tasks. Still, I do find it valuable to have another set of human eyes review your work. In the worst-case scenario, they may have nothing to add. But I recognize that this process can be both time-consuming (for you to seek readers, and for those reading your work) and challenging in terms of finding willing participants. So, make your own decision here based on your specific circumstances and goals.

If you do choose to use beta readers, their feedback can complement your AI-assisted work, potentially catching nuances or inconsistencies that AI might miss. On the other hand, if you decide to forgo this step, the comprehensive nature of AI-assisted writing and editing may well suffice for many projects. The choice ultimately depends on your personal preferences, time constraints, and the specific needs of your book.

Selecting Your Beta Readers

Selecting the right beta readers is a crucial step in refining your manuscript. It's important to choose individuals who will provide honest and constructive feedback rather than just telling you what you want to hear. To ensure a broad range of perspectives, seek diversity in your beta readers. Consider selecting individuals from different backgrounds, ages, and experiences. This variety can help ensure your book resonates with a wider audience.

It's also beneficial to include both genre enthusiasts and general readers. If you're writing in a specific genre, having readers who are familiar with that genre can offer insights into whether your book meets the expectations of that audience. Meanwhile, general readers can help you assess how well your book might appeal to those outside your target genre. Fellow writers, particularly those who are familiar with your genre, can be invaluable in providing insights into the technical aspects of your writing.

Reliability is another key factor in choosing beta readers. Look for individuals who are committed to reading your manuscript and providing feedback within your desired timeframe. It's also wise to aim for a mix of familiar faces and strangers. While friends and family may be supportive, they might not offer the most objective feedback. Including some readers who don't know you personally can provide a more balanced and honest critique.

Remember, you don't need a large number of beta readers. A group of 3-4 dedicated individuals is usually sufficient to give you a range of valuable perspectives that can help you improve your manuscript.

Questions to Ask Your Beta Readers

To get the most useful feedback from your beta readers, provide them with a set of questions to consider as they read. Here are some examples:

1. Did the opening chapters grab your attention? If not, at what point did you become fully engaged in the story/content?

187

2. Were there any parts of the book where your interest waned? Which sections and why?

3. Did you find the characters (for fiction) or arguments (for non-fiction) believable and well-developed?

4. Were there any parts of the book that confused you or seemed inconsistent?

5. Did the pacing feel appropriate throughout the book?

6. Were there any sections that felt repetitive or unnecessary?

7. Did the ending feel satisfying and appropriate to the rest of the book?

8. Did you notice any recurring grammar or spelling errors?

9. If this book were on a shelf, what other books would you expect to see next to it?

10. What do you think is the main message or theme of the book? Was it effectively conveyed?

Encourage your beta readers to be honest and specific in their feedback. Remind them that constructive criticism is more helpful than vague praise.

Balancing Beta Reader Feedback with AI Assistance

Once you receive feedback from your beta readers, you'll need to integrate it with the work you've already done, including your AI-assisted revisions. Here's how to approach this process:

1. Compile and organize feedback: Create a system to organize the feedback you receive. You might use a spreadsheet or a document where you can categorize comments by chapter or theme.

2. Look for patterns: If multiple beta readers point out the same issue, it's likely something that needs addressing. Pay special attention to these recurring comments.

3. Use AI to analyze feedback: You can use your AI assistant to help analyze the feedback. For example, you might prompt: "I've received the following feedback from beta readers about Chapter

X. Can you suggest ways to address these concerns while maintaining the overall structure and tone of the chapter?"

4. Address major issues first: Start with the big-picture problems identified by your beta readers. These might include plot holes, pacing issues, or unclear arguments.

5. Leverage AI for specific revisions: Once you've decided on the changes you want to make, use your AI assistant to help implement them. For instance, if beta readers found a character underdeveloped, you might prompt the AI: "Beta readers found the character of [Name] underdeveloped. Can you suggest ways to flesh out this character in Chapters Y and Z, focusing on their motivation and background?"

6. Maintain your voice: While incorporating feedback and using AI assistance, be careful not to lose your unique authorial voice. Use the AI as a tool to enhance your writing, not to replace your style.

7. Consider conflicting feedback carefully: If beta readers disagree on certain points, use your judgment (and perhaps your AI assistant's analysis) to decide which changes to make.

8. Don't feel obligated to make every suggested change: Remember, this is your book. If you disagree with a piece of feedback, it's okay not to act on it. However, do consider why the reader might have had that reaction.

9. Use AI to check consistency after revisions: After making changes based on beta reader feedback, use your AI assistant to ensure these changes haven't created new inconsistencies or issues in your manuscript.

10. Conduct a final read-through: After incorporating beta reader feedback and making AI-assisted revisions, read through your manuscript one more time to ensure everything flows smoothly.

Remember, the goal of using beta readers alongside AI assistance is to create the best possible version of your book. Beta readers provide the human touch — the emotional response and reader perspective that AI can't replicate. Meanwhile, your AI assistant can help you efficiently implement changes and maintain consistency throughout your revisions.

By effectively combining these two valuable resources — human insight and AI efficiency — you can refine your manuscript to a high polish, addressing both technical issues and reader experience. This dual approach can help ensure that your final draft is not just technically proficient, but also engaging and impactful for your target audience.

Rechecking Potential Legal Issues

As you approach the final stages of your manuscript preparation, it's crucial to shift your focus to potential legal issues. While your work may have been for your eyes only or shared with a close circle of friends until now, the landscape changes dramatically when you begin approaching publishers or consider self-publishing. This is the point where your potential legal liability becomes significantly more important. The transition from a private project to a public work introduces a host of legal considerations that you must carefully navigate.

We've previously discussed copyright and contractual issues, and you may have already performed initial checks. However, at this stage, it's imperative to be even more cautious, especially given the current scrutiny surrounding AI technology in both legal and publishing circles. Many publishers may harbor concerns about potential infringements and might be hesitant to publish your book because of these uncertainties. We'll explore this further in the chapter on publishing, but it's worth noting that these concerns can significantly impact your path to publication.

It's important to recognize that these legal and ethical concerns surrounding AI-assisted writing are likely growing pains in the industry. Based on my experience with legal innovations and lawsuits, I don't foresee courts completely halting this technology. The integration of AI into creative processes seems inevitable, but it will take time for copyright litigation against AI companies to be resolved and for clear legal precedents to be established. However, this doesn't negate the need for caution on your part as an author.

The primary issue at this stage is uncertainty, and much depends on how risk-averse publishers are. They will undoubtedly avoid anything that clearly infringes on copyrights or even comes close to infringement. For instance, if your book includes copyrighted characters from major franchises like Disney or Pixar, it's unlikely to be published by a reputable publisher, even if it's not a direct copy. This caution extends even to cases where you might argue for fair use, such as in parodies. Most publishers are unlikely to take chances in these gray areas, regardless of whether AI was used in the creation process.

What's crucial for you to verify is that your work, even if not intentionally copied from copyrighted materials, is indeed original. This involves a two-pronged approach: checking for textual originality and reviewing any visual elements in your book. For text, it's advisable to use software that checks for authenticity. There are several options available, ranging from free tools like Copyscape to more comprehensive paid services like Turnitin or iThenticate. These tools can help you ensure that your AI-assisted text hasn't inadvertently reproduced content from other sources, which could happen if the AI model was trained on copyrighted materials.

When it comes to images, a manual review is essential. Carefully examine any illustrations, cover art, or other visual elements in your book. Pay special attention to recognizable trademarks or copyrighted characters. While it's unrealistic to know every copyrighted image, you should be able to identify clear references or resemblances to well-known intellectual property. If you've used AI-generated images, exercise extra caution, as some AI art generators have been scrutinized for potentially using copyrighted material in their training data. To check for similarities, use tools like Google Lens to search for matching visuals online.

Contractually, ensure that you have secured all necessary rights. If you've followed the guidance provided earlier in this book about choosing AI assistants, you should be in a good position. However, keep in mind that you will soon need to disclose everything related to your AI use to the publisher. Prepare a thorough report detailing how AI was used in your writing process. This should include which AI tools you used, how you used them, and any steps you took to ensure originality and avoid copyright infringement.

It's also important to consider the evolving landscape of AI-related rights. Some AI companies now offer indemnification (protection against legal liability) for certain uses of their technology, which could provide an extra layer of protection. If this option is available for the tools you've used, it might be worth exploring. However, be sure to read the fine print carefully and fully understand what is covered under such agreements.

Another aspect to consider is the potential need for disclaimers in your book. Depending on the extent of AI assistance and the nature of your content, you might need to include a statement about AI use. This is particularly important for non-fiction works where the accuracy and origin of information are crucial.

If your book includes any interviews, quotes, or other content from real people, double-check that you have proper permissions and that your use of this material aligns with any agreements you've made. AI might have helped you organize or expand on this content, but the responsibility for its proper use still lies with you.

For those considering self-publishing, be aware that you'll need to be even more diligent. Without a publisher's legal team to back you up, the onus is entirely on you to ensure your work doesn't infringe on any copyrights or other legal protections. This might involve hiring a lawyer specializing in intellectual property to review your manuscript before publication. But this might be too costly, so just try to minimize your risks of infringement by following the thumb rules I offer.

Lastly, stay informed about ongoing legal developments in this area. The landscape of AI and copyright law is rapidly evolving, and what's acceptable today might be problematic tomorrow. Consider joining author associations or forums where these issues are discussed, and don't hesitate to seek professional legal advice if you're unsure about any aspect of your work. Remember, while these legal considerations might seem daunting, they're a necessary part of bringing your work to a wider audience. By being thorough and proactive in addressing these issues, you're not only protecting yourself but also ensuring that your AI-assisted book has the best possible chance of success in the marketplace. Your diligence at this stage can save you from significant headaches and potential legal issues down the line, allowing you to focus on what really matters: sharing your story or ideas with the world.

No let's talk publishing.

Chapter VIII: Publishing

You've finally written that book you've been dreaming about. If you're reading this for the first time, you're likely still in the learning phase (or should be!). But when you return to this part later, having completed your manuscript—well done! I hope you enjoyed the process, even though I'm sure you encountered challenges along the way, and it wasn't always smooth sailing.

Now, let's talk about the publishing part. The good news is that it's entirely doable! If you're determined to publish your book, you always have the option to self-publish (and self-promote; more on that later). This is also part of the AI revolution. We're no longer entirely dependent on traditional publishing houses or marketers. Anyone can do it themselves. However, there's still added value in having a publisher handle these aspects for you, with their expertise and industry connections. But getting chosen by a publisher isn't easy and depends on many factors, including a fair bit of luck.

The purpose of this section is to map out the possibilities once you've completed your first draft. In some fields, like academic publishing (which I cover in a different book), it's common to submit a book proposal first and then write the book after securing a contract. This approach exists in other fields too, particularly for non-fiction works where publishers want to assess market potential before committing to a full manuscript. However, for your first AI-assisted book, I advise you to write it first. Once you've established yourself as a successful AI author, you may be able to secure book deals in advance of writing.

We'll divide this chapter into three main sections: Traditional Publishing, Self-Publishing, and Hybrid Publishing. In each section, we'll discuss how AI can assist in these processes, from crafting query letters and book proposals to designing covers and marketing materials. We'll also address some unique considerations for AI-assisted books, such as disclosure, rights and royalties, and market reception.

There is an important caveat I'd like to mention. Although I have published in the past and gained some knowledge through research and from conversations with friends and colleagues who have also done so, from this point onward, the book is less about my personal experience in the field of AI authorship. I am only now beginning the publishing and marketing process myself. My suggestion is to read this section, but also engage in your own research. Depending on your specific book genre or area, this information might be more or less relevant. Maybe you'll find that certain strategies or insights apply directly to your situation, while others might not be as useful. Whatever path you choose, I'm confident that some of the information here will prove valuable. If you already have a clear direction for your publishing journey, feel free to skip directly to the final chapter and begin your writing journey. You can always return to this section later if needed. Now for the publishing part.

Traditional Publishing

Traditional publishing remains a significant path for many authors, including those using AI-assisted writing tools. This route involves submitting your manuscript to established publishing houses, who then take on the responsibility of editing, producing, distributing, and marketing your book.

Understanding the Landscape

The publishing industry is a complex and multifaceted ecosystem, with a diverse array of players each serving different niches and audiences. To navigate this landscape effectively, especially as an author of an AI-assisted book, it's crucial to understand the various types of publishers and their roles in the industry. Let's dive deeper into each category:

The "Big Five" Publishers

The "Big Five" refers to the largest and most influential publishing houses in the English-speaking world. These are Penguin Random House, HarperCollins, Simon & Schuster, Hachette Book Group, and Macmillan. These publishing giants are the result of numerous mergers and acquisitions over the years, and they dominate a significant portion of the market.

Penguin Random House, for instance, is a behemoth formed by the merger of Penguin Books and Random House in 2013. It houses over 300 imprints worldwide, publishing more than 15,000 titles annually. Similarly, HarperCollins, owned by News Corp, has operations in 17 countries and publishes approximately 10,000 new books every year. These publishers have vast resources at their disposal, including large marketing budgets, extensive distribution networks, and teams of experienced professionals in editing, design, and promotion. They often have the power to turn books into bestsellers through their marketing muscle and industry connections.

However, the "Big Five" are also the most competitive and challenging to break into as a new author. They receive thousands of submissions annually and typically accept only a small fraction. They often focus on books they believe have mass market appeal or are written by established authors with proven track records. For authors of AI-assisted books, the "Big Five" present both opportunities and challenges. On one hand, their resources could potentially catapult your book to wide readership. On the other hand, they might be more cautious about AI-assisted works, depending on their current policies and the evolving legal landscape surrounding AI-generated content.

Medium-Sized Publishers

Below the "Big Five" are a number of medium-sized publishers. These houses are smaller than the giants but still have significant reach and resources. They often specialize in certain genres or types of books, allowing them to cultivate dedicated readerships in specific niches.

Examples of medium-sized publishers include Sourcebooks, which has grown to become one of the largest independent publishers in North America, and Kensington Publishing Corp., known for its focus on commercial fiction, especially romance and mystery genres.

These publishers often offer a middle ground between the vast resources of the "Big Five" and the personalized attention of smaller presses. They may be more open to innovative concepts or emerging trends, which could be advantageous for authors of AI-assisted books.

Medium-sized publishers typically have established distribution channels, experienced editorial teams, and the ability to get books into major retail outlets. However, they may not have the same marketing budgets as the largest houses, often requiring authors to be more involved in promotion. For AI-assisted book authors, medium-sized publishers might offer a sweet spot. They may have the resources to effectively market your book while being more open to new technologies and writing methods than some of the more traditional large houses.

Small Presses

Small presses, also known as independent publishers, play a vital role in the publishing ecosystem. These houses are often independently owned and operated, publishing fewer than 10-50 books per year. Despite their size, many small presses have earned reputations for quality and innovation in specific genres or styles.

Examples include Graywolf Press, known for literary fiction and poetry, and Tin House Books, which focuses on contemporary fiction and non-fiction. Small presses often take risks on experimental or niche works that larger houses might pass on, making them potential havens for unique or boundary-pushing books.

Working with a small press often means more personalized attention throughout the publishing process. Authors might work closely with editors and have more input on cover design and marketing strategies. However, small presses typically have limited budgets and distribution reach compared to larger publishers. For authors of AI-assisted books, small presses could be particularly interesting. Many are at the forefront of embracing new technologies and innovative writing methods. They might be more willing to take a chance on an AI-assisted book, seeing it as an exciting new frontier in literature.

However, it's important to note that the financial stability of small presses can vary greatly. Some operate on shoestring budgets, while others have secured solid financial footing. Authors should do their due diligence when considering small presses, ensuring they have a track record of successful publications and fair author treatment.

Academic Presses

Academic or university presses primarily focus on scholarly works and textbooks. These publishers, often affiliated with universities, prioritize the dissemination of knowledge over commercial success, though many do publish books intended for a general audience as well.

Notable academic presses include Oxford University Press, Cambridge University Press, and MIT Press. These publishers are crucial for the publication of specialized academic works, dissertations turned into books, and cutting-edge research across various fields. I have published with Cambridge University Press in the past, and it was an excellent experience which I highly recommend for academic authors.

Academic presses typically have rigorous peer-review processes and high standards for scholarly merit. They often have strong reputations within specific academic disciplines and can lend considerable prestige to authors publishing with them. I won't dive too deeply into the details here, as those in academia are often familiar with these publishers. It's worth noting that the perceived prestige of these presses can vary between universities, and even within departments of the same institution.

For authors of AI-assisted books, academic presses could be particularly relevant if your work explores the technological, ethical, or societal implications of AI in writing and creativity. Many academic presses are actively seeking works that examine the intersection of technology and various academic disciplines.

However, it's important to consider that academic presses often have longer publication timelines and may offer lower advances compared to commercial publishers. They also typically expect authors to write in a more formal, scholarly style, which may or may not align with the goals of your AI-assisted book.

When considering an academic press, weigh the benefits of scholarly credibility and specialized distribution against potential drawbacks like longer timelines and lower financial returns. Your decision should ultimately depend on your book's content, target audience, and your personal publishing goals.

Digital-First Publishers

In the evolving publishing landscape, a relatively new category has emerged: digital-first or digital-only publishers. These publishing houses focus primarily or exclusively on ebook and print-on-demand formats, often leading the way in embracing new technologies and innovative publishing models. Their approach is a response to the growing demand for digital content and the increasing efficiency of online distribution.

Examples of digital-first publishers include Carina Press, a digital-first imprint of Harlequin, and Bookouture, now a part of Hachette UK. These publishers are known for their faster production timelines compared to traditional publishing houses, which can be a significant advantage for authors looking to bring their work to market quickly. Additionally, digital-first publishers may be more open to experimental formats or genres that might not fit the mold of conventional publishing.

Given their focus on digital innovation, these publishers might be particularly receptive to AI-assisted books, viewing them as part of the broader digital revolution in publishing. Their expertise often extends beyond traditional publishing practices to include sophisticated online marketing strategies, making them adept at reaching readers who are not only comfortable with new technologies but also actively seek out digital content.

However, it's important for authors to be aware of certain trade-offs when working with digital-first publishers. One of the main limitations is their often limited presence in physical bookstores. Because their focus is primarily on digital formats, their efforts are concentrated on maximizing online sales and visibility rather than securing shelf space in brick-and-mortar stores. This can be a disadvantage for authors who still value a strong physical presence for their books.

That said, the strengths of digital-first publishers in the digital space can be a considerable asset, especially for authors who are targeting a tech-savvy audience or are interested in leveraging the rapid distribution and marketing potential of digital platforms. As the publishing industry continues to evolve, digital-first publishers represent an exciting and dynamic option for authors looking to navigate the future of publishing.

Market Research

Before approaching publishers or deciding on a publishing path, it's essential to conduct thorough market research. This step is crucial for understanding where your AI-assisted book fits in the current market landscape and which publishers or publishing avenues might be most interested in your work. In the age of AI-assisted writing, this research takes on new dimensions and importance.

Understanding Your Book's Place in the Market

The first step in your market research should be to gain a clear understanding of where your book fits within the existing literary landscape. This involves several key aspects:

1. **Genre Analysis:** Identify the specific genre or subgenre of your book. In the case of AI-assisted writing, your book might straddle multiple genres or even create a new niche. For instance, if you've written a science fiction novel using AI, you might explore how it

fits within traditional sci-fi categories and whether it could be considered part of an emerging "AI-assisted sci-fi" subgenre.

2. **Comparative Titles**: Look for books similar to yours in theme, style, or subject matter. In the case of AI-assisted books, this might include both traditionally written books in your genre and other works created with AI assistance, if any exist. Pay attention to how these books are marketed, their cover designs, and their reception by readers and critics.

3. **Market Trends**: Analyze current trends in your genre and in publishing as a whole. Are readers showing increased interest in books that explore AI themes? Is there growing curiosity about AI-assisted creative works? Understanding these trends can help you position your book effectively.

4. **Audience Identification**: Define your target audience. Who is most likely to be interested in your AI-assisted book? This might include tech enthusiasts, fans of your genre, or readers interested in innovative storytelling methods. Understanding your audience will help you tailor your marketing approach and choose the right publishing avenue.

Leveraging AI for Market Research

Ironically, AI can be an invaluable tool in researching the market for your AI-assisted book. Here's how you can use AI to enhance your market research:

1. Data Analysis: Use AI-powered tools to analyze large datasets of book sales, reader reviews, and publishing trends. These tools can quickly process vast amounts of information, identifying patterns and insights that might be difficult to spot manually.

2. Sentiment Analysis: Employ AI to analyze reader reviews and social media discussions about books similar to yours. This can provide insights into what readers appreciate or dislike about comparable works, helping you refine your own book or marketing strategy.

3. Trend Prediction: Some advanced AI tools can predict future trends based on current data. While not infallible, these predictions can offer valuable insights into where the market might be heading, helping you position your book for future success.

4. Keyword and Topic Analysis: Use AI to identify popular keywords and topics related to your book's genre and themes. This can be particularly useful for optimizing your book's metadata and marketing materials for discoverability.

Identifying Potential Publishers

With a clear understanding of your book's place in the market, the next step is to identify publishers who might be interested in your work. This process involves several strategies:

1. **Publisher Profiling**: Create detailed profiles of publishers who have released books similar to yours. Look at their recent catalogs, submission guidelines, and any public statements about their interest in innovative writing methods or AI-related topics.

2. **Imprint Analysis**: Many larger publishers have multiple imprints focusing on different genres or styles. Identify specific imprints that might be a good fit for your AI-assisted book. For example, a science fiction imprint of a major publisher might be more open to AI-assisted writing than their general fiction department.

3. **Track Record with Innovative Works**: Research which publishers have a history of taking chances on unconventional or technologically innovative books. These publishers might be more receptive to an AI-assisted work.

4. **Conference and Event Monitoring**: Keep track of publishing industry conferences and events. Publishers often use these platforms to discuss their interests and future plans. Look for panels or talks about AI in publishing or the future of writing.

5. **Social Media Insights**: Follow publishers, editors, and literary agents on social media platforms. They often share insights about what they're looking for or their thoughts on industry trends, which could include attitudes towards AI in writing.

Analyzing the Reception of AI in Publishing

As an author of an AI-assisted book, it's crucial to understand the current reception of AI in the publishing world:

1. **Industry Attitudes**: Research articles, interviews, and opinion pieces from publishing professionals about AI in writing.

Understanding the spectrum of attitudes can help you anticipate potential reactions to your work.

2. **Legal and Ethical Considerations**: Stay informed about ongoing discussions and potential legal issues surrounding AI-generated content. This knowledge will be crucial when discussing your book with publishers or readers.

3. **Reader Perceptions**: Analyze reader reactions to known AI-assisted works or articles about AI in writing. This can help you anticipate potential marketing challenges or opportunities.

Continuous Learning and Adaptation

The landscape of AI in publishing is rapidly evolving. What's true today might change significantly in a matter of months. Therefore, market research for an AI-assisted book isn't a one-time task but an ongoing process:

1. Set up alerts for news and articles related to AI in writing and publishing.

2. Join writing and publishing communities where these topics are discussed.

3. Consider attending tech conferences that focus on AI in creative fields.

4. Regularly revisit and update your market research findings.

By conducting thorough and ongoing market research, you'll be well-equipped to navigate the unique challenges and opportunities presented by publishing an AI-assisted book. This knowledge will be invaluable whether you're pitching to traditional publishers, considering self-publishing, or exploring hybrid models. Remember, in the rapidly evolving world of AI and publishing, being well-informed is your best strategy for success.

The Submission Process

The submission process for an AI-assisted book shares many similarities with that of traditionally written books, but it also presents unique challenges and considerations. Understanding this process in depth can significantly increase your chances of success in the competitive world of publishing.

Query Letters: Your First Impression

The query letter is often your first point of contact with agents or publishers, and it's particularly crucial for AI-assisted books. Here's how to craft an effective query letter:

1. **Hook**: Start with a compelling hook that captures the essence of your book. For an AI-assisted work, this might include a brief mention of the innovative writing process, but be careful not to let this overshadow the content of your book. For example: "In 'Digital Dreams,' a novel co-created with cutting-edge AI, humanity's future hangs in the balance as a rogue AI system threatens to rewrite reality itself."

2. **Book Summary**: Provide a concise summary of your book, focusing on the plot (for fiction) or main arguments (for non-fiction). While the AI aspect of your writing process is important, ensure that the summary primarily focuses on the content and quality of the book itself. For instance: "Set in a near-future metropolis, 'Digital Dreams' follows cyber-detective Alex Chen as she uncovers a conspiracy that blurs the lines between human and AI. As the boundaries of reality crumble, Alex must confront not only the rogue AI but also her own understanding of consciousness and free will."

3. **Word Count and Genre**: Clearly state the word count and genre of your book. If your AI-assisted process has resulted in a unique genre blend, you might mention this briefly. For example: "Complete at 85,000 words, 'Digital Dreams' is a cyberpunk thriller that pushes the boundaries of the genre, much like its AI-assisted creation process."

4. **Unique Selling Point**: Highlight what makes your book stand out. While the AI-assisted aspect is certainly unique, also focus on other elements that make your book special. For instance: "Blending hard science fiction with philosophical exploration, 'Digital Dreams' offers readers a unique perspective on the future of AI, informed by cutting-edge research and brought to life through an innovative AI-assisted writing process."

5. **Bio**: Include a brief author bio. If you have relevant experience or qualifications related to AI or your book's subject matter, mention them here. For example: "As a software engineer with a

background in AI ethics, I bring a unique perspective to the world of 'Digital Dreams.' My work has been featured in [relevant publications or platforms], and this is my debut novel."

6. **Comparison Titles**: Mention 2-3 comparable titles, explaining how your book is similar yet unique. This helps agents and publishers understand where your book fits in the market. For AI-assisted books, you might compare both to traditional books in your genre and to other innovative or technologically-influenced works. For instance: "Fans of William Gibson's 'Neuromancer' and Martha Wells' 'Murderbot Diaries' will appreciate the blend of high-tech intrigue and philosophical depth in 'Digital Dreams,' while its AI-assisted creation adds a meta-layer to the exploration of artificial intelligence in fiction."

7. **AI Disclosure**: Consider whether to disclose the AI-assisted nature of your book in the query letter. This is a personal decision and may depend on the publisher or agent you're querying. If you choose to disclose, be clear about the extent of AI involvement and how it enhanced rather than replaced your creative process. For example: "While 'Digital Dreams' explores the future of AI in its plot, it also represents a step into that future in its creation. Using advanced language models as a collaborative tool, I've pushed the boundaries of the writing process itself, resulting in a novel that is as innovative in its conception as it is in its content."

Manuscript Submission: Presenting Your AI-Assisted Work

If a publisher or agent expresses interest based on your query letter, they will typically request a full or partial manuscript. Here's how to prepare your AI-assisted manuscript for submission:

1. Formatting: Adhere strictly to standard manuscript formatting guidelines. This typically includes using a standard font (like Times New Roman, 12-point), double-spacing, and one-inch margins. Proper formatting is crucial as it demonstrates professionalism and makes your manuscript easier to read and evaluate.

2. Proofreading: Thoroughly proofread your manuscript. While AI assistance can often result in clean prose, it's essential to carefully review for any inconsistencies, errors, or awkward phrasings that might have slipped through. You can use the AI to do so but also use traditional tools like spell check or Grammarly.

3. Consistency Check: Ensure consistency in style, voice, and narrative throughout the manuscript. Since AI-assisted writing might involve multiple sessions or iterations, it's crucial to maintain a cohesive feel throughout the book.

4. AI Artifacts: Be vigilant about removing any artifacts of the AI writing process. This could include repetitive phrases, inconsistent information, or any text that clearly reads as machine-generated rather than human-refined.

5. Front Matter: Include a title page with your contact information, the book's title, word count, and genre. You might also include a brief note about the AI-assisted nature of the work, depending on your disclosure strategy.

6. Synopsis: Prepare a detailed synopsis of your book. For AI-assisted works, ensure that the synopsis focuses on the content and themes of the book rather than the writing process, unless the AI aspect is integral to the book's concept.

7. Chapter Breakdown: For non-fiction works, include a detailed chapter breakdown. This should clearly outline the structure and main arguments of your book.

Book Proposals: A Comprehensive Package

For non-fiction works, and occasionally for fiction, you might need to submit a book proposal. This document is particularly important for AI-assisted books as it allows you to provide context for your innovative writing process. A comprehensive book proposal should include:

1. Overview: A detailed description of your book, including its premise, themes, and unique selling points. For an AI-assisted book, you might discuss how the AI collaboration enhances or relates to the book's themes.

2. Market Analysis: An in-depth look at your target audience and how your book meets a specific market need. Include information on comparable titles and how your book differs or improves upon them.

3. Author Platform: Details about your platform as an author, including any relevant expertise, online presence, or media connections. For AI-assisted books, highlight any experience or

knowledge you have related to AI or innovative writing technologies.

4. Marketing and Promotion: Ideas for marketing your book, including how you might leverage the AI aspect in promotion without letting it overshadow the book's content.

5. Detailed Chapter Outline: A comprehensive breakdown of each chapter, including key points and how they contribute to the overall narrative or argument.

6. Sample Chapters: One or two polished chapters that showcase your writing style and the book's content. Ensure these chapters are representative of the AI-assisted work as a whole.

7. AI Methodology: Consider including a section that briefly explains your AI-assisted writing process, how it contributed to the book, and how you ensured the final product's quality and originality.

Submission Strategy

Developing a strategic approach to submissions can increase your chances of success:

1. Targeted Submissions: Based on your market research, create a list of agents and publishers who seem most likely to be interested in AI-assisted works or innovative writing processes.

2. Simultaneous Submissions: Consider making simultaneous submissions to multiple agents or publishers, but always disclose this in your query letter.

3. Tracking: Keep meticulous records of your submissions, including dates, responses, and any feedback received.

4. Patience: The submission process can be lengthy. Be prepared to wait several weeks or even months for responses.

5. Resilience: Rejections are common in publishing, even for excellent books. Don't be discouraged; use any feedback to improve your submission package for the next attempt.

By thoroughly understanding and carefully navigating the submission process, you can present your AI-assisted book in the best possible light, increasing your chances of catching the eye of an agent or publisher. Remember, while the AI aspect of your book is unique, it's the quality of the writing and the strength of your story or ideas that will ultimately determine your success.

Working with Literary Agents

For authors of AI-assisted books aiming for traditional publishing, working with a literary agent is often a crucial step. In many cases, it's necessary, as direct access to publishers is typically limited. Agents serve as intermediaries between authors and publishers, leveraging their industry expertise and connections to place your book with the right publisher. However, the distinctive nature of AI-assisted writing introduces both opportunities and challenges in the agent-author relationship.

The Role of Literary Agents in the AI Era

Literary agents play multiple roles in an author's career, and these roles are evolving with the advent of AI-assisted writing:

1. Gatekeepers and Advocates: Agents are often the first professional hurdle your manuscript needs to clear. They sift through numerous submissions to find works they believe have commercial potential. For AI-assisted books, agents who are open to this new form of writing can become powerful advocates, helping to overcome potential skepticism in the industry.

2. Negotiators: Agents negotiate contracts with publishers on your behalf. With AI-assisted books, this role becomes even more crucial as there may be new contractual territories to navigate, such as clauses related to AI usage and rights.

3. Career Advisors: A good agent doesn't just sell one book; they help manage an author's career. For authors using AI assistance, agents can provide valuable guidance on how to position yourself in the evolving landscape of AI and literature.

4. Industry Insiders: Agents have their finger on the pulse of the publishing industry. They can provide insights into how the industry is responding to AI-assisted writing and help you navigate these changing waters.

5. Editorial Advisors: Many agents offer editorial feedback to help polish your manuscript before submission to publishers. For AI-assisted works, this editorial eye is crucial in ensuring the final product reads as a cohesive, human-crafted piece.

Finding the Right Agent for Your AI-Assisted Book

The process of finding an agent for an AI-assisted book involves some unique considerations:

1. Research Agents' Attitudes Towards AI: Look for agents who have expressed interest in or openness to technological innovations in writing. This might be evident in their social media posts, interviews, or the clients they represent.

2. Identify Agents Representing Similar Works: Look for agents who represent books in your genre, particularly those with technological themes or innovative structures. They may be more receptive to AI-assisted works.

3. Attend Literary Conferences and Tech Events: Literary conferences are great places to meet agents, and some tech conferences now include panels on AI in creative fields. These can be excellent networking opportunities.

4. Utilize AI in Your Agent Search: Ironically, AI tools can be helpful in researching and organizing information about potential agents. Use AI-powered databases or create your own system to track agent preferences and submission requirements.

5. Consider Newer Agents: Younger agents or those newer to the industry might be more open to AI-assisted works as they seek to build their client lists with innovative projects.

Approaching Agents with Your AI-Assisted Book

When reaching out to agents about your AI-assisted book, consider the following strategies:

1. Craft a Compelling Query Letter: Your query should focus on the story or content of your book, but it's also important to address the AI aspect. Explain how AI enhanced your creative process rather than replaced it.

2. Be Transparent About AI Usage: Honesty is crucial. Clearly explain the extent of AI involvement in your writing process. This transparency can help build trust with potential agents.

3. Highlight the Unique Aspects: Emphasize how the AI-assisted process contributed to unique aspects of your book. Perhaps it allowed for more complex plot structures or helped in generating diverse character perspectives.

4. Prepare for Questions: Be ready to discuss the technical aspects of your writing process. Agents may be curious about how AI assistance works and what it means for the future of writing.

5. Show Your Human Touch: Demonstrate how your creativity, editing skills, and overall vision shaped the AI-assisted content into a cohesive, compelling narrative.

Working with Your Agent

Once you've secured an agent for your AI-assisted book, here's how to make the most of the relationship:

1. Collaborative Editing: Work closely with your agent on any necessary edits. Their industry experience can help refine your AI-assisted work for maximum appeal to publishers.

2. Strategic Planning: Discuss with your agent how to position your book in the market. Should the AI aspect be a key selling point, or is it better to focus on the content itself?

3. Addressing Publisher Concerns: Your agent can help anticipate and address potential concerns publishers might have about AI-assisted writing. Work together to develop compelling responses.

4. Future Projects: Discuss your plans for future works with your agent. If you intend to continue using AI assistance, consider how this might shape your author brand and career trajectory.

5. Staying Informed: Keep open communication with your agent about developments in AI and publishing. Their industry insights, combined with your technological knowledge, can create a powerful partnership.

Navigating Challenges

Working with an agent on an AI-assisted book may present unique challenges:

1. Skepticism: Some agents may be skeptical about AI in creative writing. Be prepared to demonstrate the value and originality of your work.

2. Rights and Contracts: The use of AI in your writing process may raise new questions about intellectual property rights. Work with your agent to navigate these complex waters.

3. Market Positioning: There may be differing opinions on how to market an AI-assisted book. Be open to your agent's advice while also advocating for your vision.

4. Industry Evolution: The publishing industry's stance on AI-assisted writing is still evolving. Be prepared for a landscape that may change rapidly and work with your agent to stay adaptable.

5. Balancing Disclosure: Deciding how much to disclose about the AI assistance in your writing can be tricky. Your agent can provide valuable advice on industry norms and reader expectations.

The Future of AI and Literary Agents

As AI continues to evolve, the role of literary agents may also change:

1. **AI in Agenting**: Some agencies are beginning to use AI tools to help sift through submissions or analyze market trends. This could lead to more efficient processes but also raises questions about the human element in decision-making.

2. **Specialization**: We may see the emergence of agents who specialize in AI-assisted or AI-themed works, much as we have agents who specialize in specific genres.

3. **Expanded Role**: Agents may need to become more tech-savvy, potentially expanding their role to include advising on AI tools and techniques in writing.

4. **New Business Models**: The integration of AI in writing could lead to new business models in agenting, potentially including different commission structures for AI-assisted works.

5. **Ethical Considerations**: Agents may play a crucial role in shaping ethical guidelines for the use of AI in literature, advocating for fair practices that benefit both authors and the industry.

Working with a literary agent can significantly enhance your chances of success in traditional publishing, especially when navigating the new territory of AI-assisted books. By understanding the unique aspects of this relationship and being prepared for both the opportunities and challenges, you can forge a powerful partnership that brings your innovative work to a wide audience.

The Editorial Process

The editorial process is a crucial stage in the journey of any book from manuscript to published work. For AI-assisted books, this process takes on additional dimensions and complexities. Understanding this process in depth can help you, as an author, to better prepare your manuscript and work effectively with editors to produce the best possible version of your book.

Stages of Editing

The editorial process typically involves several stages, each with its own focus and importance. For AI-assisted books, these stages may require additional considerations:

Developmental Editing. Developmental editing is a crucial step in the book creation process, focusing on the big picture of your work - its structure, content, and overall effectiveness in conveying your message or story. This stage becomes even more critical when working with AI-assisted content, as it helps to harmonize the blend of human creativity and AI. For AI-assisted books, developmental editing takes on additional dimensions. One key aspect involves identifying and smoothing out any inconsistencies in narrative voice or style that may have resulted from the AI assistance process. As AI can sometimes mimic different writing styles, it's essential to ensure that the overall voice of the book remains consistent and authentic to your vision.

Another important focus is ensuring that the overall structure of the book is coherent and effective. AI might sometimes generate content that doesn't fit seamlessly into the larger narrative, so a developmental editor will work to integrate these sections more smoothly or recommend their removal if they don't serve the book's purpose. This process also involves addressing any areas where the AI's contributions might have led the book in directions that don't align with your original vision, helping to bring the work back to its intended path.

Developmental editing for AI-assisted books also includes identifying themes or motifs that emerged during the writing process. Sometimes, AI can introduce interesting concepts or recurring elements that you might not have initially planned. The editor will help you decide whether to develop these further, weaving them more intricately into your narrative, or to pare them back if they distract from your main message.

Throughout this process, a developmental editor might pose thought-provoking questions to guide the refinement of your AI-assisted book. They might ask, "How does this AI-generated section contribute to the overall arc of the story?" This question helps ensure that every part of your book, whether human or AI-generated, serves a purpose in your narrative. Another crucial query might be, "Are there any parts where the AI's input seems to diverge from your intended message or tone?" This helps identify areas where the AI's contributions might need to be adjusted to better align with your vision.

Perhaps one of the most important questions a developmental editor might ask is, "How can we leverage the unique perspectives provided by the AI while maintaining your authentic voice?" This question gets to the heart of the challenge and opportunity of AI-assisted writing. It acknowledges the potential for AI to bring fresh ideas and perspectives to your work, while also recognizing the importance of preserving your unique voice and vision as an author.

Content Editing. Content editing goes deeper into the substance of your book, focusing on accuracy, clarity, and logical flow. This stage becomes particularly crucial when working with AI-assisted content, as it helps to refine and validate the information generated through this collaborative process.

For AI-assisted books, content editing takes on several important dimensions. One of the primary tasks is fact-checking information generated by the AI, especially in non-fiction works. While AI can process and synthesize vast amounts of data, it's essential to verify the accuracy and currency of this information. This process helps ensure that your book provides reliable, up-to-date content to your readers.

Another key aspect of content editing for AI-assisted books involves ensuring that any speculative or creative elements introduced by the AI are consistent with the book's internal logic and your vision. AI can sometimes generate novel ideas or scenarios that, while interesting, might not align perfectly with the world or argument you're building. The content editor works to seamlessly integrate these elements or adjust them to fit your book's framework.

Refining language choices is another critical task in this stage. AI might sometimes use phrases or terms in ways that subtly alter the intended message. A content editor carefully examines the text to ensure that the language accurately reflects your intended meaning, making adjustments where necessary to preserve the nuances of your ideas and arguments.

Content editing also involves identifying and resolving any repetitive patterns or clichés that the AI might have inadvertently introduced. While AI can generate diverse content, it may sometimes fall back on common phrases or structures. The editor works to vary the language and eliminate any overused expressions, ensuring your prose remains fresh and engaging throughout the book.

Content editors working on AI-assisted books often focus on specific questions to guide their work. They might ask, "Is this AI-generated information accurate and up-to-date?" This question is crucial for maintaining the credibility of your work, especially in rapidly evolving fields where information can quickly become outdated.

Another important query might be, "Does this section maintain the level of expertise we're aiming for, or has the AI introduced any oversimplifications?" This question helps ensure that your book maintains the depth and sophistication appropriate for your target audience, avoiding any unintended simplification of complex topics.

Lastly, a content editor might consider, "Are there any unique insights or connections made by the AI that we can develop further?" This question recognizes the potential for AI to generate novel ideas or unexpected connections. By identifying and expanding on these insights, you can add unique value to your book, offering readers fresh perspectives that might not have emerged through traditional writing methods alone.

Line Editing. Line editing is a critical phase in the book creation process, focusing on the craft of writing at the sentence and paragraph level. This stage aims to refine the language for maximum impact and readability, a task that takes on unique dimensions when working with AI-assisted content. The goal is to create prose that flows seamlessly, engages the reader, and maintains a consistent, authentic voice throughout the work.

For AI-assisted books, line editing often involves smoothing out any awkward phrasings or unnatural language constructions that might be artifacts of the AI writing process. While AI can generate grammatically correct sentences, it may sometimes produce combinations of words that feel slightly off to a human reader. The line editor's job is to identify these instances and rework them to sound more natural and engaging.

Ensuring consistency in tone and style throughout the book is another crucial aspect of line editing for AI-assisted works. Different sections generated with AI assistance might have subtle variations in voice or style. The line editor works to harmonize these sections, creating a cohesive reading experience that feels like it comes from a single, consistent authorial voice.

Enhancing the rhythm and flow of the prose becomes particularly important in sections where AI-generated content is integrated with your own writing. The line editor pays close attention to how sentences and paragraphs transition, ensuring that the AI-assisted portions blend seamlessly with your original content. This might involve adjusting sentence structures, varying paragraph lengths, or fine-tuning word choices to create a more natural cadence.

Line editing also involves identifying and resolving any instances of overly formal or stilted language that AI models sometimes produce. AI can occasionally default to more formal or academic language, which might not fit the tone of your book. The editor works to adjust these sections, infusing them with more personality and making them more accessible to your intended audience.

Throughout this process, line editors working on AI-assisted books might ask several key questions. One such question is, "Does this sentence sound natural, or does it bear hallmarks of AI-generated text?" This helps identify areas where the language might need to be adjusted to sound more human and authentic.

Another important query might be, "How can we adjust this AI-assisted section to better match your unique voice as an author?" This question recognizes the importance of maintaining your individual style and tone, even in sections where AI has played a significant role in content generation.

Lastly, a line editor might consider, "Are there opportunities here to elevate the language in ways that the AI might not have considered?" This question opens the door to creative enhancements, recognizing that while AI can generate competent prose, human creativity can add layers of nuance, imagery, or emotional resonance that take the writing to a higher level.

Copy Editing. Copy editing is a meticulous process that involves a detailed review of grammar, punctuation, spelling, and adherence to style guides. When applied to AI-assisted books, this stage takes on additional layers of complexity and importance. The goal is to ensure that the final text is polished, consistent, and free from errors, regardless of whether the content was generated by AI or written by the author.

For AI-assisted books, copy editing requires extra vigilance for subtle grammatical errors or unconventional usages that AI might introduce. While AI models are generally proficient in grammar, they can sometimes produce constructions that are technically correct but stylistically awkward or uncommon. The copy editor must be attuned to these nuances, correcting not just outright errors but also refining language choices to align with natural, fluent writing.

Ensuring consistent spelling and punctuation becomes particularly crucial when working with AI-generated content, especially for proper nouns or specialized terms that the AI might handle inconsistently. AI models might draw from diverse sources, potentially leading to variations in spelling or capitalization of specific terms. The copy editor meticulously standardizes these elements throughout the book, maintaining consistency and professionalism.

Verifying that any style guide requirements are met consistently is another key aspect of copy editing AI-assisted books. AI might not always adhere to specific style conventions, such as the Chicago Manual of Style or AP Style. The copy editor must carefully review the text to ensure it complies with the chosen style guide, making adjustments where necessary to maintain consistency in elements like citation formats, number treatments, and abbreviation usage.

Checking for and resolving any instances of mixed regional spellings or idioms is an important task when working with AI-generated text. AI models might inadvertently mix American and British English spellings or use idioms from different regions. The copy editor must identify these inconsistencies and standardize the language to match the intended audience and style of the book.

Copy editors working on AI-assisted texts often focus on specific questions to guide their work. They might ask, "Are there any recurring grammatical patterns in the AI-generated sections that need to be addressed systematically?" This helps identify any quirks in the AI's language generation that might require consistent correction throughout the book.

Another crucial question is, "How can we ensure that the technical or specialized language used by the AI is consistent with industry standards?" This is particularly important for non-fiction works or novels set in specific professional contexts. The copy editor may need to research or consult experts to verify that the terminology and concepts are accurately and consistently presented.

Lastly, copy editors might consider, "Are there any unusual word choices or constructions that, while technically correct, might benefit from revision for clarity or style?" This question addresses the nuanced aspects of language use, recognizing that even grammatically correct sentences might sometimes be improved for readability or stylistic consistency.

Through this thorough process, copy editing ensures that AI-assisted books meet the high standards of professional publication, presenting readers with a polished, error-free text that seamlessly blends human creativity with AI-generated content.

Proofreading. Proofreading is the final stage of the editing process, serving as the last line of defense against errors and inconsistencies before a book goes to publication. For AI-assisted books, this stage takes on additional significance, ensuring that the final product seamlessly blends human and AI-generated content into a cohesive, polished work.

In the context of AI-assisted books, proofreading involves a final check for any lingering artifacts of the AI writing process. This might include repeated phrases or information that the AI inadvertently duplicated across different sections of the book. Proofreaders carefully comb through the text, identifying and eliminating these repetitions to ensure a smooth, non-redundant reading experience.

A crucial aspect of proofreading AI-assisted books is ensuring that all edits made during previous stages have been implemented consistently. Given the potentially extensive revisions that might occur during developmental, content, and line editing, it's essential to verify that these changes have been applied uniformly throughout the text. This includes checking that any adjustments made to AI-generated sections align with the overall style and tone of the book.

Proofreaders also conduct a last review for any formatting issues, paying special attention to sections where AI-generated content has been integrated. This might involve checking for consistent font usage, proper paragraph breaks, correct heading styles, and appropriate spacing. The goal is to create a visually consistent document that doesn't betray which sections were AI-assisted and which were not.

For AI-assisted books that involve creative elements, such as science fiction or fantasy novels, proofreaders verify that any unique elements introduced by the AI are used consistently throughout the book. This might include invented words, names of fictional places or technologies, or specific rules of an imagined world. Ensuring consistency in these elements is crucial for maintaining the integrity of the story world and preventing reader confusion.

Throughout the proofreading process, professionals working on AI-assisted texts might ask themselves several key questions. One such question is, "Are there any last traces of 'AI-ness' in the text that need to be addressed?" This helps identify any remaining quirks or patterns in the language that might hint at its AI-assisted origin, allowing for final refinements to create a more natural, human-sounding text.

Another important consideration is, "Have all the unique elements introduced during the AI-assisted writing process been handled consistently?" This question ensures that any creative contributions from the AI, whether they're speculative concepts, character traits, or world-building details, are maintained consistently from beginning to end.

Perhaps the most crucial question a proofreader might ask is, "Does the final product read smoothly as a cohesive work, regardless of which parts were AI-assisted?" This overarching query gets to the heart of the proofreading process for AI-assisted books. The goal is to create a final product that reads as a unified, coherent work, where the lines between AI-generated and human-written content are indistinguishable to the reader.

By addressing these questions and meticulously reviewing the text, proofreaders ensure that AI-assisted books meet the highest standards of professional publishing. The result is a polished, error-free manuscript that effectively harnesses the power of AI while maintaining the unique voice and vision of the human author.

The Future of Editing AI-Assisted Books

The future of editing AI-assisted books is an exciting frontier that promises to reshape the publishing landscape. As AI-assisted writing becomes more prevalent, we're likely to see a dynamic evolution in editing approaches, blending traditional literary expertise with cutting-edge technology.

AI-assisted editing tools are poised to become a significant part of this future. Just as AI currently aids in the writing process, we may soon see sophisticated AI systems designed to assist in the editing process. These tools could potentially identify issues more quickly and efficiently than human editors alone, flagging inconsistencies, suggesting improvements in pacing or structure, or even offering stylistic enhancements. However, it's important to note that these tools are likely to augment rather than replace human editors, adding another layer of refinement to the editing process.

The rise of AI in writing may lead to the emergence of specialized editors who are experts in working with AI-assisted texts. These professionals would possess a unique blend of skills, combining a deep understanding of literary craft with knowledge of AI capabilities and limitations. They would be adept at identifying the strengths and weaknesses of AI-generated content, skilled at seamlessly integrating AI and human-written sections, and capable of preserving the author's voice while maximizing the benefits of AI assistance.

As AI becomes more integrated into the writing process, the publishing industry may need to develop new ethical guidelines for editing AI-assisted works. These guidelines would likely address complex questions of authorship, originality, and disclosure. For instance, how much AI assistance should be disclosed to readers? How do we define originality in the context of AI-generated content? These ethical considerations will shape the way AI-assisted books are edited, marketed, and received by readers.

The increasing prevalence of AI in writing may also lead to evolving stylistic norms. As readers become more accustomed to AI-influenced writing, we might see shifts in what's considered stylistically acceptable or desirable. Perhaps certain AI-generated structures or phrasings that initially seemed unusual will become normalized. Editors will play a crucial role in navigating these changing norms, balancing innovation with readability and literary tradition.

Looking further ahead, we might see the development of more collaborative AI models designed to work in tandem with human editors. These advanced systems could potentially learn from editorial decisions, improving their output over time to align more closely with human aesthetic judgments and storytelling principles. This could lead to a more symbiotic relationship between AI writing assistants and human editors, each enhancing the capabilities of the other.

The editorial process for AI-assisted books represents an exciting convergence of traditional publishing wisdom and innovative technology. It challenges us to rethink our approaches to writing, editing, and storytelling while maintaining the core values of quality, creativity, and reader engagement. By understanding this evolving landscape and working closely with skilled editors, authors can harness the power of AI to create books that are not only well-crafted and engaging but also push the boundaries of what's possible in literature.

As we move forward, the key will be to embrace the opportunities presented by AI while maintaining the human touch that gives literature its heart and soul. The future of editing AI-assisted books is not about replacing human creativity, but about enhancing it, opening new avenues for expression, and potentially democratizing the writing process. It's an exciting time for authors, editors, and readers alike, as we explore the new frontiers of storytelling in the age of AI.

Self-Publishing

If the traditional publishing route makes you feel nervous, don't worry— there's another option available to you. Self-publishing has revolutionized the publishing industry, giving authors unprecedented control over their work. For authors of AI-assisted books, this path offers unique opportunities and challenges. It allows for greater flexibility in how you present and market the AI aspect of your work, but it also requires you to navigate the complexities of production, distribution, and promotion on your own. The digital age has made self-publishing more viable than ever, with numerous platforms available to help authors reach their audience directly.

When you choose to self-publish an AI-assisted book, you're taking on the responsibilities traditionally handled by publishing houses. This includes editing, formatting, cover design, distribution, marketing, and sales. While it requires more work, it also offers greater control and potentially higher royalties. For AI-assisted books, self-publishing offers several distinct advantages. You have complete control over how and when to disclose the AI-assisted nature of your book, which can be particularly important given the varying attitudes towards AI in creative works. The flexibility in production allows you to experiment with innovative formats or structures that might emerge from the AI-assisted writing process, which traditional publishers might be hesitant to support.

The fast-paced nature of AI development means that self-publishing can allow you to bring your book to market quickly, capitalizing on current trends or discussions around AI. Many self-publishing platforms allow for direct interaction with readers, which can be valuable for explaining your AI-assisted process and gathering feedback. Additionally, self-publishing typically offers higher royalty rates, which can be beneficial if your AI-assisted book targets a niche market interested in this new form of literature.

There are numerous self-publishing platforms available, each with its own strengths and features. **Amazon Kindle Direct Publishing** (KDP) stands as the giant in the self-publishing world. I choose it for this book, as you know. It offers authors a direct path to the largest online bookstore globally, with options for both ebooks and print-on-demand paperbacks. This print-on-demand model allows authors to offer physical copies of their books without the need for upfront printing costs or inventory management. For AI-assisted books, KDP's wide reach can potentially connect you with readers who are interested in innovative writing techniques.

The platform is remarkably user-friendly, allowing authors to upload manuscripts, design covers, and set prices with relative ease. KDP's royalty structure is particularly attractive, offering up to 70% for ebooks priced between \$2.99 and \$9.99. Additionally, KDP integrates seamlessly with

Amazon's powerful marketing tools, providing opportunities to leverage Kindle Unlimited, Amazon's subscription service, and even run targeted ads directly on Amazon's platform.

However, while KDP excels in online distribution, it's important to note that getting your book into physical bookstores through KDP can be challenging. The platform primarily operates within Amazon's ecosystem, and its print-on-demand nature doesn't align with traditional bookstore distribution models, which often require bulk orders and different distribution channels. Despite these limitations, KDP remains a dominant and highly effective option for self-publishing, particularly for authors looking to capitalize on the digital market and Amazon's vast customer base.

IngramSpark is another popular option, known for its wide distribution network and high-quality printing options. It's particularly favored by authors looking to get their books into physical bookstores. Unlike KDP, which primarily serves Amazon, IngramSpark can distribute your book to over 40,000 retailers and libraries worldwide. This platform offers both print-on-demand and ebook distribution services. One of IngramSpark's standout features is its professional-grade printing options, including hardcover books, which some other platforms don't offer. This makes it an excellent choice for authors planning to create high-quality physical books or those targeting the gift market.

Other platforms like **Barnes & Noble Press, Apple Books, Kobo Writing Life, and Google Play Books** each offer unique advantages. B&N Press provides access to Barnes & Noble's dedicated customer base and the potential for in-store placement. Apple Books offers direct access to the iOS user base, which can be particularly receptive to innovative, tech-forward books. Kobo Writing Life is strong in international markets, especially Canada, Australia, and parts of Europe, potentially connecting you with a global audience interested in AI and literature. Google Play Books leverages Google's powerful search algorithms, which can enhance your book's discoverability.

When it comes to editing and formatting your AI-assisted book for self-publishing, you'll face unique challenges. In the developmental editing stage, focus on ensuring coherence between AI-generated sections and your own writing, paying special attention to maintaining a consistent voice throughout the book. During copy editing, be vigilant for any unusual phrasings or errors that might be artifacts of the AI writing process, and ensure consistency in terminology, especially for any technical or AI-related terms. Proofreading an AI-assisted book may require multiple rounds to catch any subtle errors that might have slipped through the AI-assisted writing process.

Formatting your book requires careful attention to ensure consistency across different devices and platforms. Consider including a note about the AI-assisted nature of the book in the front or back matter. You'll also need to decide how to handle sections that are primarily AI-generated versus those that are more heavily edited by you. Some authors choose to include examples of raw AI output alongside their refined text as a point of interest for readers.

Creating a cover for your AI-assisted book presents another unique opportunity. Your book cover is crucial for attracting readers, and it can also serve to convey the innovative nature of your work. Consider incorporating elements that subtly hint at the AI-assisted nature of the book, such as circuit patterns or abstract digital motifs. However, ensure the cover still aligns with genre expectations while conveying the book's unique AI angle. The title and subtitle can be used to indicate the AI-assisted nature of the book if you choose to make this a selling point. You'll also need to decide how to credit yourself as the author, with some authors of AI-assisted books choosing to include a phrase like "in collaboration with AI" on the cover.

Pricing your AI-assisted book effectively is crucial for its success in the self-publishing market. Consider factors such as production costs, competitor pricing, your book's length and perceived value, and platform-specific pricing strategies. AI can assist in analyzing market trends and suggesting optimal price points based on your genre and target audience.

Marketing a self-published AI-assisted book requires a multi-faceted approach. Leverage social media platforms to engage with potential readers, explaining your AI-assisted writing process and the unique aspects of your book. Consider creating behind-the-scenes content that shows how you collaborated with AI, which can be intriguing for tech-savvy readers. Utilize AI tools to analyze market trends and optimize your marketing copy. Build an author website that showcases both your book and your unique writing process.

Distribution of your self-published AI-assisted book should utilize multiple channels to maximize reach. This might include online retailers, your personal website or blog, social media platforms, local bookstores (for print books), libraries, and book fairs or conventions. AI can help identify the most effective channels for your specific book and target audience.

Self-publishing an AI-assisted book offers exciting possibilities for authors willing to take on the challenges of production, marketing, and distribution. It allows for greater control over how the AI aspect of your work is presented and provides the flexibility to quickly adapt to the rapidly evolving landscape of AI in literature. While it requires significant effort and learning, self-publishing can be a rewarding path for authors looking to push the boundaries of AI-assisted creative writing.

This might be the most important part: use your AI not just to write, but to **understand** the entire publishing process. Let's say you've chosen KDP (Kindle Direct Publishing). Open ChatGPT—or any capable AI assistant—and explain your choice. Then ask it to walk you through a detailed, step-by-step guide: from setting up your KDP account to publishing your final book. There are countless small details you may not yet be aware of, and these AI tools are excellent at surfacing them. They can guide you through things like formatting your manuscript in Word, choosing the correct trim size, setting up the right margins, understanding bleed and gutter settings, preparing your cover to KDP's exact specifications, uploading high-resolution images, selecting keywords, pricing your book, and understanding KDP's royalty structure. If you get stuck, ask follow-up questions—AI can break things down as specifically as you need. This is one of the most transformative parts of the AI revolution: not just generating content, but demystifying the systems that bring that content to life. Embrace it.

Hybrid Publishing

Hybrid publishing represents a middle ground between traditional publishing and self-publishing, combining elements of both approaches. This model has gained traction in recent years, offering authors an alternative path to publication that balances professional support with greater control and potentially higher royalties. For authors of AI-assisted books, hybrid publishing presents a unique set of opportunities and considerations.

In a hybrid publishing model, authors and publishers typically share the costs, responsibilities, and profits of publishing a book. This approach aims to blend the quality control and distribution capabilities of traditional publishing with the creative control and higher royalties of self-publishing.

For AI-assisted books, this can be particularly advantageous as it allows for more flexibility in how the AI aspect of the work is presented and marketed, while still benefiting from professional publishing expertise.

Unlike traditional publishing, hybrid publishing usually requires an upfront investment from the author. This financial contribution can vary widely between publishers, ranging from a few thousand to tens of thousands of dollars. The investment typically covers editing, design, printing, and initial marketing costs. For AI-assisted books, this investment might also include specialized editing to ensure seamless integration of AI-generated content, or marketing strategies tailored to highlight the innovative nature of the work.

Hybrid publishers provide professional services similar to traditional publishers. These often include editorial support (developmental editing, copy editing, proofreading), cover design and interior layout, ISBN assignment and copyright registration, distribution to major retailers and wholesalers, and basic marketing and publicity services. For AI-assisted books, some hybrid publishers might offer additional services such as tech-savvy editors familiar with AI writing tools, or marketing specialists experienced in promoting innovative literary works.

One key aspect that distinguishes reputable hybrid publishers from vanity presses is their selective acquisition process. They don't accept every manuscript submitted, which helps maintain the publisher's brand quality and increases the likelihood of success for published titles. For AI-assisted books, this selectivity might involve assessing not only the quality of the writing but also the innovative use of AI in the creative process.

Hybrid publishing typically offers higher royalty rates than traditional publishing, often ranging from 30% to 70% of net sales. This is due to the author's initial investment, which offsets the publisher's risk. For authors of AI-assisted books, these higher royalties can be particularly attractive, especially if the book appeals to a niche market interested in the intersection of AI and literature.

In most hybrid publishing arrangements, authors retain the rights to their work. This allows for more flexibility in future publishing decisions or adaptations of the work. For AI-assisted books, this rights retention can be crucial, given the rapidly evolving landscape of AI technology and potential future opportunities for AI-enhanced or dynamic versions of the book.

The advantages of hybrid publishing for AI-assisted books are numerous. It offers a faster time to market compared to traditional publishing, which can be crucial in the fast-paced world of AI technology. Authors have more creative control, which is particularly important when dealing with the unique aspects of AI-assisted writing. The professional support provided can help address the specific challenges of editing and marketing AI-assisted works, while the higher royalties can reward the author's innovative approach.

However, hybrid publishing also presents certain challenges. The upfront costs can be substantial, and there's no guarantee that these costs will be recouped if the book doesn't sell well. This financial risk needs to be carefully considered, especially given the potentially niche market for AI-assisted books. The quality of hybrid publishers can vary widely, from highly reputable companies to those bordering on predatory practices. Authors of AI-assisted books need to be particularly diligent in researching potential hybrid publishing partners, ensuring they have experience with or openness to technologically innovative works.

There's also the consideration of industry perception. Some segments of the publishing industry and some readers may view hybrid-published books as less prestigious than traditionally published works. This perception might be compounded for AI-assisted books, which already face some skepticism in certain literary circles. Authors need to be prepared to advocate for the quality and value of their work.

Marketing responsibilities in hybrid publishing often fall more heavily on the author than in traditional publishing. While the hybrid publisher will provide some marketing support, authors are typically expected to be heavily involved in promoting their work. For AI-assisted books, this might involve educating potential readers about the AI writing process and addressing any misconceptions or concerns about AI in literature.

When considering hybrid publishing for an AI-assisted book, authors should thoroughly research potential publishers. Look at their track record with innovative or technologically-oriented books. Examine their distribution capabilities, understanding how they might position an AI-assisted book in the market. Carefully review all costs involved and what services they cover. It's crucial to review the contract carefully, possibly with legal assistance, paying special attention to clauses that might affect AI-generated content or future AI-enhanced versions of the book.

The integration of AI in publishing is opening new possibilities for hybrid publishers. Some are using AI tools to more efficiently evaluate submitted manuscripts, which could be particularly relevant for AI-assisted books. AI-driven data analysis can help in making informed decisions about book potential and pricing, which might be especially useful for books that don't fit neatly into traditional genres. Some hybrid publishers are exploring AI-assisted marketing strategies, which could align well with the innovative nature of AI-assisted books.

Hybrid publishing might be a good fit for authors of AI-assisted books who have a completed manuscript but limited publishing experience. It can be attractive to those who want professional support but also desire creative control, especially over how the AI aspect of their work is presented. Authors who can afford the upfront investment and are willing to be actively involved in marketing their book might find this model appealing. The faster publishing timeline of hybrid publishing can be advantageous for AI-assisted books, allowing them to reach the market while the technology and concepts are still cutting-edge.

However, hybrid publishing may not be ideal for authors with very limited funds, as the upfront costs can be substantial. It also might not suit authors who prefer complete control over every aspect of publishing, as hybrid publishers will still have some say in the process. Authors aiming for the prestige associated with major traditional publishing houses might find that hybrid publishing doesn't fully meet this goal.

As the publishing industry continues to evolve, particularly in response to technological advancements like AI, hybrid models may continue to grow and adapt. We might see the emergence of hybrid publishers specifically focused on AI-assisted or technologically innovative books. These specialized publishers could offer unique insights into marketing and distributing such works, as well as specialized editing services for AI-generated content.

In conclusion, hybrid publishing offers a unique blend of traditional and self-publishing elements that can be particularly well-suited for AI-assisted books. It provides a path to publication that allows for innovation and author control while still offering professional support and wider distribution. As with any publishing decision, thorough research and careful consideration of your goals and resources are crucial. In the evolving landscape of publishing, where AI is playing an increasingly significant role, hybrid models represent an innovative approach that may continue to grow and adapt, offering exciting opportunities for authors pushing the boundaries of AI-assisted writing.

*

As we conclude this exploration of publishing options for AI-assisted books, it's clear that we stand at the cusp of a new era in literature. The integration of AI into the writing process has opened up unprecedented possibilities, challenging traditional notions of authorship and creativity while offering exciting new avenues for expression and innovation. Whether you choose traditional publishing, self-publishing, or a hybrid approach, your journey as an author of an AI-assisted book is part of a larger narrative of technological advancement and artistic evolution.

Chapter IX: Marketing

ChatGPT, Claude, and others are basically top-tier marketers—right at your fingertips. Just use them. Upload your book, tell them you want to sell it, and let them guide you. They'll help you build a full strategy: what platforms to use (Facebook, Instagram, TikTok), how much to spend, how to set a realistic budget, and how to create and test ad campaigns. You don't need any background in marketing. They'll walk you through everything—setting up accounts, choosing the right visuals, writing ad copy, and even understanding things like conversion rates and audience targeting.

But here's the crucial part: don't trust everything they tell you blindly. AI gives confident-sounding advice, but not all of it will work for your specific book or audience. The key is role-playing and experimentation. Tell ChatGPT to "act as a book marketing expert," then try a different session where it's "acting as a social media strategist," and another where it's "a conversion optimization specialist." Compare their advice. Look for patterns and contradictions.

Then—and this is critical—test their suggestions with small amounts of money first. Start with five or ten euros a day maximum. Think of it as tuition for your personal crash course in book marketing. Every campaign you run, whether it succeeds or fails, teaches you something valuable that will make your next book launch better.

If you've published through Amazon KDP, start there first. Amazon Ads should be your primary focus—it's where your readers are already browsing for books. Ask the AI to walk you through setting up Sponsored Product ads, Sponsored Brands, and Kindle Direct Publishing Select promotions. Amazon's advertising platform can feel overwhelming, but AI can demystify everything from keyword bidding to ACOS (Advertising Cost of Sales) optimization. The beauty is that people on Amazon are already in buying mode, unlike social media where you're interrupting their scrolling.

And honestly, it's kind of amazing. Let's say you decide to spend five euros a day on Amazon ads or Facebook ads. Every morning, you can check your stats, copy and paste them into ChatGPT—even if you have no idea what they mean—and it will break it all down. It will tell you what's working, what's not, how your results compare to typical campaigns or similar books, and exactly what to adjust. It can help you change your copy, tweak your images, or rethink your landing page in real time.

We're living in an era where the most powerful marketing knowledge on Earth is built into tools that are always available, never sleep, and exist solely to help you. They don't get tired. They don't need breaks. They just keep optimizing. You used to need a team of experts to do this. Now, you just need to ask—but you also need to verify, test, and learn from each attempt.

By your second or third book, you'll have developed real marketing instincts. You'll know which AI advice to trust and which to question. You'll understand your audience better than any algorithm. The AI becomes your research assistant rather than your decision-maker.

Use them. Seriously. But use them smart. This is the revolution.

Oh yes. And what's really crucial for marketing are reviews. They're the social proof that convinces other readers to buy your book and the fuel that feeds Amazon's algorithm to show your book to more people. Without reviews, even the best book can disappear into digital obscurity.

So if this book helped you in any way—gave you useful tools, saved you time, or simply entertained you—I'd be incredibly grateful if you could take a moment to leave a review. Even a few sentences about what you found most helpful would make a huge difference. It's the best way to help other writers discover these AI tools and continue this revolution.

Thank you for reading, and thank you in advance for any review you might leave.

Final Words: Your Journey Begins Here

If you've made it this far, congratulations! You now hold the keys to a new world of creative possibilities. You're equipped with the tools and knowledge to embark on an exciting journey of writing with AI. Whether you're planning to write about a subject you're deeply knowledgeable in or a topic you're passionate about exploring, the adventure that awaits you is bound to be transformative.

But let me tell you a secret: reading this book is just the beginning. Writing with AI is a craft, and like any craft, it requires practice, patience, and perseverance. I remember when I first started this journey. I sat down, brimming with excitement, thinking the AI would magically produce a bestseller at the touch of a button. Oh, how naive I was!

The reality was both more challenging and infinitely more rewarding than I could have imagined. There were days when the words flowed like a river, and the AI seemed to read my mind, expanding on my ideas in ways I never thought possible. But there were also days when I stared at the screen, feeling stuck, frustrated, and wondering if I was cut out for this at all.

These challenges, I've come to realize, are not obstacles but steppingstones. They're part of the process, shaping you into a better writer and a more creative thinker. When you hit a wall – and trust me, you will – don't give up. Instead, revisit the chapters on overcoming writer's block and reigniting your creativity. Remember, every great writer, AI-assisted or not, faces these moments. The key is to push through.

One of the most valuable lessons I've learned is the importance of balance. At first, I wanted the AI to do all the heavy lifting. But I quickly discovered that the magic happens in the collaboration between human and machine. The more effort and creativity you put in upfront, the more remarkable the results. It's not about letting AI write your book; it's about dancing with it, leading sometimes, following other times, but always moving forward together.

And oh, what a dance it can be! There are moments when I find myself grinning ear to ear, marveling at the ideas that emerge from this partnership. My mind races with possibilities – books I want to write, stories I want to tell, knowledge I want to share. It's intoxicating and liberating all at once.

This is why I often find myself juggling multiple projects. When one book starts to feel challenging, I pivot to another that ignites my passion anew. This approach has led me to complete books I never thought I'd write, while also teaching me valuable lessons from the projects I set aside. Who knows? Maybe one day I'll return to that half-finished self-help book and turn it into something extraordinary.

But here's the thing – it's not about the number of books you finish or even if you publish them. It's about the journey, the growth, and the sheer joy of creation. This book you're reading now? It wasn't born from a desire for accolades or bestseller status. It came from a place of genuine excitement, a desire to share what I've learned in this new frontier of writing.

As a law professor, my daily writing usually revolves around legal theories and case analyses. But exploring AI-assisted writing has opened up a whole new world for me. It's pushed me out of my comfort zone, challenged my preconceptions about creativity and authorship, and ultimately made me a better writer in all aspects of my life.

Now, I'm passing the baton to you. Your journey with AI-assisted writing will be uniquely yours. You'll discover techniques that work brilliantly for you, which might be different from mine. You'll face challenges I never encountered and find solutions I never imagined. And that's the beauty of it all – we're pioneers in this new realm of creative expression.

So, I encourage you – no, I challenge you – to take that book idea that's been simmering in your mind and bring it to life. Start writing, even if it's just for yourself. Share it online if you feel so inclined. Or keep it private as a personal achievement. The choice is yours. I do hope you send me a copy.

Yes, there will be frustrating moments. Yes, there will be times when you question why you started this journey in the first place. But I promise you, the rewards are worth it. The feeling of completing a chapter, of bringing a new idea to life, of expressing yourself in ways you never thought possible – it's nothing short of exhilarating.

Remember, every great book starts with a single word. Every groundbreaking idea began as a fleeting thought. You have within you the potential to create something remarkable. And now, with AI as your collaborator, the only limit is your imagination.

So, my fellow writer, are you ready? Your blank page awaits. Your AI assistant stands ready. And a world of infinite possibilities stretches out before you.

What story will you tell?